The Thistle

THE THISTLE
A Chronicle of Scottish Rugby

DEREK DOUGLAS

MAINSTREAM
PUBLISHING

EDINBURGH AND LONDON

First published in Great Britain in 1997 by
MAINSTREAM PUBLISHING COMPANY (EDINBURGH) LTD
7 Albany Street
Edinburgh EH1 3UG

ISBN 1 85158 737 3

A catalogue record for this book is available from the British Library

Designed by Jenny Haig
Typeset in Bembo
Printed and bound in Great Britain by Butler and Tanner Ltd, Frome

The Thistle

The thistle has been an important symbol in Scottish heraldry for over 500 years . . . The first use of the thistle as a royal symbol in Scotland appears to have been on silver coins issued by James III in 1470, and the Order of the Thistle was founded by James VII in 1687. . . The motto *nemo me impune lacessit* (loosely translated as 'No one attacks me and gets away with it') is usually associated with the Scottish thistle badge.

From *Collins Encyclopedia of Scotland*

The Scottish XX which defeated England in the world's first rugby union international at Raeburn Place, Edinburgh, on 27 March 1871, wore the thistle on the left breast of their blue jerseys. Scotland's national emblem has undergone numerous redesigns and transformations since then; but it still remains the instantly recognisable symbol of the Scottish game.

For Sheila

Contents

Acknowledgements

Much of this book was written at home in Edinburgh. However, rugby having taken off so spectacularly in a global sense, and my being chief rugby writer with *The Herald* newspaper, various sections were roughed out and some completed in locations as diverse and exotic as Pretoria and Cape Town in South Africa; Dunedin and Auckland in New Zealand; Pau and Paris in France; Dubai, Hong Kong and London. Truly, a journey from the sublime to the ridiculous. Rugby used to be a winter game. Now it is a game of perpetual motion played seamlessly and ceaselessly, without regard to season or national boundary. It's tough on the scribes who make the journey into endless winter and tougher still on the players, coaches and administrators who are at the heart of the action. My thanks are due to all of them – from the early pioneers to the professional players of today. Without them there would be no story to tell.

Along the way many, many individuals have endeavoured to make the venture slightly easier. First of all I wish to acknowledge the pioneering work done by the Rev. F.P. Marshall, who compiled the first genuine compendium of the game published in 1892 and, again, in 1894. Those two volumes, which not only provided contemporary accounts of the game but also surveyed the development of rugby from the first international match in 1871, have marked the starting point for generations of rugby historians. We are all indebted to Marshall and his contributors.

Secondly, and nearer to home, there is the debt owed to Scottish historians of the game. R.S. Phillips set the trend in 1925. The torch was taken up by the late Sandy Thorburn, honorary historian and librarian of the Scottish Rugby Union, with his invaluable record of every match which the Scottish national side played between 1871 and 1980. That was, truly, a labour of love and an irreplaceable chronicle of the Scottish game. Sandy was also responsible for the official history of the Scottish Rugby Union, another invaluable source of information – now sadly out of print – for all those interested in Scottish rugby.

Sandy's work was carried on by John Davidson, his successor at Murrayfield. Here I wish to record my thanks to John for the interest he has shown in this book. He very kindly agreed to read the manuscript; he also put at my disposal the resources of the SRU library, which include many of the photographs that appear between these covers. A work of this scale and scope has a capacity for error which is quite frightening to contemplate. John has endeavoured to keep me on the straight and narrow. The opinions expressed herein, however, are mine not his, and if the odd knock-on, dropped pass or downright fumble have crept into the text, then they are down to me and no reflection on John's encyclopaedic knowledge of the Scottish game.

I wish, too, to acknowledge the painstaking work done by an army of club archivists and historians. Those who compiled Jubilee histories in the 1920s and Centenary accounts in the '50s, '60s and '70s are due special thanks for their diligence. Without those accounts much of the grassroots' history of the game would have been lost forever.

There are many others in the rugby community who have been unstinting and uncomplaining in their response to my requests for assistance. I wish to record my thanks to them all.

I am especially grateful to, in no particular order: John Light, rector of Edinburgh Academy; Brian Cook, secretary of the Academical Club; Magnus Moodie and Rob Steadman, Edinburgh Academicals FC; Jennifer Macrory, former archivist of Rugby School, and Rusty McLean, current holder of the post; John Dunn, Langholm RFC; Malcolm Jack, Loretto School; Jock Dewar, historian of Royal High School FP; Ralph McNaught, Stirling County RFC; Harry Pincott, Boroughmuir RFC; David Edwards and Peter O'Malley, Heriot's FP; Willie MacTaggart, Hawick; Alasdair Reid and photographers Mike Wilkinson, Jim Galloway, Paul Clements, Gordon Lockie and Stan Hunter.

Matthew Gloag & Son Ltd, producers of The Famous Grouse whisky and team sponsors of the Scotland national side, kindly agreed to lend financial support to this book. The Famous Grouse and Scottish international rugby combine to produce a uniquely attractive 'double'. I raise a glass to them.

I wish also to thank my publishers Mainstream for the patience shown when the manuscript failed to appear for three years in succession; and The Royal Bank of Scotland for permission to reproduce the two Grand Slam paintings commisioned from Ronnie Browne. Finally, but most importantly, I wish to express the debt of gratitude which I owe to my wife, Sheila, who has endured with smiling good grace my absences around the world on rugby business and the endless hours, days, weeks and months listening to the tap-tap-tap from the word processor as this latest offering took shape.

My sincere thanks go to them all.

Prologue

Rugby union football is a game played by two million people in just over 100 countries throughout the world. It has become a multi-million-pound business which has spawned three World Cup tournaments with the fourth to be headquartered in Wales on the eve of the millennium, in 1999.

It is a game whose roots are buried deep in antiquity and whose antecedents were for much of the Middle Ages banned by royal command. The game we recognise today was fashioned in the great public schools of England, with Rugby School to the fore. It was adopted with alacrity in Scotland's leading houses of learning – although there is compelling evidence to suggest that the kernel of the game was there already – and spread far and wide by graduates from the British universities and by the builders of Empire who turned the world map imperial red throughout the nineteenth century.

Others, better qualified, have already documented in detail the statistical development of the game in Scotland and elsewhere. In the following pages I shall attempt to chart the evolution of rugby union football in Scotland, but not exclusively so. It is simply not possible to produce a historical narrative which fails to take account of the intertwined and symbiotic national relationships and rivalries which have produced the game we know today. However, the story which is about to unfold is most certainly and unapologetically told from a Caledonian perspective.

Scotland, Scottish clubs and the Caledonian founding fathers were present, if not in at the birth, then certainly in good time to hear the stripling babe utter its first forceful cries. The leading Scottish schools of the time – Edinburgh Academy, Glasgow Academy, Loretto, Merchiston Castle, Fettes and Royal High – played a hugely significant role in the development of the game not just in Scotland but, through their Oxbridge connections, in England as well.

Scotland hosted, too, the world's first rugby-rules international match, which was played against England on 27 March 1871 at Raeburn Place – the Edinburgh Academical cricket and playing field. This plot of land, then on the outskirts of Edinburgh in the village of Stockbridge, can rightly be termed the cradle of rugby union football in Scotland. It will figure often in this story.

At that first international match Mr J.H.A. Macdonald – a former pupil of the Academy and later the Court of Session judge Lord Kingsburgh – sat at the gate at a baize-covered deal table on which stood an earthenware bowl. Into this modest receptacle the 2,000–4,000 spectators who attended the match (estimates vary) placed their one-shilling entrance money. After expenses had been deducted – and according to the Edinburgh Academical Club's official history of its playing field published almost half a century ago – the princely sum of £5 was handed over.

Now, each Test match at Murrayfield attracts gross revenue of well over £1 million and the 1995 World Cup in South Africa amassed a profit thirty times that amount. Commercial support for the 1999 tournament is expected to be in the region of £60 million. From £5 in 1871 to million-pound matches at Murrayfield – and in just over a century and a quarter – is an astronomical leap and underlines in startling fashion just how a game designed for schoolboys in keeping with the Victorian values of muscular Christianity, and with the Graeco-Roman concept of a healthy body promoting a healthy mind, has mushroomed into the global business it is today.

But what kind of a game is this rugby union football? What are its values? What is its appeal, and will that appeal survive the professional revolution which swept aside the amateur ethos that had been its guiding light for well over a century?

As the twentieth century draws to a close, the game is stumbling through uncharted territory. It has been in turmoil. No other word can properly describe the quite fantastic upheaval which engulfed the sport when amateurism was consigned to the sidelines at that watershed International Board meeting in Paris on 27 August 1995.

On the French Mediterranean coast in a graveyard in the village of Menton, there is some corner of a foreign land which is forever England. There lies buried the Rev. William Webb Ellis. As befits a man of the cloth, his spiritual remains are no doubt with his Maker. Even in the after-life – or so those who believe in such things will fervently wish – pastoral needs have to be catered for too. Webb Ellis is probably engaged right now in a game of football on the Elysian Field. And no doubt he will be cheating!

Before embarking upon a largely undistinguished career as a churchman, Webb Ellis was the Rugby School pupil who achieved posthumous fame as the only true begetter of what we now know as rugby union football.

As we shall see as our story unfolds, Webb Ellis's role in the creation of the carrying game in 1823 was a myth perpetrated – without sinister intent – by Old Rugbeians. It may well have been that Webb Ellis 'with a fine disregard for the rules of the game as played in his time' ran with the ball in his hands on the Close at Rugby School. But as the defining moment in the creation of the carrying game, the story is a fable. It is a myth, however, which has gained common currency; in any vox pop, nine times out of ten, William Webb Ellis will be paraded as the one and only true begetter of the game. The World Cup trophy – the highest honour which the game can bestow – is named in honour of the charlatan Rugby schoolboy. How preposterously ironic that a boy who was never particularly liked at school, and who was damned by his contemporaries as someone who was prone to 'take unfair advantage at football', should have the highest tangible prize that the rugby world can offer named after him.

According to Rugby School, Webb Ellis was the boy first documented as having flouted the rules by running with the ball. But this Big Bang notion that the game was created – like the Universe – in a single instant, is too outrageously fortuitous to be true.

William Webb Ellis may well have been a fraud in so far as being the inventor of the game is concerned – not his fault, others made the claim on his behalf – but the values that he encountered at Rugby School (or at least some of them, as he was also accused of having cheated in a Latin examination) are still those of the game which took the school's name.

The public schools, with their focus on muscular Christianity, were where what eventually turned out to be rugby was born. These great seats of learning were a completely new educational phenomenon. They were not intended as an exercise in egalitarianism or as a means of educating the masses. They were private boarding-schools designed exclusively for the education of the sons of the ruling class and the new, upwardly mobile mercantile classes. They replaced the practice of education by private tutor and, soon, these new educational establishments were consumed by a quite remarkable games cult.

These Victorian values equipped rugby with a special ethos. It was an ethos which held true for 150 years and which, as the game underwent its conversion to professionalism, made rugby especially attractive to the media moguls and millionaire paymasters who filled the fiscal void created when amateurism was scrapped. What were those values? Fair play, self-discipline, respect for opponents, respect for authority in the form of the referee, and a willingness to take your knocks without grumbling.

At least, those are the values which the game strives to uphold and, by and large, succeeds in so doing. Rugby is a hard, physical contact sport which is potentially dangerous

and in which bloodlust could so easily rule. The fact that it hardly ever does owes everything to that set of values bequeathed to the game by its Victorian founding fathers.

Association football and rugby union are divergent streams from the same reservoir and not so long ago they were as one. But to those of us who are not adherents of the 'People's Game', its universal appeal is a mystery. The tribalism and triumphalism of association football are concepts with which we have difficulty coming to terms. This is not élitism, because in the Scottish Borders, Wales, the north of England (where it co-habits uneasily with rugby league), in southern France and in New Zealand, rugby union is very much the 'People's Game'.

It would take a sociologist to explain why rugby union fans – and to an even more significant degree rugby league fans – from the same background as association football fans have not over the years behaved in the same manner. There is at least a prima-facie case for suggesting that it must be something to do with the values held dear by the rival codes.

Money probably has something to do with it as well. What effect money is going to have on professional rugby union is still the great unanswered question. Early indications have not been encouraging. Throughout the year which followed that epochal International Board meeting in Paris the game was riven and disfigured by bitter disagreements over money.

The Five Nations championship, one of the world's truly great sporting institutions, came within an ace of being sacrificed on the altar of the great god Mammon. The Rugby Football Union had incensed its Five Nations partners by negotiating its own £87.5 million television broadcasting deal with the media mogul Rupert Murdoch – selling games at

13

Twickenham despite the fact that it takes England and one other to put on a show. The championship was saved only after a partial climbdown by the RFU and the implementation of a compromise deal which saved face all round. In Scotland, England and Wales – but particularly in England – the first, full year of professionalism was further disfigured by a quest for financial self-determination among the leading clubs; in England it was accompanied by such rancour that it seemed for a long time that outright revolt and breakaway from the RFU was a certainty. These were not great exemplars of what money will do for the sport and it may well be that the commendable Victorian values which have made the game what it is are not compatible with what the game has become.

Certainly those who run the game found it impossible to engineer a seamless transition from amateurism (or shamateurism) to professionalism. But an 'open' game was the only feasible route to follow. The International Board, which cast the game to the wolves at that meeting in Paris, could have agreed a transitional period with a moratorium on full-blast professionalism until some definite date in the near future. By then, however, they were no longer masters in their own house; they were ranged against external forces over which they had no control. There was no alternative to immediate, full-blown professionalism. Unless the game proceeds warily, however, the very values which give rugby union a virtually unique place in the sporting world – values which made the game such an attractive proposition for blue-chip sponsors and advertisers in the first place – will be lost for ever. Babies, bath-water and the disposal thereof are the words which come readily to mind.

Amateur rugby is the game that was. Now all players can be professional if they are good enough and they want to be. In future the game will almost certainly be administered by professionals – the days of the amateur 'blazeratti' are numbered, though they should be commended for handing on a sport generally sound in body and mind – and it will be financed by TV moguls who know the price of everything and the value of nothing. It has taken 150 years for the game to get where it is today. Trading values for money is not a good deal. The new men had better take good care of their inheritance or they will never be forgiven.

ONE

The Impossible Quest

In search of the forbidden game

The quest to discover the true origins of the game which became rugby union football is destined always to end in failure. The fact of the matter is that, from ancient times, men and boys – and perhaps women too – have kicked and carried a ball of some sort or other.

The Greeks and the Romans played ball games. The Romans delighted in *harpastum*, based on a Greek game (its name derived from the Greek word to 'snatch'), in which two teams on a properly delineated pitch attempted to score 'goals' by forcing a small, hard ball over their opponents' line. There was handling and passing and kicking and tackling, not altogether unlike the game we know as rugby today. But rugby it wasn't. The Romans also played *pila paganica*, or village ball, with a small feather-stuffed ball. They spent their leisure time, too, in pursuit of a ball which they called the *follis* which was an inflated animal bladder contained in a leather case.

Perhaps the real hero in our odyssey to pin down the origins of the game is not the Rugby School pupil William Webb Ellis, who will feature later in our tale, but the anonymous individual who first had the imagination – not to mention a fine disregard

for the niceties of life – to put his lips to the bladder of a farmyard beast in order to provide his chums with that vital component without which all ball games would have foundered at birth – a properly inflated ball.

Circumstantial evidence suggests that the Romans spread the concept of playing games with a ball throughout their Empire, which at that point was the most far-flung and powerful the world had ever seen. Here there is an echo of the ball-playing explosion which would occur nearly 2,000 years later when the British Empire was at its peak and the colonisers took with them to the four corners of the globe all the comforts of home. Those comforts, of course, included the games they had played at school. Hence, rugby and football and cricket took root and prospered wherever the Union Flag flew; juvenile pastimes born on the playing fields of Eton and Harrow, on The Close at Rugby, the Yards at the Royal High School of Edinburgh and at Edinburgh Academy's Raeburn Place, were exported throughout the world.

So, in the absence of compelling evidence to the contrary, let us proceed on the basis that the notion of 'playing ball' in all of its multi-faceted shapes and forms can trace its lineage to the games that Romans played when the duties and business of Empire were sufficiently slack to allow the odd moment of relaxation.

The 400 years in which Rome held sway over most of Britain – Wales and the unruly Picts inhabiting the land north of the Antonine Wall, which stretched from Forth to Clyde, proved more difficult to subdue – were more than enough for the habits and pastimes of the occupying forces to rub off on the natives.

In a Scottish context it is tempting to make the connection between the existence of various forms of hand ba' throughout the Borderland, certainly from medieval times, and the fact that the area between the Cheviots and the important Roman garrison and administrative centre at Trimontium, on the Tweed near Melrose, would almost certainly have been the most Romanised tract of land in the northernmost territories of the Roman Empire. Dere Street, the Roman highway intended, as they all were, to lead from the most remote corners of Empire directly to Rome, bisected the eastern Borders *en route* from the Corbridge settlement at Hadrian's Wall to Trimontium and then Inveresk on the Firth of Forth. Living and working astride the main north-south artery of Roman rule, the Dere Street dwellers would certainly have suffered, or enjoyed, more exposure than most to the ways of the occupying forces. That would undoubtedly have included the games they played.

Hand ba', played with a hard, leather-covered ball just slightly larger than a modern cricket ball, has existed since time immemorial throughout the Borders, though it was played elsewhere in Scotland, too. And until relatively recently hand ba' games were played throughout the Border parishes of Hawick, Hobkirk, Lilliesleaf, Denholm, Ancrum, Selkirk, Galashiels, St Boswells, Melrose, Kelso, Duns, Morebattle and Yetholm. The game, between Uppies and Doonies, where the object is to hail the ball by fair means or foul in opposition territory, is still a feature of life in Jedburgh where Border reiving lore has it that the original was played with the head of an unfortunate Englishman. Maybe, but I for one am happier to believe that the hand ba' played now in the Royal and Ancient Burgh owes more to Rome than to a headless Englishman. Perhaps the outbreak of Jethart Justice came later!

Nevertheless, by the time that the Roman Empire had disintegrated, as all empires ultimately must, there existed a tradition for ball-playing throughout Britain. Just as in Scotland, where hand ba' held sway, in England there are numerous historical references to variations on the theme – camp ball in the eastern counties centred around the hitherto Roman strongholds of Lincoln, Colchester and St Albans; hurling in Cornwall; *cnapan* in Wales; and the carrying game in the neighbouring parishes of St Peter's and All Saints in Derby, which provides us with the expression 'local derby'.

Football, whether of the carrying or kicking kind, and references throughout this chapter make no distinction between the two, was generally a rustic pursuit. In the larger conurbations it was mainly the province of the lower orders. The games which developed in the cities were accompanied by 'much shouting and hallooing', which so disturbed the genteel merchant classes that there were soon moves to have the games banned. Football hooliganism, which so disfigured the Association code throughout the '70s and '80s, is apparently not a new phenomenon.

Shrove Tuesday was traditionally the high day and holiday on which football was a popular distraction from the grind of everyday life. On that day in 1175 in London – on a site identified without absolute certainty as Smithfield – one William Fitzstephen, a monk of Canterbury who was also the biographer of the murdered Archbishop Thomas à Becket, becomes the first sportswriter in the history of British football.

The morning was spent in cock-fighting and other boyish pastimes. Then, after dinner, all the youth of the city proceeded to a level piece of ground just outside the town for the famous game of ball. The students of every different branch of study had their own ball as did the various tradesmen. The older men, the fathers and the men of property, arrived on horseback to watch the contests and, in their own way, shared the sport of the young men. These elders were filled with excitement at seeing so much vigorous exercise and participated, vicariously, in the pleasures of unrestrained youth.

However, these pleasures did not last long. Football was not a pastime enjoyed by the ruling classes, who favoured field sports – principally hunting and hawking – and who, in any case, considered that it was not within the remit of the lower orders to have fun. They considered, too, that aimless kicking and running with a ball on the few occasions that the populace obtained release from the toil of simple survival was keeping them from more honest and worthwhile tasks like practising their archery and keeping their martial arts in good order.

Therefore, the first recorded instance of a ban was not long in coming; it came from King Edward II of England, who obviously had other things on his mind when he was vanquished by Robert the Bruce at Bannockburn in 1314. Before embarking on his ill-fated expedition north he issued a proclamation, through his Lord Mayor of London Nicholas de Farndonne, which put football out of bounds in the metropolis.

Medieval football was frowned upon by the Establishment which sought, for centuries, to proscribe the game. Kirk and Crown considered that the unruly masses had far better things to do with their time.

'Forasmuch as there is great noise in the city caused by hustling over large footballs in the fields of the public, from which many evil spirits might arise, which God forbid, we command and forbid, on behalf of the king, on pain of imprisonment, such game to be used in the city in future.'

Without the endorsement of the ruling élite, football had a struggle to survive. Further proclamations on the 'eviles of the footballe' came from King Edward III, who ordered all able-bodied men to practise with bows and arrows or pellets or bolts in their leisure time.

In Scotland, football was met with the same official disapproval. King James I set the trend with a proclamation issued from Perth in 1424 in which condign punishment was threatened to any man found playing at the 'fute ball'.

The principal concern of the House of Stewart was that football was being used as an excuse for the ordinary folk not to attend the regular 'wapinschawings' – literally showing the weapons – in which military skills and drills were practised. Thirty-four years after that initial blast from James I, another Stewart got in on the act. In a decree issued from Edinburgh in 1457, King James II extended the regal disapproval from football to golf. 'It is decreyit and ordanyt that the wapinschawings be haldin be the lordis and the barronis spirituall and temporal foure tymis in the yeir. And that the futball and golf be utterly cryit downe and not to be usit.'

The English kings Richard II and Henry IV were similarly discomfited by the prospect of their feudal men-at-arms letting their martial skills fall into abeyance by playing football. Both rulers issued further decrees banning the game, with Henry invoking the penalty of a stinging 20 shilling fine on all mayors and bailiffs in towns where the ban

was not observed. In fact, so insistent and shrill had the official proclamations against football become that, from this distance, it appears that the monarchs in both Scotland and England spent almost the entire fifteenth century fighting a losing battle against this insidious threat to the safety and well-being of both realms.

In 1471, in a royal proclamation issued in Edinburgh, James III had joined the crusade against football and, in this case, also against golf. 'Ilk sherif, steward, bailze and other officiares should mak wapinschawing within the bondes of thar office eftir the tenor of the Act of Parliament. Swa that in defawt of the said wapinschawing our souvran lordes leiges be nocht destitut of harnes quhe that neid and at the futball and golf be abusit in tym cumyng.'

Similarly, in 1491, King James IV hammered home the message that there was no place in Scotland for football or golf if the wapinschawings were not to suffer. 'It is statute and ordanit that ilk schiref, steward or baillie of the realm gar wapinschawyings be maid foure tymes in the zeir in all placis convenient within his Baillierie ... and attour that in na place of the realme there be usit futball, golf or other sic unproffitabill sportis.'

This preoccupation with martial matters and sixteenth-century civil defence was, of course, no idle foible on the part of the Stewart court. Scotland was forever on her guard against invasion from England and James IV did, indeed, come to an extremely gory end along with the cream of Scottish nobility on Flodden Field in 1513. Ironically, this catastrophe, which touched every noble house in the land and every household throughout southern Scotland, was presaged by Scottish invasion of England in support of the Auld Alliance with France. James and his court would have done better by far to have remained at home engaged in 'unproffitabill sportis'.

But there were those who recognised the attraction of football. Just one year after the disaster at Flodden Field, Andrew Barclay, a Benedictine based at Elie, was waxing lyrical about the delights of ball-playing sports. And note, too, that Barclay was telling us that 'football' in sixteenth-century Fife was not a game played exclusively with the feet.

> The sturdie plowman, lustie strong and bold
> o'ercometh the winter with driving the
> football.
> Forgetting labour and many a grievous fall.
> In the winter, when men kill the fat swine,
> They get the bladder and blow it up great
> and thin
> With many beans and peasen put within.
> It ratleth, soundeth and shineth cleare and
> fayre
> when it is throwen and casteth up in the
> ayre.
> Each one contendeth and hath a great delite
> with foote and with hand the bladder for to
> smite.

Despite Barclay's deposition in favour of football, it seems that he was still in the minority. In 1511 the Privy Council of Scotland had adjudicated on a complaint that in Perthshire, under cover of a game of football, the 'ball green of the lands of Campbell' had been inundated by gangs of heavily armed youths. Similarly, in the Borders, games of football and horse-racing meetings were utilised by the Mosstroopers as cover for their freebooting activities.

At a time when the mass of the population was still living in the countryside the authorities became extremely anxious at anything which enabled foregathering by large numbers of people when subversion

might be plotted and insurrection fomented.

By 1572, Queen Elizabeth I was still railing in irate and regal fashion about the iniquities of football; more than 250 years after the first royal decree banishing the game from the streets of London she threatened, still, a jail sentence for any miscreant found in breach of the ban. 'No foteball player be used or suffered within the City of London and the liberties thereof upon pain of imprisonment.'

It was, however, to take more than royal decree against such 'unprofitable sports' to blunt the appetite of the populace for the game, in all its forms, which they chose to call their own. Even blasts from the pulpit failed to shake the hold which football exerted though not for the want of ecclesiastical trying. The Kirk in Scotland, under the zealous influence of John Knox, was not much in favour of anything that involved having fun, whilst the Puritan pamphleteer Philip Stubbes, writing in 1583, went straight for the jugular.

> Football is a devilish pastime and hereof groweth envy, rancour and malice and sometimes brawling, murther, homicide and great effusion of blood, as experience daily teacheth. They have the sleights to meet one betwixt two, to dash him against the hart with their elbowes, to butt him under the short ribs with their griped fists and, with their knees, to catch him on the hip and pick him on his neck, with a hundred such murthering devices. Lord, remove these exercises from the Sabbath. Any exercises which withdraweth from Godliness either upon the Sabbath or any other day, is wicked and to be forbidden.

But the forbidden game would not disappear. This was a period when the working man laboured for six days a week and when the

Sabbath, emphatically, was to kept holy and as a day of rest. It mattered not to those who made the rules, and who could engage in leisure pursuits on any day they chose, that the Sabbath was the only day on which the ordinary man could seek distraction from his weekday toil.

The anti-sabbatarians found an unlikely ally in King James I and VI. In 1618 he courted the popular vote, and at the same time delivered a regal rebuke to the extremist Presbyterians and Puritans, with a declaration read from every pulpit in Scotland and England which gave official sanction to the playing of games on Sundays – after Kirk – and on holy days.

He considered that if the Establishment maintained its disapproval of playing games on Sundays then the masses would be turned away from the church. He believed, too, that sport honed a nation's fitness for war and that if the working people were to be denied their pleasures then they would simply turn to the ale-house as an alternative. Most significantly of all, James VI realised that Sundays and holy days provided the only opportunities for diversions from work. When, he asked, would the common people have leave to exercise if not upon Sundays and holy days, seeing that they must apply their labour and win their living in all working days?

Gradually, and inevitably, the forbidden game was winning official acceptance. In truth, the Kirk and the Crown would have been on safer but equally fruitless ground trying to prohibit adultery. Football had captured the public imagination in a manner that is virtually unique in its all-pervasive power. Quite simply, football was here to stay.

TWO

Life is Itself but a Game of Football

The Carterhaugh Ba' Game

The great game of football – or, more properly, hand ba' – played at Carterhaugh on Monday, 4 December 1815, is in all probability a cul-de-sac along the road to chart the development of rugby football in Scotland. Nevertheless, it is such a romantic tale that it deserves re-telling and, because its principal instigator Sir Walter Scott had connections with two Edinburgh schools which were soon to be among the first and leading proponents of the game in Scotland, it might not be quite the dead-end that it first appears.

Young Walter, the son of an Edinburgh lawyer, had been stricken by poliomyelitis at the age of 18 months and was sent to recuperate in the bracing air on his grandparents' farm at Sandyknowe, just a few miles south of Kelso. Thereafter, he became a scholar at the High School of Edinburgh. He was a kinsman of the Scotts of Buccleuch, who had their principal residence at Branxholme Castle, near Hawick. He may have been a city child but he was a Borderer at heart, and he knew all about the hand ba' games which in his time were still part and parcel of Border life.

Scott was sheriff of Selkirkshire and a poet of European renown but had not yet been unmasked as the author of the first of his novels, *Waverley*, when plans were put in hand for the grand football match which was to be staged between the Shepherds of Yarrow, representing the Earl of Home, and the Souters of Selkirk, representing Charles, fourth Duke of Buccleuch. Scott was distantly related to the Duke, whose sister had married the Earl of Home, and it was over dinner at Bowhill, the Buccleuch residence on the outskirts of Selkirk, that preparations for the Great Gathering were put in place.

From the outset Scott saw it not just as a game of football but as a re-enactment of the Mosstrooping days when the Reivers would gather by family name under the direction of the family chief and ride with the family standard at their head. Scott was an incurable romantic. Seven years later, as chief organiser for the visit of King George IV to Edinburgh, he would swathe the capital in a madness of tartan tomfoolery and set the fashion trend for generations of Scots to come.

Carterhaugh was, and is, the flat open plain at the confluence of the rivers Ettrick and Yarrow, near the Covenanting battlefield of Philiphaugh and, coincidentally but fittingly, the home of Selkirk RFC. There is some cosmic synchronicity at work here!

Although we shall probably never know for sure, the origins of the Carterhaugh game dwell in all likelihood in Border folklore. Certainly the composition of the two 'teams' indicate that this is so.

It's up wi' the Souters o' Selkirk
An doon wi' the Earl o' Home
An' up wi' a' the braw lads
That sew the single-shoed shoon.

That song, still sung at the Selkirk Common Riding, is reckoned to depict the contrasting behaviour of the men of Selkirk and those supporting the Earl of Home at the Battle of Flodden. Tradition has it that of the Selkirk contingent who fought with King James at Flodden all were slain save one, who brought the tidings of disastrous defeat back to the Royal and Ancient Burgh. By contrast, the Earl of Home and his followers had quit the battlefield, it was said, in cowardice.

A conflicting interpretation of the song, however, is given by the Rev. Thomas Robertson in the *Statistical Account of Scotland 1791–1799,* a central register compiled by Sir John Sinclair in which parish ministers (generally but not exclusively) filed a sociological snapshot of their parishes. Robertson maintained that the ditty had nothing whatsoever to do with Flodden.

Some have very falsely attributed to that event, that song 'Up with the Souters of Selkirk and down with the Earl of Hume'. There was no Earl of Hume at that time, nor was this song composed until long after. It arose from a bett betwixt the Philiphaugh and Hume families; the Souters (or shoemakers) of Selkirk against the men of Hume, at a match of football, in which the Souters of Selkirk completely gained, and afterwards perpetuated, their victory in that song.

Robertson's interpretation was immediately contested by the sheriff-depute of Selkirkshire Andrew Plummer, who maintained that he had lived all of his life in the area and had never heard tell of what he termed the 'imaginary contest' of football until he had read the Rev. Robertson's account.

In passing, it is worth noting that the minister not only called into question the probity of a slice of local folklore held dear, still, by the Souters of Selkirk, but also passed a damning judgement on the morals of his flock. 'The only additional circumstance tending to the depopulation of this part of the country is the dissipation of the lower ranks which makes them afraid of marriage and desirous of enjoying the pleasures without the burdens of matrimony.'

Sir Walter was undoubtedly aware of the controversy over the origins of the song because he succeeded Plummer as sheriff of Selkirkshire. In his 'Minstrelsy of the Scottish Border' he publishes a version of the song with a footnote, recounting the competing verdicts as to its origins from Robertson and Plummer.

The germ of an idea had been planted in Sir Walter's fertile imagination, and it seems that over dinner at Bowhill, Scott, Buccleuch and Home decided that, while the Rev. Robertson's interpretation was suspect, the concept of just such a football match between the houses of Home and Buccleuch was rather a good one.

Sir Walter was charged with the organisation, and he fell to the task with great energy. Ever the great romantic, he obviously felt that he could not let the occasion pass simply on the level of a sporting contest. The Great Gathering would be used as a modern re-interpretation of the medieval wapinschaws and of the trysts whereby the freebooting Border families of

Sir Walter Scott – Border Laird, author, poet, sheriff of Selkirkshire and incurable romantic – organised the Carterhaugh Ba'
Game not just as a game of football but as a re-enactment of the great Mosstrooping days in the Border country. It ended in
near riot with Sir Walter making his way home to Abbotsford only after dispensing largesse to the crowd which had gathered in
the market square at Selkirk.

old would foregather before setting out on their Mosstrooping missions. The event was to be celebrated, too, in song and verse. In terms of general organisation and on the

literary front the 'Shirra' was tremendously busy, as contemporary letters indicate.

I cannot write to you any more at present,

being very busy with preparations for a grand football match at which we are to hoist the old Banner of Buccleuch which has been produced to the air for the first time this hundred years and more. Your young friend Walter [Sir Walter's son] is to bear it to the weapon-show where we expect to muster many hundreds – Lord have mercy on their necks and legs – their shins are past praying for.

Sir Walter commissioned music to accompany the verse which he was writing to celebrate The Gathering and he enlisted the literary talents of his friend James Hogg, the Ettrick Shepherd. Scott's poem was entitled *The Lifting of the Banner* and focused upon the standard of the House of Buccleuch which was embroidered with golden crescent moons and stars and other heraldic bearings on a blue background and bore the word Bellendaine, the Scotts' battle-cry.

From the brown crest of Newark its summons extending,
Our signal is waving in smoke and in flame;
And each Forester blithe, from his mountain descending,
Bounds light o'er the heather to join in the game.

Chorus: Then up with the Banner, let forest winds fan her,
She has blazed over Ettrick eight ages and more;
In sport we'll attend her, in battle defend her,
With heart and with hand, like our fathers before.

When the southern invader spread waste and disorder,
At the glance of the crescents he paused and withdrew,

For around them were marshall'd the pride of the Border
The Flowers of the Forest, the bands of Buccleuch.

A stripling's weak hand to our revel has borne her,
No mail glove has grasp'd her, no spearmen surround.
But ere a bold foeman should scathe or should scorn her,
A thousand true hearts would be cold on the ground.

We forget each contention of civil dissension,
And hail, like our brethren, Home, Douglas and Car;
And Elliot and Pringle in pastime shall mingle,
As welcome in peace as their fathers in war.

Then strip lads, and to it, though sharp be the weather,
And if, by mischance, you should happen to fall,
There are worse things in life than a tumble on heather,
And life is itself but a game of football.

And when it is over we'll drink a blithe measure
To each Laird and each Lady that witnessed our fun,
And to every blithe heart that took part in our pleasure,
To the lads that have lost and the lads that have won.

May the Forest still flourish, both Borough and Landward,
From the Hall of the Peers to the Herd's ingle-nook;

The title-page illustration from the 'Ettrick Garland' pamphlet printed by Sir Walter for the Carterhaugh game. The gothic artwork includes a pennant with the Scotts of Buccleuch war cry 'Bellendaine' and the pamphlet contained the text of the two songs written for the occasion by Scott and his friend James Hogg, the Ettrick Shepherd.

And huzza! my brave hearts, for Buccleuch
and his standard,
For the King and the Country, the Clan and
the Duke.

With the big day fast approaching, and with communication with James Hogg proving troublesome, Scott enlisted the aid of the Duke of Buccleuch in his efforts to secure the Ettrick Shepherd's literary contribution to the proceedings. 'My Dear Lord, I wish Hogg to give me a little of his best assistance to celebrate the Lifting of the Banner and enclose a note to this purpose which some of your Grace's people must get up to him without loss of time as it would lie too long at Selkirk.'

On 24 November – less than a fortnight before the match – Hogg came up with the goods. He sent Scott a poem entitled *To The Ancient Banner of Buccleuch* which, he said, had been composed in haste, as he judged that there was 'no time to lose'. He advised Scott that, since the poem had been made up very quickly, he should feel free to 'lop and add' as he saw fit. In the finished article Hogg, like Scott, focused on the Buccleuch Banner as the centrepiece of the day's events.

And hast thou here, like hermit grey,
Thy mystic characters unrolled
O'er peaceful revellers to play,
Thou emblem of the days of old?

25

Or comest thou with the veteran's smile,
Who deems his day of conquest fled,
Yet loves to view the bloodless toil
Of sons whose sires he often led.

I love thee for the olden day,
The iron age of hardihood
The rather that thou led the way
To peace and joy through paths of blood;
For were it not the deeds of weir,
When thou wert foremost in the fray,
We had not been assembled here,
Rejoicing in a father's sway.
Then hail! memorial of the brave,
The liegeman's pride, the Border's awe!
May thy grey pennon never wave
On sterner field than Carterhaugh!

So, the stage was set for the grandest game of football that Scotland had ever seen. The Souters of Selkirk, led by their chief magistrate Dr Ebenezer Clarkson, wore twigs of fir in their bonnets while the Shepherds of Yarrow, led by the Earl of Home with James Hogg as his deputy, were distinguished by sprigs of heather in theirs. The Souter ranks were swelled by about 50 braw lads from Galashiels and about 100 callants from Hawick. The contest played with many hundreds on each side, was essentially a match between townsfolk and country dwellers, and although Scott referred to it throughout as a game of football, he was taken to task at the time by participants and onlookers, who declared that it was, in fact, handball that was being played.

The balls themselves, which were to be hailed at 'goals' set a mile apart and marked by pennons set in the riverbed at either end of the Carterhaugh, were fashioned from leather with a wool interior. They were somewhat larger than the type of hand ba' still in use in some parts of the Borders today, but smaller than a modern football.

The huge crowd which gathered at Carterhaugh began arriving on the Sunday night before kick-off. Scott was delighted and surprised at how popular the event was proving to be. 'We had not reckoned on half the numbers that came and found grave difficulty in settling which should play on each side. Selkirk and Yarrow were the districts named but all the other dalesmen joined in.'

The Hawick contingent arrived in high spirits and a contemporary account records the nature of their preparations.

The Drums and Fifes paraded the streets early in the morning, arousing those who intended to enter the lists. A large muster was quickly made up under the leadership of Rob Reid, thereupon and ever after known as General Reid. At Haining Wood they stuck in the fir twig and marched green and grand to the residence of Bailie Clarkson, who asked 'Who commands these men and where are they from?'

'It's me and we're thrae Hawick,' was the prompt and emphatic reply of Reid. 'Then,' said the lieutenant of the Souters, 'I don't give o' my thumb for a' Ettrick and Yarrow.'

Bailie Clarkson entertained the Hawick men to a drop of the 'mountain dew' and the Selkirk Burgh accounts for 1815 contain the entry: 'paid to George Young for whisky for Hawick football players, £1 11s 4d.' It is reckoned that such a sum in those days would have purchased over two gallons of whisky.

The Carterhaugh Ba' Game was a notable talking point not just in the Borders but also further afield. The *Edinburgh Journal* carried an account of the proceedings, the author of which was suspected to have been Scott himself. As we shall soon see, he was not an altogether truthful, or accurate, correspondent.

The appearance of the various parties marching from their different glens to the place of rendezvous, with pipes playing and loud acclamations, carried back to the coldest imagination to the old times when the [Ettrick] Foresters assembled with the less peaceable purpose of invading the English territory, or defending their own. The romantic character of the scenery aided this illusion, as well as the performance of a feudal ceremony previous to commencing the games.

The feudal ceremony to which Scott, if indeed he was the writer, alluded was the rather contrived entrance on horseback of young Walter – dressed in forest green and buff, with a green bonnet complete with eagle feather and a gold chain and medallion around his neck – prior to receiving the Bellendaine Banner from Lady Anne Scott, a daughter of the Duke.

Young Walter of Abbotsford, who was then 14 years old and, like his father before him, a pupil at the High School of Edinburgh, paraded the banner before the crowd, some of whom reacted rather scornfully and irreverently. Nevertheless, Sir Walter was happy and his biographer J.G. Lockhart recorded that the Shirra would rather have seen his heir carry the Banner of Bellendaine gallantly at a football match at Carterhaugh than hear that he had attained the highest honour from the first university in Europe.

Sir Walter was a great man for traditions – even if he had to invent them himself. Next, the crowd of many thousands were issued with a pamphlet, entitled 'The Ettrick Garland', in which were printed the words of the songs composed for the occasion by Scott and Hogg, and soon it was time for the proceedings to get underway.

The Duke of Buccleuch started the first game by throwing the ball into the air in the centre of the field. The two sides – and contemporary accounts put the total number of players at 750 – rushed together and the field was engulfed in a sweating mass of heaving bodies. For a long time the game was locked in stalemate.

The *Hawick Archaeological Society Transactions* of 1863, quoting the reminiscences of a local minister, the Rev. Henry Scott Riddell, provide an eyewitness account of what happened next.

The state of the game at length was altered by two of the Yarrow men, considered among the best runners of the district – Walter Laidlaw, younger, of the Gair on Tema, and William Riddell, shepherd at Bellendean. Having watched for an opportunity, Laidlaw, according to agreement, lifted the ball and threw it to Riddell, who . . . immediately sped off with it towards the only open space – the woods of Bowhill – intending, by eluding his pursuers and making a circuit, to carry it eventually to the opposite hail. That, his fleetness might have enabled him to accomplish but that he was pursued and ridden over by a farmer on horseback who no doubt thought he was performing a commendable deed, although nothing could exceed the wrath and fury of the Yarrow contingent at his conduct.

The voices of many farmers . . . assailed the Earl of Home, asking if horses were to be allowed, signifying that they were as ready and willing to play the game on horseback as in any other way. Lord Home, with an oath, replied that if he had a gun, he would shoot the perpetrator of the deed, and that unfortunate interferer, suddenly convinced of the state of feeling towards him, left the field at full gallop amid a volley of stones and other missiles.

The initiative was then gained by the Souters and Robert Hall, a Selkirk mason reckoned to be one of the strongest men on the field, gained possession of the ball and rushed into the River Ettrick to win the first game for the townies. The hail was disputed by the Earl of Home, who considered that a foul had taken place and that the game should be replayed. It had taken the Souters nigh on 90 minutes to make the first hail and they were having none of it. Jamie Inglis, sheriff officer of Selkirk and convener of the town's trades guild, warned the Earl that if the hail was not allowed to stand, then he would take his tradesmen off the field and the match would be over. The noble lord bowed to trade union power and, after a suitable break for refreshments, the participants made ready for the second game.

But before Buccleuch could throw the ball into the air, the Galashiels contingent suddenly changed sides. The defection of the Braw Lads – who had a particularly useful tradition of playing hand ba' and were no mean exponents of the game – caused consternation. The Souters of Selkirk and the Teries from Hawick were incensed. The specific reason for the change in allegiance of the Gala men has been lost in time but it is reckoned that during the interval one of the Buccleuch daughters had expressed disappointment at the outcome of the first game and Sir Walter and the local Laird of Torwoodlee had each played a part in persuading the Braw Lads to desert their recent allies. The switch made for an even more closely contested game. The Gala men gave the Shepherds a more than useful advantage and after three hours they equalised with a hail by George Brodie from Greatlaws, upon Ale Water.

Sir Walter and Buccleuch immediately set in hand preparations for a third game, but the Selkirk and Hawick men considered that the Braw Lads had behaved extremely disgracefully and refused to have anything further to do with them. Sir Walter, obviously deciding that discretion was the better part of valour, threw his hat in the air and challenged the Shepherds to a deciding match which was to be played between Christmas and New Year. The Shepherds' captain, the Earl of Home, accepted; but before the arrangements could be made, he was called back to his regiment and the game never took place.

It was just as well. Feelings were running high in Selkirk that night. The Gala men were not flavour of the month and according to contemporary reports the Souters 'wreaked their vengeance on such stragglers from the Galashiels contingent as fell into their hands.' It seemed that all of Sir Walter's best laid plans were gang aglay.

> On one hand there could be seen stalwart country men waging an unequal contest with equally stout and more numerous natives of the burgh town. In another part of the field men were flying for their lives and many a rush was made into the Yarrow after opponents, which generally terminated into a complete ducking, and not seldom a broken head into the bargain, while stones were flying in all directions and causing the more peaceably disposed to retire to a respectful distance from the strife. The blood of both parties was fairly up, and it was well when darkness put an end to a most unseemly contest.

Sir Walter himself did not escape the wrath of the outraged Souters. As his carriage left for Abbotsford that night it was surrounded by a large and angry crowd in the Market Square, just in front of his very own courthouse. He listened patiently to their complaints and managed to soothe their ire, eventually winning them over by producing two guineas which, he said, were to be used for refreshment purposes.

However, no record of these angry and unseemly scenes found its way into the *Edinburgh Journal*'s report of the Carterhaugh Ba' Game. Bear in mind that Sir Walter was reckoned to be the journal's correspondent and contrast the account deemed suitable for the eyes of the city gentry with what really took place.

It was impossible to see a finer set of active and athletic young fellows than appeared on the field. But what we chiefly admired in their conduct was that, though several hundreds in number, exceedingly keen for their respective parties, and engaged in so rough and animated a contest, they maintained the most perfect good humour, and showed how unnecessary it is to discourage manly and athletic exercises among the common people under the pretext of maintaining subordination and good order.

No doubt Sir Walter was keen that his metropolitan friends and colleagues got no hint of what he got up to when he traded life in Edinburgh for the bucolic existence in the Borders. His life was compartmentalised to an extraordinary degree. He was a lawyer by profession, an advocate and sheriff of Selkirk. He was, even at the time of the Carterhaugh match, a literary lion – the Wizard of the North – whose epic poems had taken Europe by storm. He was a townsman, with a handsome dwelling in Edinburgh, and a would-be Border laird, with a baronial-style pile at Abbotsford, on the Tweed near Galashiels. He was also what we would term nowadays a workaholic. His literary output was prodigious and he became a rich man on the strength of his penmanship. It was also the source of his undoing. He became insolvent in 1826 after the financial collapse of his printers and publishers. Thereafter, with the ever-present threat of losing everything, Sir Walter set himself the task of writing his way out of debt. Future literary earnings went to his creditors and, eventually, the effort killed him. He died in 1832 at what for the time was the relatively respectable age of 61.

However, returning once again to the theme of our quest. Walter Scott had been a pupil at the High School of Edinburgh, which had existed since 1578 on a site in what is now Infirmary Street. That the High School scholars played football there is no doubt; they did so on the nearby School Yards and there is hearsay evidence that from 1810 or thereabouts there was already in existence a form of football which owed more to the handling than the kicking code. The High School of Edinburgh had been founded elsewhere in the city in 1128, making it one of the oldest established, and still existing, educational establishments in the British Isles. It moved from its site in The Pleasance to the neoclassical building on Calton Hill in 1829 and again in 1969 to its present location in Barnton.

Sir Walter was a pupil at the school between 1779 and 1783. Because of his physical disability which was a legacy of his infantile paralysis, he was never much of a sportsman but would, no doubt, have been perfectly aware of the ball games played on the School Yards. In addition, his son followed him to the High School and, by then, we are well into the era where the pupils were said to be playing a form of hand ball on the Yards. Scott's knowledge of the numerous Border hand ba' games allied to what was going on at his old school, may well have played a role in determining the nature of events at Carterhaugh.

Who knows? It is interesting to speculate

nonetheless. But Sir Walter's links – tenuous or not – with the development of what became rugby football in Scotland do not end there.

Another seat of learning in Scotland's capital city – Edinburgh Academy – can, with the Royal High School, genuinely be said to have been in the vanguard of the movement which established rugby union football north of the Border. The Academy was founded in 1823 by a group of former High School pupils who considered that their alma mater was not the place it had been in their day. The founding fathers included Lord Cockburn, James Skene of Rubislaw – and Sir Walter Scott, lawyer, author, self-styled Laird of Abbotsford and organiser of the grandest football match the world had ever seen.

THREE

Muscular Christianity

The public school games cult

The Carterhaugh Ba' Game, which took place in 1815 – the year that Napoleon finally met his Nemesis in the form of the Iron Duke at Waterloo, was just a single, early symbol of the new vogue for organised games-playing which was about to sweep Great Britain. Did not the Duke of Wellington attribute his victory over Bonaparte to the forging of character accomplished on the playing fields of Eton? He was referring, of course, to his officer corps; his army he compared to the scum of the earth.

The nineteenth century encompassed a period of unparallelled change in Britain, which was set to become the most powerful imperial power that the world had ever seen. Truly, the nation of shopkeepers as Napoleon dubbed Britain, was about to establish an Empire on which the sun never set. It was the epoch of the industrial revolution, the age of the railways and an era in which, for the first time in history, more people lived in towns than in the countryside. By the time that Princess Victoria succeeded King William IV in 1837 the stage had been set for Britannia to rule the waves.

For the first time a prosperous middle-class began to make its presence felt. Trade was no longer the dirty word it had been when leaders were born, not made. Victorian Britain was by no means an egalitarian society – very far from it – but the scions of the emergent mercantile, middle-classes were becoming a force to be reckoned with; their appearance on the scene was accompanied by a boom in a new educational phenomenon, the public boarding school where the new juvenile meritocracy were sent to be fashioned into gentlemen.

For virtually the first time in history – ecclesiastical, monastic, military and penal life notwithstanding – herds of fit, young men, with a surfeit of leisure time, were domiciled together for months on end during which the devil could well find work for idle hands to do. It is no wonder, then, that very soon a games cult enveloped these Victorian educational establishments. The fashion for organised games began with the boys – the masters had very little to do with it. However, as the diversion of games kept the boys from engaging in more illicit and unsavoury pursuits such as poaching – which was a very real problem in the early days of the public school system – they played their ball games with the wholehearted blessing of headmasters and teaching staff.

A Big-Side at Rugby School. The game which took the name of the school undoubtedly has its roots there. However, the claim that it emerged in a single defining moment when William Webb Ellis ran forward with the ball in his hands is a much more controversial proposition.

The wheel had turned full circle. Football, which the Establishment had sought to ban for nigh on 500 years, was suddenly respectable. A pastime which hitherto had been the province of the lower orders was embraced with a vengeance by the new, upwardly mobile mercantile class and its offspring.

At Eton, Winchester, Harrow, Charter-house, Marlborough, Shrewsbury, Westminster, Rugby and so on, and so on, ball games developed and were nurtured; each was as individual in character as that of the schools in which they were played and each was jealously defended as being the one true footballing game. Rules were formulated by the boys and, because inter-school contests were unheard of,

each game prospered in isolation.

In Scotland, or so we are told, the Royal High School in Edinburgh was playing its own particular brand of the handling code in the School Yards around the year 1810. At Edinburgh Academy, for certain, they were playing football 'in the primitive Scottish fashion' in the 1820s. In the early 1840s there still existed 'a game of the most primitive kind; crude and devoid of regulation and rule . . . the most cruel hacking with iron-toed and heeled boots was allowed and suffered in what was called a muddle, the ball being composed of a raw bladder, fresh from the butcher's hands, and enclosed in a leather case.' Football, in its myriad forms and applications, was here to stay. It had won acceptance from the

movers and shakers of Victorian society and, by process of dissimilation and distillation, it would evolve into the game that we know today.

The brand of football played at Rugby School proved to be the most virile and enduring. The Rugby Rules were those which gained common currency because Old Rugbeians were the most dogged propagators of the game they had known and loved at school. The ascendancy of the Rugby Rules, in a kind of ball-playing process of natural selection owes nothing whatever to the William Webb Ellis myth. As I have said already, Ellis was an impostor. He was not the 'inventor' of rugby union football or anything like it. His 'running with the ball' misdeed of

1823 went virtually unremarked at the time and it was another 20-odd years, even at Rugby School, before handling became even remotely acceptable. The codification of the game, which is when, effectively, the school gave its name to the game we know today, did not occur until the first set of printed rules emanated from the school in 1846. At that point there was no mention of Ellis as having been the one and only true begetter of the game. It was not until almost the turn of the century before the William Webb Ellis myth grew like Topsy and it is a fallacy which Rugby School has had to live with ever since. The real sadness is that Rugby's place in the conception, nurturing and rearing of the game was, and is, safe. The school had no need of a mythological creation to cement its position at the forefront of the game's development. In fairness, that was never the intention of those who by their actions gave birth to the myth. But born it was and myth it is still.

The genesis of the William Webb Ellis myth is to be found in an attempt by an Old Rugbeian, Matthew Bloxham, to correct an earlier published account which declared that the handling game had found early acceptance at the school. This account suggested that the handling game had taken root at Rugby because that school, contrary to the case elsewhere, had long possessed a wide, open, grass play-ground of ample dimensions. Hence, declared the author of the erroneous account, Montague Sherman, the original game had survived almost in its primitive shape.

Bloxham, a solicitor and antiquarian in the town of Rugby, maintained that, until he left the school in 1821, football and not handball was the pupils' game of choice. Even in the 1870s the debate was raging as to the origins of the game and, in reply to a declaration that the Rugby game was of great and unknown antiquity, Bloxham wrote to the *Meteor*, the Rugby School magazine, in which first mention was made of William Webb Ellis. That was in 1876. The controversy has raged ever since.

Bloxham, whose brothers had also attended the school, and probably were contemporaries of Webb Ellis, declared that the first recorded switch from a kicking to a handling game had occurred in 1823, and that he had ascertained it had originated with a Town boy or Foundationer by the name of William Webb Ellis. It must have been in the second half of 1823 says Bloxham, that the change from the former system, in which the football was not allowed to be taken up and run with, commenced.

Now, the cat had well and truly been set among the pigeons. Eventually, a committee of Old Rugbeians conducted an inquiry into the origins of the handling game at the school and the part that Ellis might have played. They sought written evidence from a number of Old Boys and, having considered the evidence, published their conclusion in the form of a pamphlet in 1897.

> That at some date between 1820 and 1830 the innovation was introduced of running with the ball and that was, in all probability, done in the latter half of 1823 by Mr W. Webb Ellis. To this we would add that the innovation was regarded as of doubtful legality for some time, and only gradually became accepted as part of the game but obtained customary status between 1830 and 1840 and was duly legalized first in 1841-42.

Jennifer Macrory, a former archivist of Rugby School, in her excellent book *Running with the Ball: The birth of rugby football*, points out that it had never been the intention of the Old Rugbeian Society to lionise Ellis. In fact, she writes, he was more anti-hero than hero. Macrory was able to access the Rugby School archives to first-rate effect and her 1991 publication remains the foremost account of the role played by Rugby School in the birth and development of the game.

The main objective in publishing their report had been to correct Montagu Sherman's mistake in suggesting that the Rugby game was the lone example of 'primitive' football surviving in a school. This done, the report attempted to provide some account of how the carrying game developed. In seeking corroboration for the Webb Ellis story, the committee were prompted by no more sinister a motive than a desire to expand their knowledge of the matter through the recollections of contemporary witnesses, while there were still one or two alive to consult.

The big mistake made by the Old Rugbeian Society was in the wording of the plaque which they decided to erect on the Close in 1900 to pronounce their understandable pride in the game which had developed there. They intended to celebrate the game, but instead created a myth.

The popular history of Rugby Football was written in 1900, quite literally in a tablet of stone. The report of the committee carefully noting the gradual acceptance of the carrying game was forgotten and the 'Big Bang' story was born.

THIS STONE
COMMEMORATES THE EXPLOIT
OF
WILLIAM WEBB ELLIS
WHO WITH A FINE DISREGARD
FOR THE RULES OF FOOTBALL
AS PLAYED IN HIS TIME
FIRST TOOK THE BALL IN HIS
ARMS AND RAN WITH IT
THUS ORIGINATING THE
DISTINCTIVE FEATURE OF
THE RUGBY GAME
AD 1823

The birth of the game, and Rugby School's role as midwife, had already been given a boost by the publication in 1851 of the hugely popular *Tom Brown's Schooldays* by Thomas Hughes. The author had based the book on his own days at the school which began in 1834, and he had been one of those called to give evidence by the Old Rugbeians committee of inquiry. Hughes was disinclined to believe that running with the ball in an effort to score was accepted practice in his day. In *Tom Brown's Schooldays* however, we are provided with an extended and evocative account of a Big Side game at Rugby. That work of fiction, which was a massive bestseller when it was first published, and which has remained popular to this day, brought the day-in, day-out life of the public schools — warts and all — to a widespread readership. Undoubtedly, it informed a wider audience of the fact that a games cult revolution was underway in the great public schools. That revolution was underway in Scotland, too, where the leading revolutionary was the magnificently monikered Hely Hutchinson Almond. He has a starring role to play in the development of the Scottish game and deserves a chapter to himself.

FOUR

Visionary, Rebel and Reformer

Hely Hutchinson Almond

Hely Hutchinson Almond was born in Glasgow on 12 August 1832. He was the second son of George Almond, incumbent of St Mary's Episcopal Chapel in the city, and he was precociously clever. He began to read at the age of 16 months and was poring over his multiplication tables by the time he was three.

He attended the collegiate school in Glasgow and in 1845 entered Glasgow University. He distinguished himself in Greek, Latin, mathematics and logic, and in 1850 he won a Snell Exhibition which took him to Balliol College, Oxford. In 1853 he obtained a first-class degree in classical and mathematical moderations and graduated with an MA in 1855. He had also shown athletic prowess and won a place in the Balliol rowing eight. However, and despite his all-round success, he was not much enamoured of his undergraduate days and could not leave Oxford soon enough.

His original intention had been to join the Indian civil service but he failed to gain entry; while in Torquay, where his father was living in retirement, he was encouraged by a friend to assist him in his tutorial establishment. The civil service's loss was education's gain. Almond had found his true vocation. In 1857 he accepted the offer of a teaching post at Loretto School in Musselburgh where three brothers, Charles, Thomas and Alexander Langhorne – Charles was an Oxford contemporary – were running a tutorial establishment which at that time was, merely, a preparatory for the English public schools.

Hely Hutchinson Almond, headmaster of Loretto School, was a hugely significant figure in the development of the Scottish game. He was a rebel, a visionary and a reformer who brought the ethos of muscular Christianity to the shores of the Forth at Musselburgh and turned his small school into one of the leading rugby establishments of its day.

Loretto School, which Almond purchased in 1862.

Almond remained at Loretto for a year before moving to Merchiston Castle School in Edinburgh as second master. Both schools would be at the forefront of rugby in Scotland. In 1862 Almond purchased Loretto and he set about implementing the ideal of muscular Christianity pioneered in England by the likes of Dr Thomas Arnold at Rugby, and G.E.F. Cotton at Marlborough.

The co-existence of academic learning and regular physical exercise was the foundation upon which Almond set about building the reputation of Loretto. He began with only 14 boys and one of the first steps he took along the road to achieving what he termed his 'science of health' was to acquire for the school a playing-field at Pinkie Mains. There, as much as in the classroom, he pursued the five ideals by which he believed he could turn out a properly rounded boy – character, physique, intelligence, manners and information.

The game-playing ethos of his school was simple. He wanted team games which built camaraderie and team spirit.

Games in which success depends on the united efforts of many, and which also foster courage and endurance, are the very life-blood of the public school system. And all the more self-indulgent games or pursuits contain within themselves an element of danger to school patriotism and might, if they permanently injured the patriotic games, cause public schools to fail in their main object, which we take to be the production of a grand breed of men for the service of the British nation.

Football and cricket fitted the Almond bill. Golf, presumably, he would have dismissed as self-indulgent and dangerous.

Almond pursued his idiosyncratic Lorretonianism with unflagging vigour and uncommon zeal. He was a man ahead of his time. He prescribed fresh air and exercise as a cure for virtually every ailment known to mankind. Fresh air, personal cleanliness, proper and regular diet, plenty of sleep and exercise, exercise, exercise were his watchwords. He did away with linen shirts with collars, and suits of close material for everyday schoolwear. He favoured tweed knickerbocker suits of loose texture and flannel shirts worn open at the neck without neckties. He pioneered the appearance of today's athlete with particular clothes worn especially for the sporting occasion and, in terms of physical well-being nurturing psychological and academic contentment and attainment, he was many decades ahead of his time. Almond was implementing a Fit for Life campaign at Loretto almost a century before the government sought to improve the health of the general population with something not entirely dissimilar.

Although he was exceedingly bright, Almond was essentially an anti-intellectual. His Loretto boys never skimped on the book-learning side of their schooling, but he brought to Musselburgh the attitudes of the dons he had encountered at Oxford, who believed that sport – rowing, football and cricket – were as much a part of the educational experience as the hours spent in the classroom or lecture theatre. The prevailing view among the Scottish educational establishment at the time was that sport was a childish pastime and a distraction from the serious business of education. Sport was to be tolerated but not encouraged. By contrast, Almond encouraged sport, and rugby football in particular, with a vengeance.

Although he passed on to the great playing field in the sky nigh on a century ago, Almond's guiding credo survives in the form of a lengthy article 'Rugby Football in Scottish Schools' which is included in a seminal work entitled *Football: the Rugby Union game*, edited by the Rev F.P. Marshall and published in 1892. Today we must be grateful that Almond proved incapable of sticking to his editorial brief. As well as a detailed summary of the game in Scotland, and Scottish schools, in the last decade of the nineteenth century Almond provides a first-hand testimony of the regime which he was implementing at Loretto.

> It has come to be understood, even by the smallest boys, that a place in any of the teams cannot usually be gained without a good deal of trouble and self-denial. Small schools also become aware that they cannot hope for football eminence unless they bring not only a select few but the whole mass of their boys into the fittest possible condition. The desire to do this, therefore, gives rise to sanitary rules of various kinds. Regular exercise in all weathers is insisted upon; boys are encouraged to sleep with open windows and schoolrooms are kept fresh and airy. And perhaps above all, the importance of a proper dietary [regime] becomes evident; and the detestable and loathsome habit of 'grubbing' all sorts of unwholesomes, even between meals, becomes warred against not only by masters, but by prefects and public opinion.

> Why so many public schoolmasters permit unlimited 'grubbing,' and yet regard the less injurious vice of smoking as one of the gravest of school offences, is more than I can comprehend. I think also that it is becoming evident to the more far-sighted men in my own profession, that attention to matters of this kind produces benefits of a higher order than any football excellence. And this very fact serves to strengthen and perpetuate the foundations on which really good school football rests. On the indirect bearing of all this upon school morality I need scarcely enlarge to all who know anything about schools.

Elsewhere in his treatise Almond pays specific attention to the role that schools have played in the development of the game. He considered that he was fighting a personal crusade against sloth and indolence. Football – and at Loretto they played to the Rugby School rules right from the outset – was his principal strike weapon in this struggle to keep the nation from degeneracy and decay.

> The schools are the nurseries of the game; it began with them; it is, perhaps, under all modern circumstances their best instrument of education in the true and wide sense of the word; for I cannot conceive of any school making a good stand-up fight against the soft and self-indulgent ways of living in which town boys, at all events of the richer classes, are usually brought up, in which football is not a flourishing institution; nor is the Association game a possible refuge for the Scotch schools. We are all Rugby, and Rugby, I hope, we shall remain; for the defect of the Association game is that it gives no exercise for the upper limbs and thereby does not tend to the strengthening of the

lungs, and the equal development of both sides of the person, as the Rugby game does.

A word or two ought to be said as to the organisation of football in a school. As it is obvious that the available players are not likely to be an exact multiple of thirty, there ought to be considerable elasticity, on the lower sides at least, as to the numbers playing on a side. The best practical plan for ordinary sides, as distinct from school matches, is to divide the number of available players into a number of nearly equal sides 'Big Side' being the smallest and having about 34 on its list. Two boys should be made heads of each side and great care should be taken in their selection – knowledge of the game, and power of enforcing orders and obedience being the most necessary qualities.

They should have printed school lists, with the boys on their sides ticked off, and either the medical officer or some other competent master should look through these lists to see that no boy is placed on a side for which he is too small or too delicate. It is easy for the captains to arrange exchanges, or to let boys who can be spared off to play fives or take some other exercise . . . A certain number of 'crocks' or 'slackers' are a necessary evil; but if not looked after they constitute a great source of danger.

They are far more liable than football players to take any epidemic, and they are apt to get into lounging, lethargic habits, which are also a most infectious malady if the 'crock' or 'loafer' is unfortunately a boy of any influence.

Great care should be taken that no favouritism is shown in choosing the school teams. My experience is that it is easy to show boys what a dishonest thing it is to use any public office, such as that of captain of a team, for private purposes; and surely any headmaster or school chaplain who gives his boys anything worth calling religious teaching, will speak often and strongly about the right use of responsibility of any kind.

Certainly, to take the lowest ground, the excellence of school football greatly hinges on the certainty felt by every boy that he will get absolutely fair play, and that any mistake made about him will be one of judgement. One cannot aim at too high a standard of school morality in such matters.

Another very important point is that of referees at sides. Masters who know the game will of course help in this way, and where the cricket professional resides, refereeing should be part of his duties. Members of the XV also, who are temporarily 'crocked' should, if capable, be sent to referee, and at the same time to coach the lower sides.

Much more, however, may be done to prevent 'crocking' than is usually supposed. The most common cause of it is that a boy gets a slight sprain or twist about the knee or ankle, hobbles home with it, and thinks little more about it till the next morning, when the joint has swollen and water probably set in. He should have been carried home and then immediately had the place fomented with water rather hotter than he can bear; he should then lay up until seen by the medical officer. About two-thirds of the ordinary sprains will be arrested at once if treated in this way. Boys should, of course, be frequently spoken to about these and kindred matters. They are a most important, but too often neglected, part of their education.

Lastly, no idle spectators should be allowed to stand looking on at school sides. The very sight of loungers takes the spirit out of players, and the loungers should be doing something else if they are too feeble for football. 'Spectating' generally is, in fact, the greatest of all football dangers. When boys are allowed to look on at a big match they should all be sent a run of a couple of miles afterwards to quicken their circulations and to prevent that deadliest of dangers – ' a chill'.

The first recorded official match against Merchiston took place in 1867. Loretto lost by three goals and five tries to a solitary goal. Almond – who continued to play alongside his pupils until a ripe old age – kicked the goal.

Almond's influence on the Scottish game extended to a much wider constituency than his school at Loretto. He was instrumental in the emergence of rugby from the schools into the community at large. He was, too, an umpire in the first international match, between Scotland and England, at Raeburn Place in 1871.

In addition, he is credited with 'inventing' – although as we have seen with William Webb Ellis that is a dangerous noose to hang around the neck of any man – the passing game. He encouraged his boys to pass the ball in order to 'baffle the opposition' at a time when a player would normally run until 'collared'. It was a tactic which did not meet with general approval as, in some quarters, it was considered 'unmanly' to get rid of the ball until the inevitable tackle, or hacking-over, had occurred. A contemporary had this to say about the Lorettonian innovation of passing the ball:

If by the modern game is meant the present fast, open game with its quick passing, kicking and breaking up, I am inclined to think that Dr Almond was perhaps the real inventor. At any rate, most Lorettonians who were at school in the latter '70s and early '80s have vivid recollections of Almond, in his quintuple capacity as headmaster, captain, forward, umpire and coach, rushing about the field crying out to his boys 'Pass, pass, pass' and 'Kick, kick, kick' and there can be no doubt whatever that much of the

The Oxford University XV of 1884 which contained seven former pupils of Loretto.

phenomenal success of the Oxford teams of the early '80s was due to the Old Lorettonians in those teams.

Certainly, under Almond's influence, Lorettonians were making quite a name for themselves in the rugby world. In the autumn of 1880 six Lorettonians were at Oxford, five of them gaining their Blues against Cambridge. In 1881 and 1882 four Lorettonians were in the team. In 1883 there were five and the following year seven played in the Varsity match. Almond's disciples had transferred the passing game to Oxford. That 'magnificent seven' accomplishment of 1884 is a record for the largest-ever number of players from a single school to play in a Blues match. Almond's strictures, too, on dressing properly for the game made their mark at Oxford. Under Lorettonian influence the Oxford XV abandoned knickerbockers for shorts. Simultaneously, but not to the same amazing extent, Loretto former pupils were making inroads into the Cambridge XV and between 1879 and 1907 there was not a Varsity match played without a former pupil from the small Musselburgh school present.

Almond's adherence to a strict regime of rigorous and regular exercise stood him in good stead. He remained for much of his life an active participant in the sporting regime at the school which so reflected his pioneering personality. He had, though, achieved the biblical span of three-score years and ten at a time when life expectancy was nowhere near what it is today. Nevertheless, time and tide stand still for no man and in the last few years of his life he suffered from failing health. Hely Hutchinson Almond died of a bronchial infection on 7 March 1903. He is buried at Inveresk churchyard.

A cartoon which appeared in the Public Schools magazine, under the heading Triumph of Loretto, depicting the two Lorettonian captains of Oxford and Cambridge universities meeting before the 1900 'Varsity match.

Almond, who espoused the cause of open-neck shirts and sensible clothing for sport, is seen here in old-age with Loretto's head-boy of 1901 Sandy O'Neill.

FIVE

A Great and Noble Winter Game

The Crombie brothers arrive in Edinburgh

Hely Hutchinson Almond and his Lorretonians may well have been in the vanguard of the rugby revolution which swept Scotland in the latter years of the nineteenth century but they were merely tending seeds which had been sown some 50 years earlier by another great Scottish educational establishment. The names of Edinburgh Academy and the Crombie brothers, Alexander and Francis, are linked for ever as the institution and the personalities credited with bringing the game, codified under the terms of the Rugby School rules, to Scotland.

In his 1892 exposition on the game as played in Scottish schools, Almond declares that the elder of the brothers, Alexander, was the founding father of the game in Scotland.

So far as I know, Rugby football was introduced into Scotland in 1855 by a small knot of men connected with the Edinburgh Academy. Mr. Alexander Crombie, of Thornton Castle, may fairly be said to be the father of the game in Scotland, for he was the chairman and organiser of the club. The hon. secretary was Mr William Blackwood, the well-known publisher.

The brothers, whose family hailed from Kincardine, had arrived in Edinburgh from Durham Grammar School – where the game was already established – in 1854 and Francis, then 16, had enrolled as a scholar at the Academy. Francis became the first recorded captain of the school side a year later while Alexander fulfilled a similar function with the former pupils club, a post he was to hold for eight years. More than a century later the family association with the game was preserved in fitting manner when young Alex Crombie, the great-grandson of the Rev. Francis Crombie, played a prominent part in the nationwide relay which preceded the 1991 World Cup.

The Academical Football Club – the oldest in Scotland and, along with Blackheath, Guy's Hospital and Trinity College, Dublin, the longest established in the world – was officially founded in 1858 at a meeting in the accountancy offices of Robert Balfour CA at 21 St Andrew Square in Edinburgh. The exact date is not known, but it was certainly in the January of that year that the first general meeting took place although actual play had commenced before the turn of the year. At its formation, the Academical FC – note the absence of Edinburgh, because there were no

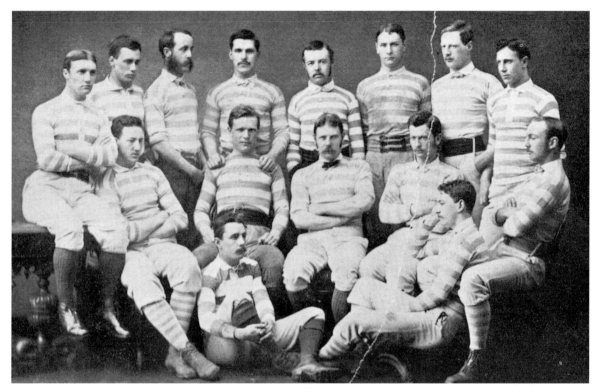

Edinburgh Academy and the Academical Football Club are indelibly linked with the development of the game in Scotland. The Academical XV of 1878-79 contained a host of 'weel kent' faces who would make their mark with the national side. Back row – G.W.L. McLeod, C.E. Wood, J.P. Bannerman, N.J. Finlay, L.J. Aitken, E. Ross Smith, T.W. Tod, P. Russel. Middle row – W.E. Maclagan, R.W. Irvine, J.H.S. Graham (captain), D.R. Irvine, P.W. Smeaton. Front row – G.Q. Paterson, J. Younger.

rivals of the same name and the absence, too, of RFC because at that time the rift between Association and Rugby football had not yet occurred – was intended for the enjoyment of present and former pupils of the school.

Although the Crombies brought with them from Durham the Rugby School rules, as we have already seen, football was already a regular pastime for the young Academicals as this account from J.H.A. Macdonald (later Lord Kingsburgh), whom we have already met as the gateman at the first International match in 1871, confirms. Macdonald was a pupil at the school from 1846 to 1852.

[The first rector of the school, Archdeacon Williams] was a kindly man and popular with us all. He kept up the dignity of his office, but being no prig, I have seen him when crossing the yards, if a football came towards him – which happened probably by intention – run his two or three paces towards it, and with a smile on his face, put all the momentum of his ponderous form into his kick, drawing a cheer from all in sight. [Football at that time] was not a game of much elaboration, but it was vigorously engaged in and enjoyed.

The arrival of the Rugby Rules at the Academy acted like a pebble cast into a pond. The ripples lapped outwards and onwards. Other schools liked what they saw and the game began to achieve widespread acceptance. Almond gives a graphic illustration of the problems which beset those seeking to legislate the new game and the manner in which it took off in popularity.

Very slowly the game spread. There was a kind of mongrel 'Rugby' at Merchiston in 1858. Some of the rules were very funny. 'Off-side' was voted 'rot'; but if a player lay on the ground with the ball, no one might touch him till he chose to move. A closer conformity to the game was, however, enforced by an approaching match with the Edinburgh Academy; but so little did any of us, masters or boys, then know about it, that I remember how, when Lyall ran with the ball behind the Merchiston goal, the resulting try was appealed against on the ground that no player might cross the line while holding the ball. The previous rule at Merchiston had been that he must let go of the ball and kick it over before he touched it down. It must be said in excuse for this and other similar sins of ignorance, that the only available rules were those printed for the use of Rugby School [1846]. They were very incomplete, and presupposed a practical knowledge of the game.

Gradually, however, the game approached, with local variations and resulting disputes, to that then played at Rugby. Clubs were formed in the West of Scotland, at the Scotch universities, and at various schools, but for a long time, in fact until well on in the 'seventies', the only schools able to play each other on even terms were the Edinburgh Academy and Merchiston, and occasionally the Royal High School.

So far as I am aware, the first attempt anywhere made at concerted action was the meeting of a committee of three schools in Edinburgh [1868] to codify the rules. The 'Green Book' which was the result of our deliberations, was assented to by the other then existing Scotch clubs.

Edinburgh Academy had set a trend which was to be followed by day schools all over the country when, in 1854, it had acquired for sporting purposes a plot of land at Raeburn Place. The two men who were instrumental in the school setting out upon this pioneering route were the then Rector, the Rev. John Hannah (later to become warden of Trinity College, Glenalmond), and the aforementioned Robert Balfour. The decision to acquire a plot of land on which boys could exercise their bodies as well as their minds was in keeping with the mores of the period whereby educationalists were paying more heed than ever before to the requirements of a properly rounded schooling.

The quest for the plot of land which was to achieve eternal fame as the location of the world's first rugby international appears in the record books as a minute from an Academical Club committee meeting of 18 April 1853. The meeting was convened in Balfour's St Andrew Square offices.

Mr Balfour (secy) reported that he had summoned this meeting in consequence of a letter which he had received from the Rector of the Academy who was anxious to secure a field for the use of the pupils for cricket and should wish to know whether the club would be disposed to aid in accomplishing this object. After some conversation the committee were of the opinion that the object was a desirable one and that they should aid the Rector, and a subcommittee was appointed.

Balfour was obviously not a man to hang around because just ten days later the committee had reconvened and the minutes reported that Raeburn Place had been identified as the location which best suited the needs of the school.

The committee appointed at the last meeting had waited upon the Rector as regards the cricket field, that along with a committee of masters and pupils various fields had been examined, that the most suitable appeared to be a field on the Estate of Inverleith immediately behind Raeburn Place which extended to ten Imperial acres, the rent being £53 17s 6d, and that from enquiries made at the present tenant, and at the agent for the proprietor, it appeared not improbable that arrangements might be made for getting immediate entry, and for a lease for several years.

The deal was done by August 1853, and the minutes from the Academical Club annual general meeting for that year record:

After an examination of the different fields in the vicinity of the Academy, one of them, situated between Comely Bank and Stockbridge and within a few minutes walk of the school, seemed so suitable that, although considerably larger than was required, a lease of it was taken for six years. About six acres were set apart for a cricket field and the remainder was sub-let. Being sensible of having the cricket field in the most excellent order possible, it was carefully levelled, cleaned, fenced and resown with grass, a portion in the centre being laid down with turf for bowling. Although these operations were conducted at some disadvantage owing to the advanced season of the year at which they were commenced . . . the field was ready to play this summer [1854], having been opened on 17 May.

No doubt the school's cricketing fraternity viewed with horror the prospect of their newly re-sown field and carefully laid wicket being trampled upon by 'muddied oafs' during the winter months, but it was not long before Raeburn Place was the scene of all-year-round sporting activity by both present and past pupils of the Academy. It seems, too, that the composition of the Academical FC was not confined to Old Boys and pupils rubbed along contentedly with those who had quit school for university and employment. It is interesting to note, by way of an aside, that Alexander 'Joe' Crombie, the first captain of Academical rugby, had never been a pupil at the school. He qualified, presumably, because he knew the rules and because his younger brother was on the Academy roll. However, once again, we are indebted to Lord Kingsburgh for a first-hand account of footballing activities, and in particular the changing facilities, at Raeburn Place in the middle years of the nineteenth century.

[We changed] in a small loft over an outhouse in the garden of a villa in the corner of the field, approached by a wooden ladder . . . no basins, no lockers . . . the only thing we could do after we had played our match (we came out quite as dirty as you do now) was to go up into that loft and smoke until it was sufficiently dark and we could go through the streets without being mobbed.

Raeburn Place itself, the street from which the ground takes its name, was built in 1814–25 as a mixed development of tenements and villas. Three handsome villas stood on the northern side of the street at what was then the absolute edge of the city. Two were demolished to make way for tenements and just one survives as the Raeburn House Hotel. It was constructed around 1832 and was formerly known as

Somerset Cottage. It may well have been in an outhouse connected to this villa that Lord Kingsburgh and his team-mates lurked, smoking and muddied, until darkness had fallen.

Raeburn Place, complete with the burn which ran along its northern boundary and a mound which arose from its centre (levelled in 1946), can truly be said to have been the cradle of the Scottish game and it is a great pity indeed that more is not made of its historic links with the birth of the Scottish game. There are, apparently, plans in hand to create a heritage centre at the ground and the sooner these can be brought to fruition the better. Such an important site, and not just in Scottish terms, is deserving of more than simply the inscribed granite boulder which commemorates Raeburn Place as the location of the world's first International match.

Although the Edinburgh Academical ground was the cradle of the Scottish game, it was not the venue for the first recorded game between two Scottish schools. That accolade is reserved for the match played on 13 February 1858 between Merchiston and the High School. A boy called Hamilton had, reportedly, brought the Rugby School rules to the High School in 1856.

Ten months later, on 11 December, Merchiston were guests of the Academy at Raeburn Place and the inaugural match in what must be the world's most venerable continuous fixture ended in a draw despite the Academicals scoring two tries without reply. Neither was converted and because, under the terms of the scoring system of the time, only goals mattered (tries counted from 1875), the historic encounter ended in stalemate. *The Merchiston Magazine*, in the first match report to appear anywhere in Scotland, carried a full account.

Football at Merchiston this year is, we are happy to say, very different and superior to the game as played last year. For this improvement we have to thank the Rugby rules and those who introduced them. Last year there was no order in the game whatsoever; it was each for himself, each kicking recklessly straight ahead, very little running with the ball, and 'off-side' scarcely heard of. Now it is far different, each one has a place assigned to him for which he is most suited, whether goal-keeper, muddler, dodger, or as a member of that useful body, the light-brigade. Last year we were disappointed in playing the Academy; but now, to our great delight, it was fixed as the first match of the season. Accordingly, at about 11am of Saturday, the 11th of December last, an omnibus drew up at the gate of the Academy field and discharged the twenty Merchistonians eager for the fight, and a few who had come as spectators.

The match did not commence at once, and the twenty sauntered over the field examining the ground, and now and then kicking the ball over the goals; and, though comparisons are odious, yet we could not help observing that the Academy goals were a good deal easier to kick over than ours, being both lower and broader. However, we shall see whether this availed us anything. And now, taking advantage of the few minutes before the game commences, we may as well present to our readers a list of the players on each side – those of the Academy being kindly given us by their captain, D. Lyall, a second 'Old Brooke'. [a reference to the footballing hero in *Tom Brown's Schooldays*].

Merchiston – Burlton, Campbell (captain), Crawford, Crum, J Ewing, P. Ewing, Glassford, Gray, Keswick, McCallum, McFie, McLean, Richard, Riddell, Rowand,

Tennant, Hugh Tennent, Hector Tennent, William Tennent, Wray.

Academy – A. Cheyne, H. Cheyne, Chiene, Findlay, Forman, Gordon, Gore-Booth, Jackson, Lloyd, D Lyall (captain), W. Lyall, Maclure, Melville, Moncreiff, Moore, Simpson, Smith. [Just 17 names provided].

About 11.30 the match commenced, and the Academy winning the toss, the kick-off was taken by Lyall. In a very short time the players were the 'colour of mother earth'; for, the ground being wet and slippery with the rain, falls were of more frequent occurrence than usual. Every now and then a shower came on, but this so far from damping their ardour, seemed only to refresh them; but it was not so with the spectators, who found the greatest difficulty in keeping themselves warm. Up to 12.30 no advantage had been gained on either side; but, all of a sudden, Lyall made a rush, and to our great astonishment, runs into 'touch' right behind our goal. Here, an expostulation was made on the plea that the rules prohibited running into 'touch' but, finding that it only related to side-touch, we were obliged to yield and allow the 'try at goal'. Fortunately for us the wet had so completely saturated the cover of the ball and made it so slippery that, when kicked, instead of going between the goal-posts, it flew out to the side. Our goal is saved! and now a few words on side-touch.

We had always been accustomed to play over the area of the whole field, our only boundaries being the goals, and the school wall on one side, and the paling at the bottom of the field on the other. Hence, having never played with side-touch, we lost several good chances. McLean and Wray each made a splendid run, which gave great hopes of success, but were alas! lost by their running into side-touch. A little after one the game is all at the Academy's goal; and here

we thought we had a goal when the great McFie kicked the ball easily over; but it stood for nothing as it was handed to him 'off his side'.

A little before two, the Academy had another 'try at goal' and again missed. Shortly after, Lyall made a furious rush which might have been successful had not Hector Tennent, with the greatest pluck, sprung upon him, stopped him, and brought him down, not, however, without hurting his head severely, which, notwithstanding, he cared nothing for in the glory of having stopped Lyall. A few minutes after, time, 2pm, was called and the match was over without a goal being scored by either side.

Almond, who was a master at Merchiston at the time, has already given us his explanation of the disallowed Lyall 'try' – he should have kicked ahead before touching down – but the confusion then surrounding the laws of the game, even when Rugby School rules were being played, is very evident in this partisan, yet splendidly restrained, account of one of the earliest properly organised games of rugby in Scotland. Significant, too, is the two and a half hours' duration of the game with no mention of an interval or of independent umpires. It is no wonder that, until the standardisation of the laws contained in the Green Book ten years later – and even then it did not always help – newspaper accounts of matches often reported that the proceedings had ended in dispute.

The game in these days was still played 20-a-side and the main focus of a match was the heaving, sweating mass of bodies which constituted a scrummage. The aim was to kick the ball through the scrummage to the other side, not to heel – or 'scrape' as it was termed at the time – the ball backwards. The vast majority of the players were forwards –

sometimes there was just one back but, with the passage of time, the number of backs on parade was increased to three on each side!

The *Merchiston Magazine* is responsible, too, for a graphic description of the game as played around 1859 which was published – or, so it was claimed – because many of its readers, which might include a large majority of parents and guardians of Merchiston boys, would never have seen a football match.

[The posts] are two very portentous-looking erections . . . facing each other at a distance of about 150 yards. Each of these consists of two poles about 13 feet high, and 14 feet apart, with a horizontal ball across, at a distance of almost 10 feet from the ground. An Oriental visitor, it was suggested, who was only partially acquainted with our manners and customs, might consider these well adapted for stringing up refractory pupils, and he would probably prefer being hung up on one of them at once, to sharing for a month or two in the daily encounters which take place between them.

At the beginning of the matches the ball, consisting of a tightly-blown India rubber bladder, with a leather covering of an oval shape, is placed half-way between the goals. The players are divided into two bodies, each attacking their opponents' goal, and protecting their own, the ultimate object of each side being to kick the ball over one of the cross bars spoken of above. This, it is evident, is a feat of no easy accomplishment, as the space to be defended is very narrow, and indeed, the weaker side, though 'penned' close to their goal the whole time, can often manage to stave off actual defeat during a match of several hours' duration.

The ball being kicked off by one side or the other in the direction of the opposite goal, the two sides, which have been drawn up in battle array, like miniature armies, rush together, each leaving a reserve behind, and then comes the tug of war. Each player must keep with his own side as much as he can, for when in front of the ball, he is debarred by the rules of the game from taking any part in it whatever till he has become 'on-side' again. The beauty of this rule is, that it makes a side keep together, and work hard, and prevents games being won by some good-for-nothing 'loafer' waiting with his hands in his pockets in the enemy's quarters till the ball happens to come his way.

And now the ball, carrying the tide of battle with it, surges from side to side, and our Oriental, unlike Ibrahim Pasha, when seeing a cricket match, has no doubt that the game has begun, but cannot make it out at all why we don't pay some people to undergo such violent exertions, instead of undergoing them ourselves. He has, however, a lurking suspicion, that we are losing our tempers, and that our sport is becoming earnest, a suspicion which soon becomes a certainty, for a 'stalwart youth' who has been keeping rather out of the thick of the fight, catches up the ball, and runs off with it bodily, evidently resolved to put an end to the quarrel by removing its cause.

But, alas! his good intentions are nipped in the bud by that lithe, active little fellow, who springs on him like a mad wildcat and pulls him right down on the top of himself, with his struggling arms, legs and body twined around him in such desperate contortions that the petrified spectator asks in ill-disguised alarm which might be the warrior's body, which his leg, and which his arm.

But the fury of both sides will not permit the issue to be decided by single combat. All the bravest and the best rush like bull-dogs on the prostrate combatants, and immediately the ground is covered by a struggling, rolling heap, two or three deep, and evidently bent on mutual extermination.

The anonymous writer, no doubt fearful that the picture of mayhem and near riot which he had painted would alarm the Merchistonian 'parents and guardians', breaks off from his account to deliver a soliloquy on the merits of robust participation in schoolboy sport. We have no way of knowing, but the sentiments expressed provide more than a hint as to the writer's identity. The reader is asked to compare the boy who took a keen and active interest in school football with the 'listless loafer' who had not one unselfish pursuit, who felt no thrill or joy at the success of his school, and would not have moved a finger to ensure it, but who preferred to kill his golden hours with novels and pastry, poking over fires to warm his chilly extremities or 'swaggering about Princes Street to display his half-fledged puppyism'. Do we detect here the pen of Hely Hutchinson Almond? Nevertheless, and whoever the author might have been, the account continues:

> Ultimately there emerges [from the maul] our wiry friend . . . with the ball under his arm. Brushing past the outsiders before the 'maul' is fairly disentangled, he knocks over some small boys in the middle of the field, dodges past one goal-keeper, slips like an eel from the embraces of the other, and pitches down the ball right behind the adversaries' goal-posts.
>
> But the game is not won yet, and now is the time for a sure foot and a steady nerve. All the side whose goal is threatened have to retire behind it while the ball is carried out

some distance to the front, and the surest kicker on the attacking side prepares to 'try at goal'. One of his own side holds the ball an inch or two from the ground and puts it down as the kicker runs at it. Woe-betide him if his nerve fails for as soon as the ball touches the ground, the besieged, as we may call them, sally forth with an Indian yell. But if the goal-kicker is fit for his post of honour, the ball sails away over the adversaries' heads and goal bar, and the goal is won.

> Chapters might be written on different kinds of 'tries at goal', on drop-kicking, punting, placing a field, keeping a reserve, and other delicate points of the game, on which the winning and losing of a match often turns. We have merely endeavoured to sketch some of the leading features of our great and noble winter game, for which it is now developed perfection, we are indebted to Rugby School.

Lord Kingsburgh, too, has left his own graphic account of the mass scrummages then such a feature of the game during his schooldays at the Academy. Writing around the turn of the century he had this to say about the game of his youth:

> We then played 20-a-side and a scrum was a scrum indeed – fifteen pushing against fifteen in a tight maul, which often was immovable for 15 minutes. The steam rose from the pack like the smoke from a charcoal-burner's pile. It was much more straining and fatiguing than the more open game of today. During the years of my football work I was never able to cross one leg over another on a Sunday if I had been playing a match on the previous Saturday, and, as for shins, the breaking up of a maul when it came meant vigorous kicking ahead, on the chance that ball and toe might meet.

The Lord Justice Clerk, Lord Kingsburgh, played at Raeburn Place as an Academical schoolboy, took the money at the gate for the first International in 1871 and played a pivotal role in the machinations which led to the formation of the International Board. SCOTTISH RUGBY UNION

The mass scrummages of his schooldays must, indeed, have had a profound effect on the noble Lord because at the Academical Club jubilee dinner in 1908 he was still extolling the masochistic virtues of the game as played in his day.

> Very few of you have ever seen a real scrum. Have you ever seen a haycock that was put up when the hay was wet, and the smoke or steam was rising from it fourteen or fifteen feet in the air? That was just what a scrum was in those days – absolutely still and steaming. Our chairman [W.E. Maclagan, capped 26 times between 1878 and 1890 and captain of the 1891 British Lions in South Africa] expressed the opinion that we enjoyed being in that scrum, that we were

taking a rest. He is very much mistaken. The chairman says he withdraws. I thank him.

At that same dinner, in a contribution from John Chiene, who had been an Academy boy when the Academical club was founded, and who was to become one of the six founding fathers of the Scottish Football Union (SRU from 1924) and its first president, we catch a glimpse of the evolution of the game into the more open style of play witnessed today.

> I can remember the days when there were twenty players – nineteen in the scrummage and one back; and I remember very well asking Arthur Cheyne [Academy captain 1859–60] to allow me to go out and become what you would now call a quarter or half-back; and I remember we won that match. We won it very easily. I watched and whenever that ball came out of that steaming heat you had only to pick it up and run behind the goal.

By the end of the 1860s the game was well established in all of the leading Scottish schools. Edinburgh Academy, Loretto, Merchiston and the High School of Edinburgh were in the van. Among others, Fettes College, Glenalmond and Glasgow Academy were not long in following suit. Former pupils of Glasgow Academy, perhaps spurred by the traditional rivalry between themselves and their eastern counterparts, moved to form a Glasgow Academical Club, with a footballing component, in 1866. Hitherto, many Glasgow Academical FPs who wished to continue their schoolboy pastime had enlisted with the West of Scotland club which had come into existence the previous year. There is, too, an interesting link between the Academy and Blackheath FC which, as we have seen, lays

Stewart's College was another Edinburgh school which was early on the rugby-playing scene. This is the College first XV from 1887.

The Edinburgh Academy side from 1894. The practice of handing out caps originated at Rugby School and was followed, too, at national level where it continues to this day. EDINBURGH ACADEMICAL FC

justifiable claim to being the most senior rugby club in the world.

The Blackheath club finds its roots in the London school of the same name. One Alexander Sinclair, who had been a pupil at Glasgow Academy until moving to London with his parents, enrolled at Blackheath School. After two years as a closed club, Blackheath declared itself 'open' in 1860 and the four founding members included the Glasgow Academical Alexander Sinclair. The Neath club in Wales was founded by a former Merchistonian who set up a medical practice in the town and it was another Merchistonian, this time a schoolteacher in the local high school, who took rugby football to Kelso. The ripples created by the Crombie brothers when they arrived in Edinburgh, armed with the Rugby School rules, in 1855 were beginning to lap the furthermost shores. The pastime for boys was beginning to break out of the groves of academe and into the wide world beyond. The spreading of the rugby gospel was underway with a vengeance and it was a sporting crusade which was unstoppable.

SIX

To Hack or Not to Hack

The dividing of the ways

Throughout the 1860s the game was gaining a foothold and exerting itself on the sporting consciousness of the nation – but no more than that. Football was still a pastime for schoolboys and for those who had just recently left school to find their way in the world.

In England at the beginning of that decade the first steps had been taken which led to the parting of the ways between the Association and Rugby codes. On Monday, 26 October 1863, at a meeting in the Freemason's Tavern, Great Queen Street, London, a handful of clubs based in and around the capital had met to form the Football Association. There were the customary disagreements over the rules as interpreted by different clubs but, strange as it may seem, the rule which led to the schism between the handling and dribbling codes, had little or nothing to do with running the ball, that one glaring difference which now distinguishes the two branches of the game.

The Blackheath club was adamant – to the point of resignation – that the practice of hacking should be retained. It may well be that the issue of hacking had been seized upon by opponents of the handling code as the chink in its armour and that Blackheath had been manoeuvred into a defence of what

many felt was the indefensible. The principal aim of the meeting had been to establish a universal code. The Cambridge University FC had drawn up a set of rules which outlawed running with the ball and hacking. With some amendments, and in the course of several meetings throughout the winter of 1863, these were the rules eventually adopted by the Football Association. Blackheath FC quit the fledgling Football Association and became the focus for clubs which wished to continue with the carrying game. The two codes had gone their separate ways.

Hacking, as we have seen, meant kicking a player on the shins. No frills, just a substantial blow to the shin-bone as a deterrent to any fancy play or over-exuberance in the mass scrummages of the day. Hacking was distinct from the contemporary practice of *hacking over* inasmuch as the latter meant, essentially, tripping up your opponent.

The Blackheatheans demanded that two specific clauses be included in the Football Association rules. They insisted that a player should be entitled to run with the ball towards his adversaries' goal if he made a fair catch. Fair enough. That is rugby, almost, as we know it today. However, the second and irresolvable difficulty which Blackheath had with the Football Association was its refusal to accept their second amendment to the rules which sought to legalise hacking, which had been an accepted part of the game right from Rugby School days onwards. 'If any player shall run with the ball towards his adversaries' goal, any player on the opposite side shall be at liberty to charge, hold, trip or hack him, or wrest the ball from him.'

The 1846 Rugby School rules had been quite specific on the matter of hacking, which, they declared, was permissible so long as the unfortunate victim was not held and hacked at the same time. Neither, they said, was hacking with the heel, or unless below the knee, considered to be fair.

The great hacking controversy became a minor *cause célèbre* with newspapers and sporting journals opening their columns to debate the issue. The fact that hacking was, in reality, a side-show and that what Blackheath had been trying to do was to preserve the distinctive, handling feature of the Rugby game, was lost in the general brouhaha which developed. A correspondent to *The Field* in 1863 indicated that, so far as he was concerned, if hacking were to be abolished then the very moral fibre of the Empire would be under threat.

> Our game is abused because it permits running with the ball. In our opinion this forms one of the most striking as well as one of the most attractive features of our game. It is said our game is barbarous because brute force forms such an important an ingredient. It is not because of brute force that no nation can face us at the bayonet. Our game is said to be barbarous because it permits hacking, or shinning! For my own part, sir, this is the point above all others concerning which I am most positive that we are in the right. I do uphold hacking because it develops that quality of which every Englishman ought to be most proud – his pluck.

In Scotland, too, the rugby-playing community was split on the efficacy of hacking. It was part and parcel of the game played at Edinburgh Academy for many years. A former pupil from the period, James Wallace, recalled that it was a practice which, quite literally, left its mark.

> We played 20-a-side and hacking and tripping [hacking over] were part of the game, while it was unlawful to pick up a ball unless bounding. Perhaps the less said about hacking the better, although I don't think that the effects, though painful at the time, were very serious. Tripping, however, was a fine art and in my day George Chiene and Andrew Gemmell were past masters of it, while the Hon. James Moncreiff was a good third.
>
> The skill in tripping consisted of catching the heel of the runner with the toe of your boot and bringing him to the ground. As a rule he fell quite gently to mother earth, but sometimes the toe of the boot caught him on the shin . . . and many of us were in the habit of walking to church on Sunday with a limp. Serious accidents, however, were few. A maul, with 20-a-side all playing forward with the exception of one full-back and two halves, was a serious affair and as they occasionally lasted for ten or 12 minutes, till the ball was 'put down' the condition of exhaustion was considerable, especially if you happened to be on the ground in the middle of the seething mass of humanity. Back play was not so much in evidence as now and 'passing' was unknown, but we had many good backs and drop-kickers.

The *Edinburgh Academy Chronicle* also noted that J.H.A. Macdonald, was wont to lie on the ball if his side needed a breather, all the while 'ignoring the hacking' which was being perpetrated on his prostrate form.

By the end of the decade, the debate was still rumbling on and in November 1869 *The Scotsman* newspaper reported on a schools' match between Merchiston and Edinburgh Academy and the correspondent left no room for doubt upon where he stood in the great hacking debate of the day. 'The semi-barbarous habit of hacking we are glad to see getting out of fashion in this part of the country. Though it was indulged in last Saturday by Craigmount [a now defunct boys' school on the south side of Edinburgh] and Merchiston in their match, the game at Raeburn Place on Saturday, was conspicuous for its nearly entire absence.'

However, the newspaper correspondent may well have left before the end because, elsewhere, it was reported that in the final ten minutes during which Merchiston had posted the winning score, the practice of hacking was 'indulged in somewhat freely'.

To hack, or not to hack, aye that was the question and the issue led to the cancellation of at least one of Edinburgh Academy's games that same year when the Academy boys declared that they would and their Craigmount opponents said that they wouldn't. The fixture was cancelled and the two schools did not play each other again for six years.

The following season the Academical Football Club decided at its annual general meeting that hacking would be allowed in FP games but for school matches it would be left to the discretion of the combatants.

In England on 26 January 1871, at a meeting held at the Pall Mall Restaurant in London, some 21 of the Rugby-playing clubs, under the chairmanship of Old Rugbeian E.C. Holmes, met to draw up a unified set of rules. Holmes was a Richmond man and it was under his captaincy that the Rugby Rules had been adopted there. This was, essentially, the formation of the Rugby Football Union and one of their first pronouncements was to prohibit the practice of hacking, which had led indirectly to the great schism eight years previously.

The parting of the ways between rugby and the Association game in the 1860s was not then associated with the kind of class distinction which today implies that rugby is for the toffs and soccer for the working man. In the Borders, Wales, the West Country and in the north of England rugby was, and is, a classless pastime. When the schism came, those who went with soccer were from the same kind of public school backgrounds as their brethren who stuck with the handling code. In Scotland Queen's Park from 1867 onwards were the standard bearers for the Association game and they played the likes of Oxford University and other sides packed with Old Etonians, Wykehamists and even Old Rugbeians. In fact, they were so adept at the game that when the first official international match (Association rules) was played between Scotland and England in 1872 it was virtually a Queen's Park select which upheld Scottish honour. The first rugby clash between the two Auld Enemies, however, had taken place the previous year and, as we are about to discover, the route towards the world's first international encounter was more tortuous than the Devil's Elbow and twice as steep.

SEVEN

At Last Flodden is Revenged

The first international match

The residual resentment between adherents of the two footballing codes – like competing disciples of a schismatic creed – had simmered throughout the 1860s. When the Football Association, under its first secretary, Harrovian Charles Alcock, arranged an 11-a-side game at The Oval in March 1870, and had the audacity to bill it as an England versus Scotland encounter, footballers north of Hadrian's Wall were sent into paroxysms of indignation. It was bad enough that the 'Scotland' XI was composed entirely of players from the London area but when Alcock, bolstered by the success of his first tentative steps into the international arena, arranged a second match for November of that year, the dander of Scottish footballers was really up.

As Alcock saw it, he was fighting his corner and the interest engendered by these so-called international matches could only bring the Association game to a wider audience. He had learnt, though, from his previous mistake and for the November match he sought to introduce to the Scotland side players with credentials which were more bona fide than a passing interest in a 'wee dram' which had been the allegation levelled at the side which represented Scotland in March. A letter to the *Glasgow Herald* newspaper was designed to stoke the patriotic fires. 'In Scotland, once essentially the land of football, there should still be a spark left of the old fire, and I confidently appeal to Scotsmen to aid to their utmost the efforts of the committee to confer success on what London hopes to found, an annual trial of skill between the champions of England and Scotland.'

Alcock's plea fell largely on deaf ears. In reality, there were not very many people listening. There were only four clubs playing to the Association code – Queen's Park, Thistle, Hamilton and Airdrie, all of them operating in the Glasgow area – at the time the letter was written, and just one Scotsman, who was in any case domiciled in London, took up Alcock's offer. Nevertheless, the game went ahead and Scotland were defeated one goal to nil.

The Oval game had, though, engendered a spirited correspondence in the newspapers and sporting publications of the time. It was suggested in one letter that the rugby-playing clubs of Scotland might like to select ten home-based Scots to join forces with ten exiles for a 20-a-side game. Alcock dismissed the notion with high-handed scorn. 'More than 11 we do not care to play as with greater numbers it is our opinion that the game becomes less scientific and more a trial of charging and brute force.'

This provoked a rejoinder from a correspondent to *The Scotsman,* who was identified by R.J. Phillips in his 1925 *History of Scottish Rugby* as H.H. Almond of Loretto. 'Mr Alcock is a very leading supporter of what is called the "association game" which is to Rugby football, or whatever its detractors may please to call it, as moonlight unto sunlight and as water unto wine.'

Nevertheless, within a month of the second Oval match, adherents of the rugby game in Scotland were gathering their forces for a challenge upon the rugby-playing might of England. The seeds of the world's first international encounter were sown following a game between Merchistonians and Edinburgh Academicals. It was agreed that a challenge should be issued, through the columns of *The Scotsman* and *Bell's Life* and that the gauntlet should be thrown down in the names of the captains of the five leading rugby-playing clubs in Scotland.

There is a pretty general feeling among Scotch football players that the football power of the old country was not properly represented in the late so-called International Football Match. Not that we think the play of the gentlemen who represented Scotland otherwise than very good – for that it was so is amply proved by the stout resistance they offered to their opponents and the fact that they were beaten by only one goal – but that we consider that Association rules, in accordance with which the late game was played, not such as to bring together the best team Scotland could turn out. Almost all the leading clubs play the Rugby code, and have no opportunity of practising the Association game even if willing to do so. We therefore feel that a match played in accordance with any rules other than those in general use in Scotland, as was the case in the last match, is not one that would meet with support generally from her players. For our satisfaction, therefore, and with a view of really testing what Scotland can do against an English team we, as representing the football interests of Scotland, hereby challenge any team selected from the whole of England, to play us a match, twenty-a-side, Rugby rules, either in Edinburgh or Glasgow, on any day during the present season that might be found suitable to the English players. Let this count as the return to the match played in London on 19th November, or, if preferred, let it be a separate match. If it be entered into we can promise England a hearty welcome and a first-rate match. Any communication addressed to any one of us will be attended to.

We are etc.

A.H. Robertson, West of Scotland FC

F. Moncrieff, Edinburgh Academical FC

B. Hall Blyth, Merchistonian FC

J.W. Arthur, Glasgow Academical FC

J.H. Oats, St Salvator FC, St Andrews

The challenges went unremarked by Alcock and the Football Association; but it was picked up by the rugby-playing sides in London. Arthur Guillemard, an Old Rugbeian who played in that first game, has left a detailed account of the impression that the challenge made south of the border.

It is not too much to say that in the year 1870 there were but very few English players who were aware that Rugby football had taken hold upon the affections of Scotsmen; a twelvemonth later we all knew it only too well. Certain of the leading Scottish clubs,

Edinburgh Academy, Edinburgh Academicals, Merchistonians, St Andrews and West of Scotland – declining to recognise a so-called England v Scotland match under association rules at the Oval as an international meeting, the dribbling game being almost unknown north of the Tweed, published a challenge in *Bell's Life* to play a picked twenty of England under Rugby School laws, during the winter of 1870–71. The challenge saw the light a few weeks before the Rugby Football Union was founded, and there was a little doubt as to who should pick up the Scottish glove. However, F. Luscombe, the energetic captain of the Gipsies, who was 'spoiling for a fight', suggested to Fred Stokes, then captain of Blackheath, that his club, as the oldest point of foundation, ought to take the lead and accordingly, B.H. Burns, the Blackheath secretary, promptly wrote accepting the challenge.

The principal clubs in London, Liverpool and Manchester were communicated with, and a committee formed to select the players, choose a uniform and make the necessary arrangements. The task was a difficult one, but the co-operation of the chief Northern clubs was enlisted, and a strong detachment of their best men joined forces with the Southern Division.

In Scotland similar arrangements were under way. It was decided to stage trial matches in Glasgow and Edinburgh before the set date for the international, Monday, 27 March. An organising committee consisting of H.H. Almond (Loretto), J.W. Arthur (Glasgow Academicals), B.H. Blyth (Merchistonians), Angus Buchanan (Royal High School FP), Dr John Chiene and F.J. Moncreiff (Edinburgh Academicals) was also set in place. The committee entered into negotiations with Edinburgh Academy for the use of their cricket field at Raeburn Place. The Academical Cricket Club committee, only 'by a majority', decided that the request would be granted and the Academical ground was assured of its place in the history of the game.

Dr Robert Irvine, who was to play in that first game, has also left us a contemporary account of the events which led up to that historic first match.

Scottish rugby football may be said to have sprung up from boyhood into robust manhood with the first international match in 1871. In saying this there is no disparagement to the earlier players. Far from it. *Vixere fortes ante Agamemnona multi.* Many of us can recall to mind Rugby players, heroes of our boyhood, who flourished before international matches were dreamed of, and the idea of a football Union had not yet taken shape, players who would have made many of our cracks of the present day look small. The Rugby game was played, and played well, by school and club . . . but in those days inter-scholastic matches were very local and comparatively few, while inter-club matches were even fewer. Except in Edinburgh and Glasgow there were very few properly organised Rugby clubs in Scotland. There was one, and a good one – St Andrews – a club whose prowess was known far and wide, and which made up for the paucity of its matches by the fervour with which it entered into those it did play.

Provincial Rugby football hardly existed. There is no evidence of any provincial Rugby club out of Edinburgh (and district), and Glasgow (and district), St Andrews and Aberdeen University, playing regularly as a club, before 1870. For some years prior to that, however, signs of greater activity and enterprise were becoming visible in the Scotch Rugby world. Edinburgh and

Glasgow clubs were playing more matches among themselves and journeying more frequently to each other.

But what gave the great impetus to the game had to do with our neighbours across the border. For some years previous to 1871 [Irvine was mistaken in that the first games had been played in 1870] an annual match had been played in London – an international match it was called – it was played according to the laws of the dribbling game. England usually won, but the Scotch made a good fight always. This match at first attracted only a sort of curiosity in Scotland, and a languid sort of interest.

But in course of time, as the Scotch were beaten time after time, and it was quite an accepted truth that Scotland was in football, as in cricket, wonderfully good for its opportunities, but far behind England, the souls of certain Scotch past and present players stirred within them. The idea dawned upon them, 'If there is to be an international match let it be a real one, and don't let the relative merits of England and Scotland in football matters be decided purely by Association football, let us ask them to send a Rugby team north and play us on our native heath.'

The Scotch leaders felt that they could not be very far behind their opponents, and at all events, better to know the truth than to be set down as inferior, as it were, by proxy. At last, after much consultation, and in some trepidation, but not at all in despair, the missive was despatched. Scotland did not undertake to play only Scotsmen residing in Scotland. She reserved to herself the right to get them from wherever she found them, and it was to be a really representative team; and she would admit that if it was beaten . . . A team was selected without wrangle and without jealousy, and invitations were sent to the team to play in a great match, and responded to with alacrity.

The fine detail of organisation was left to Hall-Blyth of Merchistonians, and Scotland appointed as umpire Hely Hutchinson Almond. Two days before the match the *Glasgow Herald* reported that it would be played by the terms of Rugby School rules with two alterations. The ball, on going into touch, was to be thrown into the ground from the spot it crossed the line, and not from where it first pitched into touch; secondly, for a try at goal the ball was to be brought out from where it was touched down. This meant that the original Rugby School rule whereby the ball was punted back into the field of play from the point where it was touched down in-goal, in order to establish the place for the goal kick, was not being adhered to.

The game had already aroused a great deal of interest and on the morning of the match a correspondent to *The Scotsman* took a last-minute opportunity to exhort his countrymen to deeds of derring-do.

Our Scottish team is a very heavy one and the play of the backs and half-backs is very fine. Will you allow me a corner of your columns to remind some of the rest of the Twenty that their proper place is 'forward' and that habitually. Assuming the positions as they did last Wednesday [at the Edinburgh trial] of quarter-backs and threequarter-backs is an annoyance to the best players and very bad play. The business of a forward is not to hang about promiscuously waiting for something to turn up but to FOLLOW UP.

The Scotsman reported that weather conditions for the day of the big game were delightful, with the exception of a slight breeze. It said, too, that the ground for the

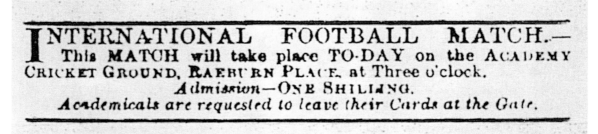

The advertisement which appeared in The Scotsman *newspaper on Monday, 27 March 1871. The first International match acted as a catalyst for the development of the game throughout Scotland.*

players was all roped in, the line nearest the pavilion being reserved for the Academicals and the Academy while the field and the hill beyond the paling on the other side [where North Park Terrace now stands] was reserved for spectators. The account left to us by Irvine reports that the Scotch side – in the terminology of the day – was selected from Edinburgh Academicals, Edinburgh University, Royal High School FP, St Andrews, Merchistonians, Glasgow Academicals and West of Scotland.

> The men were requested to get into training and did it. It was twenty-a-side, and the Scotch forwards were heavy and fast. We were ignorant what team England would bring, of what sort of players they had, and of how they would play; and though assured by Colville, a London Merchistonian – and a rare good forward, too – that we would find their size, strength, and weight not very materially different from our own, many of us entered that match with a sort of vague fear that some entirely new kind of play would be shown by our opponents, and that they would out-manoeuvre us entirely. The day of the match soon settled that uncertainty. The English twenty were big and heavy – probably bigger and heavier than ours, but not overpoweringly so.
>
> Before we had played ten minutes we were on good terms with each other. Each side

had made a discovery – we that our opponents were flesh and blood like ourselves, and could be mauled back and tackled and knocked about just like other men; they that in this far north land rugby players existed who could maul, tackle and play-up with the best of them.

Guillemard reports that no fewer than ten of the English XX were, like him, Old Rugbeians. He tells us, too, that the weather was fine and that the turf was in excellent order. An attendance, he said, of some 4,000 spectators showed that rugby football had attained considerable popularity north of the Tweed. The ground he reported as being 120 yards in length by 55 yards in breadth and that its narrowness, compared with English grounds, materially handicapped the excellent running of the English half-backs. (The modern-day pitch measures 100 metres by 70 metres, so Guillemard was correct in saying that the 1871 pitch was relatively narrow.)

> It was arranged before kick-off that the match should be played for two periods of fifty minutes each, that no hacking-over or tripping-up should be allowed, and that the ball should not be taken up for a run unless absolutely bounding, as opposed to rolling. There were other points, too, upon which the Scottish fashion of playing the game had to be followed.

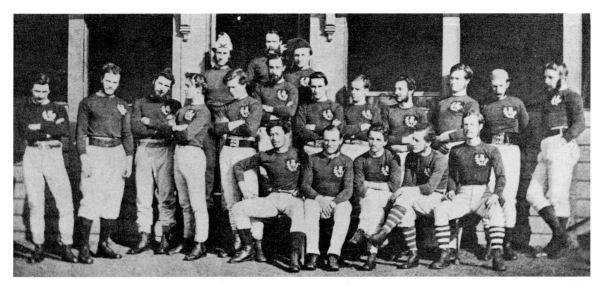

The Scotland XX which competed in the world's first rugby international at Raeburn Place. They were in at the start of something big. Angus Buchanan, who was to become the first man to score a try in international rugby, is standing on the extreme left of the picture. Back row: R. Munro (St Andrews University), J.S. Thomson (Glasgow Academicals), T. Chalmers (Glasgow Academicals). Middle row: A. Buchanan (Royal High School FP), A.G. Colville (Merchistonians), J. Forsyth (Edinburgh University), J.A.W. Mein (Edinburgh Academicals), R.W. Irvine (Edinburgh Academicals), J.W. Arthur (Glasgow Academicals), W.D. Brown (Glasgow Academicals), D. Drew (Glasgow Academicals), W. Cross (Glasgow Academicals), J. F Finlay (Edinburgh Academicals), F.J. Moncreiff, captain, (Edinburgh Academicals), G. Ritchie (Merchistonians). Front row: A. Clunies-Ross (St Andrews University), W.J.C. Lyall (Edinburgh Academicals), T.R. Marshall (Edinburgh Academicals), J.L.H. McFarlane (Edinburgh Academicals), A.H. Robertson (West of Scotland). SCOTTISH RUGBY UNION

From this distance in time, his account of the game – elegant though it is – does read rather in the manner of a justification for what turned out to be an English defeat. Scotland won by a goal and a try to a single try by England. Both Scottish scores were disputed, the first on the basis that, after the umpires had ordered that the ball be put down for a 'hack-off' in a scrummage five yards from the English line, the Scots had mauled it over the try line instead of, first, putting it down on the ground. However, the try stood and to Angus Buchanan of Royal High School FP goes the honour of scoring the first try in Test match rugby. In those days, as we have already seen, tries counted for nothing. As the name suggests they merely proffered the opportunity to have a try at goal. Therefore the first tangible (there really is no other way of describing it) points scored in international

rugby came from the boot of the ex-Merchistonian and Glasgow Academical W. Cross. A contemporary report declares: 'Many considered that the kick was an impossibility to succeed. Mr Arthur (Glasgow Academicals) placed the ball in position and the kick was entrusted to Mr Cross of Glasgow, an Old Merchistonian. Cool and collected he went at it and amidst ringing cheers he sent the ball over the goalposts.'

James Wallace, the Edinburgh Academicals captain of 1868–69, described the goal as the finest it had ever been his good fortune to witness. 'I was standing behind the goalposts with my old master and friend James Carmichael, and as the ball came sailing over, he threw his tall hat up and shouted out, "Flodden is at last revenged."'

The second Scottish try was deemed by the English to have been illegal because it

61

The vanquished England XX which participated in the first International, won by Scotland by the margin of a goal and a try to a single try.

followed a 'knock-on' by the Glasgow Academical J.W. Arthur. The ball had gone into touch near the England try line. A long throw went over the heads of the forwards and Arthur, in trying to catch it, sent the ball forward whereby his Academical colleague Cross touched down for the try. The English players immediately protested that the ball had, indeed, been knocked-on. However, the laws of the period – or certainly those in Scotland under whose jurisdiction the game was being played – deemed a knock-on to be an offence only if it was intentional. The umpires, Almond of Scotland and Ward of England, ruled in favour of the Scottish side. Cross failed to convert his own try and Scotland won by the margin of one goal scored in the game from Buchanan's earlier

try. The try which England had scored through R.H. Birkett of Clapham Rovers had not been converted by their captain Fred Stokes.

Almond has left his own account of the onerous umpiring duties which were undertaken that Monday afternoon in Edinburgh. Not only did the two officials have to adjudicate on the disputes over the tries but they were also obliged to rule on the long-vexed issue of hacking once it had, again, reared its ugly head. On the dispute over the first try, though, he waxes particularly eloquent and has bequeathed us a leitmotif for referees which holds good to this day.

I do not know to this day whether the decision which gave Scotland the try from which the winning goal was kicked was correct in fact. The ball had certainly been scrummaged over the line by Scotland and touched down first by a Scotchman. The try was, however, vociferously disputed by the English team but, upon what ground, I was then unable to discover. Had the good rule of the 'Green Book' been kept, viz. that no one except the captains should speak in any dispute unless appealed to, I should have understood that the point raised was that the ball had never been fairly grounded in the scrummage but had got mixed up among Scottish feet or legs. This I only learned afterwards, and my fellow umpire was at a distance from the scene of action. Indeed, when the game was played twenty-a-side, the ball, at the beginning of a scrummage, was quite invisible to anyone outside, nor do I know how I would have decided the point had I known what it was. I must say,

however, that when an umpire is in doubt, I think he is justified in deciding against the side which makes most noise. They are probably in the wrong.

The account left by Irvine makes it plain that patriotic passion on both sides was, at times, running at fever pitch. This was when the controversy over hacking came to the fore once again.

There was one critical time during the match. Feeling was pretty highly strung. It was among the first no-hacking matches for many of the players on both sides. Now, hacking becomes an instinctive action to one trained to it; you hack at a man running past out of reach as surely as you blink when a man puts his finger in your eye. There were a good many hacks-over going on and, as blood got up, it began to be muttered, 'Hang it! Why not have hacking allowed? It can't be prevented – far better have it.' The question hung in the balance. The teams seemed nothing loth. The captains (Moncrieff and Stokes) both looked as if they ought to say 'no' but would rather like to say 'yes', and were irresolute, when Almond, who was umpire, vowed he would throw up his job if it were agreed on, so it was forbidden and the hackers were ordered to be more cautious.

Although many matches have been played since between the two countries, there has not been one better fought or more exciting than this, the first one. The Scotsmen were exultant and the winning ball hung for many a day in the shop of Johnnie Bowton, at the Stock Bridge, adorned with ribbons like the tail of a Clydesdale stallion at a horse show. With this match and victory the life of rugby football as a national institution fairly commenced.

Robert 'Bulldog' Irvine, who was a member of the first Scotland XX, went on to captain his country. A general practitioner by profession, he left a comprehensive series of recollections concerning the early days of rugby in Scotland.

The cap and thistle badge belonging to J.W. Arthur, the Glasgow Academical who was a member of the victorious Scotland side at Raeburn Place in 1871. Early caps did not have a peak. Early players bought their own caps and paid to have them dated and embroidered.

Arthur Guillemard provides us with a run-of-play summary of the game which had been remarkably even throughout the first half during which there had been no scoring.

The match was very evenly contested until half-time, after which the combination of the Scotsmen, who knew each other's play thoroughly, and their superior training, began to tell a tale, and after a maul just outside the English goal line the umpires ordered the ball to be put down in a scrummage five yards outside the line. It was taken out accordingly, but, instead of putting it down, the Scottish forwards drove the entire scrummage into goal, and then grounded the ball and claimed a try. This, though illegal according to English laws, was allowed by the umpires, and a goal was kicked by Cross. England then penned their opponents for some time, and ultimately R.H. Birkett ran in close to touch, but the captain's place-kick, a long and difficult one across the wind, failed.

Scotland gained another try just before 'no side', Cross touching the ball down after an unintentional knock-on by one of his own side. His place-kick, however, was unsuccessful. The English twenty in this match averaged 12st 3lbs per man, and the Scotch probably the same. J.F. Green and F. Tobin for England and F. Cross for Scotland played splendidly behind the scrummage. The Scotch forwards were distinctly quicker on their feet, and in better training than their opponents.

In this match an extraordinary charge was made by Osborne [R.R. Osborne, Manchester]. Finlay [J.F. Finlay, Edinburgh Academicals] had got well away with the ball, and was sprinting towards the English goal at a hundred yards' speed, when Osborne, folding his arms across his chest, ran full tilt at him, after the fashion of a bull charging a gate. Both were very big, heavy men, and the crash of the collision was tremendous, each reeling some yards and finally falling on his back. For a few seconds players and spectators held their breath, fearing terrible results but the two giants promptly resumed their places. Burns [B.H. Burns, the Blackheath secretary] played as substitute for F.W. Isherwood, one of the best English forwards who was unable, owing to an accident, to fulfil his promise to play.

SCOTLAND: W.D. Brown (Glasgow Academicals), T. Chalmers (Glasgow Academicals), A. Clunies-Ross (St Andrews University); T.R. Marshall (Edinburgh Academicals), J.W. Arthur (Glasgow Academicals), W. Cross (Glasgow Academicals); A. Buchanan (Royal High School FP), A.G. Colville (Merchistonians), D. Drew (Glasgow Academicals), J.F. Finlay (Edinburgh Academicals), J. Forsyth (Edinburgh University), R.W. Irvine (Edinburgh Academicals), W.J.C. Lyall (Edinburgh Academicals), J.L.H. Macfarlane (Edinburgh University), J.A.W. Mein (Edinburgh Academicals), F.J. Moncreiff, (captain, Edinburgh Academicals), R. Munro (St Andrews University), G. Ritchie (Merchistonians), A.H.Robertson (West of Scotland), J.S. Thomson (Glasgow Academicals).

ENGLAND: A.Lyon (Liverpool), A.G. Guillemard (West Kent), R.R. Osborne

Six survivors from the 1871 game photographed at Inverleith before the Calcutta Cup match in 1921. Back row: A S Gibson (Manchester), Dr J Forsyth (Edinburgh University), C W Sherard (Blackheath). Seated: R R Osborne (Manchester), A Buchanan (Royal High School FP), Sir J H Luscombe (Gypsies). To Angus Buchanan, seated in the middle of the front row, went the honour of scoring the first ever points in international rugby. SCOTTISH RUGBY UNION

(Manchester); W. McLaren (Manchester); F.Tobin (Liverpool), J.E. Bentley (Gipsies), J.F. Green (West Kent); R.H. Birkett (Clapham Rovers), B.H. Burns (Blackheath), J.H.Clayton (Liverpool), C.A. Crompton (Blackheath), A. Davencourt (Ravenscourt Park), J.M. Dugdale (Ravenscourt Park), A.S. Gibson (Manchester), A. St G. Hamersley (Marlborough Nomads), J.H. Luscombe (Gipsies), C.W. Sherrard (Blackheath), F. Stokes (captain, Blackheath), D.P. Turner (Richmond), H.J.C. Turner (Manchester).

Umpires: H.H. Almond (Scotland) and A. Ward (England)

EIGHT

Union Power Arrives

The Scottish Rugby Union

Since the earliest days, the game of rugby football has congratulated itself on its deserved reputation of being a peculiarly sociable, hospitable kind of pastime. Whether that continues to be the case as the sport charges further along the path to professionalism, remains to be seen. However, with that reputation for congeniality in mind, is it any wonder that the groundwork which led to the formation of the Scottish Football Union – it did not become the SRU until 1924 – should have been done at a convivial gathering of six friends over a good meal and, maybe, a bottle or two of claret?

As 1872 was drawing to a close, Dr John Chiene, James Wallace, R. Craigie Bell and Harry Cheyne – all of them Edinburgh Academicals – along with B. Hall-Blyth (Merchistonians) and Albert Harvey (Glasgow Academicals) partook of dinner at the University Club in Edinburgh. All were graduates of that university except Harvey, who was a well-heeled Glasgow merchant. No doubt they had noted that in January of the previous year the rugby men of England had banded together to form the Rugby Football Union. That congregation, too, had conducted its business like good trenchermen, in the Pall Mall Restaurant,

Regent Street, London. Thirty-two representatives from London and suburban clubs adhering to the Rugby School rules, meeting under the chairmanship of E.C. Holmes (Richmond), had formed their union and had set themselves the task of drafting a set of bye-laws for the game. Later these bye-laws became the subject of heated and acrimonious debate between the RFU and its sister unions, but in 1871 the standard of the Rugby Football Union, under its inaugural president Algernon Rutter, was the first to be planted on the virgin turf belonging to the rugby union game.

Since the first match between Scotland and England at Raeburn Place the two nations had met again, at the Kennington Oval cricket ground on 5 February 1872, and England had avenged the earlier defeat with a comprehensive victory over the Scots. With the third game due to take place at the West of Scotland cricket club ground at Hamilton Crescent on 3 March 1873, the University Club diners saw the ideal opportunity, when the Scottish rugby community would be foregathered for the game, to advance their plans for the formation of a Scottish Union. Accordingly, on the morning of the match, an advertisement signalling their intentions was placed in the *Glasgow Herald*:

> A meeting will be held on Monday, 3 March, in the GLASGOW ACADEMY, ELMBANK STREET, GLASGOW at half-past four o'clock (immediately after the conclusion of the International Match) to consider as to the propriety of forming a FOOTBALL UNION IN SCOTLAND on a similar basis to the Rugby Union in England. All members of Clubs playing the Rugby Union Rules are invited to attend.

The bye-laws which the Rugby Football Union had drawn up after its inaugural meeting in the Pall Mall Restaurant were formally adopted at the RFU's first annual general meeting in October, 1871 and, in the absence of anything similar in Scotland, six Scottish clubs (West of Scotland, Glasgow Academicals, Edinburgh Academicals, Edinburgh University, Royal High School FP and Edinburgh Wanderers) had thrown in their lot with the fledgling RFU.

Hall-Blyth, a leading civil engineer of his day, acted as the Scottish umpire at the Hamilton Crescent match. It was played in atrocious conditions with heavy rain falling throughout and it ended in a no-scoring draw. The England team, mindful of the underfoot conditions, had sent their shoes and boots (backs normally played in shoes) to a local cobbler before the match to have bars fixed to the soles. However, (and whether this was due to patriotic fervour or incompetence is still a moot point) a couple of the English players were a boot short when the consignment was returned and they were forced to play with a dress shoe on one foot. When the game was over, Hall-Blyth and his University Club pioneers repaired to the Academy. The meeting was well attended and, with Dr Chiene in the chair, the objectives of

a Scottish Football Union were relayed to the gathering. Essentially, they were: to provide the necessary funds for the provision of a Cup; to facilitate closer co-operation between all of the clubs then playing in Scotland; and to form a committee which would have the task of selecting Scottish international sides.

The objectives met with the approval of the meeting and eight clubs were immediately proposed as members of the new Union – Edinburgh Academicals, Glasgow Academicals, West of Scotland, Royal High School FP, Merchistonians, Edinburgh University, St Andrews University and Glasgow University. The captains, and one other nominee, from each of these clubs formed a steering committee and plans were laid to stage the first general meeting in Edinburgh the following October.

That meeting duly took place, in the rooms of Keith and Co at 65A George Street, on Thursday, 9 October 1873. John Chiene, who later became president of the Royal College of Surgeons of Edinburgh, was elected to the presidency and the bye-laws of the organisation, which was to be called the Scottish Football Union – again, it was not thought necessary to include the word 'rugby' – were adopted. Edinburgh Wanderers and Warriston FC were admitted as members; membership was set at one guinea with an annual subscription of five shillings.

It was agreed at the meeting that all clubs in Scotland playing the Rugby rules were eligible for membership and that the main objectives of the new body were: the encouragement of football in Scotland; co-operation with the Rugby Football Union; and selection of the international team. The notion of providing funds for a Cup had been dropped since the steering committee meeting in Glasgow, and for the following 123 years the Union would, for a variety of reasons, turn its face against the prospect of a national Cup competition.

In its early days the Union's affairs were run to a large extent by players still active in the game. This led to committee members essentially selecting themselves for international duty. Probably, they were the best men for the job but it was not an ideal situation. With the increasing popularity of the game, a burgeoning membership and more paper-work to be dealt with, the composition of the general committee gradually changed to encompass older men.

Just 11 years after its formation the SFU became embroiled in a bitter dispute with the RFU which was to have far-reaching and lasting consequences for the worldwide game. The date was 1 March 1884 and Scotland were playing England at Blackheath. By half-time Scotland were leading by an unconverted try to nil. In the second half R.S. Kindersley (Exeter), scored a try, which the Scots immediately disputed on the grounds that a Scottish player had beforehand knocked the ball back with his hand. In Scotland at the time a knock-on in any direction was considered unlawful. The Scots shouted the appeal 'fist' and the Scottish umpire, the SFU president J.H.S. Graham, raised his stick to indicate that he at least considered the appeal to be valid. Most of the players on each side stopped in their tracks but Kindersley pounced on the ball and ran in to score at the posts. The game was halted for half an hour or so while a vigorous debate ensued. The goal kick, which the Scots sanctioned under notice of protest, was successful and Scotland lost by the margin of a goal to a try.

That was the start of what 'Bulldog' Irvine, in his 1892 account in the Marshall history, refers to as the 'Great Dispute' – and great dispute it certainly was. Two contemporary accounts of the central issue – one from an English perspective and the other from a Scotsman who participated in the match – set the tone for what was to follow.

The RFU secretary Rowland Hill declared that in the course of play the ball had been 'knocked back' by a Scotsman whereby Kindersley secured possession and a try was scored. 'The Scots claimed that 'knocking back' was illegal; the English held that it was not an illegal act and even though it had been, the act was done by a Scotsman and as no Englishman claimed for it, the Scotsmen could not claim for, or profit by, their own infringement.'

A.R. Don Wauchope, who was a member of the Scotland side, maintained that the huge row which was about to unfold came about because of that ongoing problem over universal interpretation of the laws. Before we hear evidence on behalf of the Scots' case it is worth bearing in mind that the Advantage Law was not introduced until two years later.

In those days there were two umpires who carried sticks, not flags, and a referee without a whistle. The ball was thrown out of touch, an appeal was made, the umpire on the touchline held up his stick, all the players with the exception of four Englishmen and two Scotsmen, stopped playing and England scored a try. The only question of fact decided by the referee was that a Scotsman knocked the ball back. This, according to the Scottish view of the reading of the rule, was illegal and the whole question turned on the interpretation. The point that no Englishman had appealed was never raised at the time and to judge by the fact that eleven of the English team ceased play, it would appear that it was their idea that the game should stop.

The affair now assumed the stature of a

'diplomatic incident' and at the heart of the matter was the Scottish perception that the RFU was determined that it, and it alone, should be the sole custodian and arbiter of law. The SFU annual general meeting of 1884 determined that the English could not be allowed to ride roughshod over the rights of Scotland, and it would soon turn out Wales and Ireland as well. The SFU resolved as follows:

> That the recent match in March between Scotland and England may be held null or a draw, or be satisfactorily settled by reference; that the independence of the Scottish union be fully recognised and arrangements be made for the settlement of future disputes by reference; and that when these points are settled the Secretary shall either issue or accept a challenge for the ensuing season.

What the SFU was suggesting was something along the lines of an international board to which disputes could be referred and which would, effectively, become the governing body for the international game. But England would have none of it. There was no match between the two nations in 1885 and, once again, at the AGM of that year the Scots were underlining their independence. They were willing to have the dispute terminated but not, they said, by an unconditional surrender to England.

The Irish and Welsh unions were then approached in an attempt to determine whether a unified approach to England might meet with more success. The Irish RFU suggested that the four Unions should meet to discuss the affair and also to consider the efficacy of an international board which would adjudicate in future disputes.

The four unions met in Dublin on the day that Ireland played England on 6 February 1886. Scotland offered a compromise whereby they would concede victory to England in the 1884 game if the RFU would agree to join the others, on the basis of equal representation, on the proposed international board. Initially, that compromise seemed to do the trick and Scotland played England, once again, at Raeburn Place in 1886 in a match which ended in a nil–nil draw and at which the 36-strong police contingent was strengthened for the first time by a squad of officers mounted on horseback.

Soon, though, it became clear that England was not willing to budge from its position that the RFU should enjoy primacy among the four Home Unions. The International Rugby Football Board was officially formed in 1887 with the RFU boycotting proceedings. As a result, for seasons 1887–88 and 1888–89, England were cast into the wilderness and played no international matches. Towards the end of 1889, and following peace talks between the Scottish and English unions, the whole, sorry mess went to arbitration; the RFU was represented by their president Major F.A. Marindin and the IB called upon the services of Scotland's leading judge, Lord Kingsburgh, the Lord Justice Clerk, the Edinburgh Academical who, as plain Mr Macdonald, acted as gateman at the inaugural international match between Scotland and England in 1871. The result of their deliberations, which all parties accepted, was that England would join the new IB but with six representatives compared to two each from the other three Unions. The disparity of representation was explained by the fact that England had more clubs than the other three Unions and this was but an early shot in a battle which has raged intermittently throughout the history of relations between the RFU and its Northern Hemisphere counterparts. It never did so more

The men who forged the shape and form of Scottish rugby. Past presidents and office-bearers photographed at Inverleith in 1909. The diminutive figure of James Aikman Smith, who was to play such a leading role in Union affairs as honorary secretary and as a seemingly ever-present member of the General Committee, is seated on the extreme left of the front row. Standing: A.B. Flett 1907–08 (Edinburgh University), J.W. Simpson 1904–05 (RHSFP), R.C. Greig 1903–04 (Glasgow Academicals), D.S. Morton 1892–93 (West of Scotland), B Hall-Blyth 1875–76 (Merchistonians), W.H. Kidston 1876–77 (West of Scotland), R.S. Davidson 1902–03 (RHSFP), T. Ainslie 1891–92 (Edinburgh Institution FP), G.T. Neilson 1901–02 (West of Scotland). Seated: J.A. Smith, Hon Secy 1890–1914 (RHSFP), J.D. Boswell 1898–99 (West of Scotland), M. Cross 1884–85 (Glasgow Academicals), D.G. Findlay 1896–97 (West of Scotland), A. Harvey 1874–75 (Glasgow Academicals), D.Y. Cassels, president 1908–09 (West of Scotland), A. Buchanan 1879-80 (RHSFP), L.M. Balfour-Melville 1893–94 (Edinburgh Academicals), R.D. Rainie 1897–98 (Edinburgh Wanderers), I. McIntyre 1899–1900 (Fettesians-Lorettonians), A.S. Blair, vice-president 1908–09 (Fettesian-Lorettonians). SCOTTISH RUGBY UNION

significantly than throughout 1996 when the Five Nations championship itself was in grave danger of disintegration after England's unilateral settlement of a separate broadcasting contract and the contention that, in any case, the RFU deserved more money than the rest because it had more 'mouths to feed'. History does, indeed, repeat itself – often with farcical results.

Maybe the Victorian gentlemen who ran the SFU in its formative years were representative of their time and it is a worthless exercise to attempt to endow them with late-twentieth-century personalities and attitudes. More than a century later, though, they do seem to have been a particularly stern

bunch. In particular their protection of the amateur ethos of the game was conducted with such zeal that it might have made the Inquisition wince.

They were operating, of course, at a period when the game in England was experiencing the Northern Union crisis over 'bona fide broken-time payments'. That dispute rumbled on from 1893 to 1895 when at a meeting in the George Hotel, Huddersfield, on 29 August those Yorkshire and Lancashire clubs which wanted to compensate their players for wages lost through playing, broke away to form the Northern Union – later to become the Rugby League.

The 22 rebel clubs were immediately

ejected from the RFU and the Scottish union resolved that no clubs north of the Border should have any further contact with them. In addition, Scottish clubs were warned in forthright manner to check the credentials of any 'foreign' clubs before accepting fixtures with them and it was determined that any Scottish player who enlisted with the Northern Union would be considered a professional and banned *sine die* from the Union game. The effects of this decision would be long-lasting and, for those involved, embarrassing and injurious. It would be another 100 years before Rugby League professionals would be welcome once again not just within the Union game but, on a more mundane level, even within the premises of Union clubs.

Within two years of the Northern Union breakaway the issue of perceived professionalism would result in a cessation of international rugby against Wales. The Welsh RFU had decided to mark the retirement of their great centre and captain Arthur Gould by means of a testimonial fund, the proceeds of which would be used to buy a house. The International Board warned the Welsh Union that they considered this to be in contravention of the rules governing professionalism. However, the fund was a great popular success in Wales and the cash was handed over. The IB reprimanded the Welshmen and the WRU withdrew from the Board. Thereafter, Scotland would not play Wales again until 1899.

The SFU had also become much exercised in 1889 by an unofficial British Isles tour to Australia and New Zealand organised by two English professional cricketers, Messrs Arthur Shrewsbury and Alfred Shaw. Three Hawick players, the Burnett brothers and A. J. Laing, formed part of the 24-strong squad that took part in the first-ever tour outwith the UK.

The warning bells were ringing loud and clear even before the tourists departed on their eight-month sojourn to the other side of the world. An English player admitted to the RFU that he had received £15 expenses to kit himself out for the adventure and he was declared a professional. He went on tour but was never played for fear of tainting his team mates. However, on their return the RFU demanded signed affidavits from the English players to the effect that they had not infringed their amateur status. The SFU interrogated the Burnetts and Laing but, in the absence of compelling evidence that money had changed hands, decided that nothing should be done. Nevertheless, the SFU's findings indicated that even a 'not proven' verdict was arrived at grudgingly: 'Their assurances being satisfactory, the matter was dropped until such time as direct evidence might be adduced in support of any alleged professionalism.'

The SFU's stand against the supposedly corrosive effects of professionalism – or anything that smacked remotely of it – was all-encompassing. Scottish clubs were ordered not to accept fixtures with Newport as one of their players was alleged to have signed Northern Union forms. The Border clubs were ordered to cease the practice of providing gifts for prizes at their seven-a-side tournaments and Pontypridd were told that they could not mark the selection of one of their players for the Scotland side with a suitable gift. Players and club members were prevented from accepting payment for newspaper articles on rugby and, again in the Borders, many players were suspended for having taken part in Northern Union trial matches. In the 1920s, Newport were back in the SFU 'bad books' when they decided to mark an undefeated season by making the gift of a £21 watch – an expensive timepiece in those days – to each of their players. Their Scottish internationalist Neil Macpherson was among the recipients and the SFU ordered him to hand back the gift. Macpherson refused and he was banned *sine die*. The International Board became involved and ruled that in future such gifts had to be limited to a value of £2. Honour, satisfied as they saw it, the SFU lifted the ban on Macpherson. Significantly, though, after having been capped on seven occasions, he never wore the Scotland jersey again.

In Scotland, even the numbering of players was considered to be in some way deleterious to the Corinthian spirit. Elsewhere the practice of numbering jerseys, as an accommodation for spectators, had been widespread since 1897. However, the practice was frowned upon by the SFU. Numbered jerseys first appeared at international level in the match between Wales and England in 1922. The Irish RFU were keen to fall into line and four years later asked the Scottish Union – which had become the SRU in 1924 – what they thought. The answer was still 'no'. The Union had relented by 1928 when the Scottish players were numbered for the game against France at Colombes. However, the committee had, apparently, asked the senior 'cap' John Bannerman to elicit the views of the players and the message which he sent back was that they were not in favour. The numbers were removed for the subsequent games against Wales and Ireland which led to the RFU inquiring if the numbers could be sewn back on for the Calcutta Cup match at Twickenham.

The SRU were affronted. As they saw it here, once again, was another example of the English union seeking to dabble in Scottish affairs. The RFU was informed that the Scottish players would not be numbered for Twickenham and the issue was taken up by the English Press. It was against such a backdrop that one of the most influential figures in the annals of the SRU – and hence Scottish rugby – uttered the immortal line with which he has become indelibly linked.

James Aikman Smith, small in stature, Napoleon by nickname, and considered variously as a tyrant – benign or otherwise – or a stalwart and stout-hearted defender of the principles of amateurism, dominated Union affairs from his appearance on the scene as a committee-man in 1887 until his death in 1931. He died in harness, having

James Aikman Smith, nicknamed 'Napoleon' on account of his diminutive stature and commanding personality, was at the heart of Union affairs from 1887 until his death, still in harness, in 1931. He was the arch apostle of the amateur creed and fearlessly chided King George V at Twickenham when the monarch asked why the Scottish players were not numbered. This portrait hangs in the Murrayfield library.
SCOTTISH RUGBY UNION

become unwell on the train taking the Scots to the Welsh match in Cardiff. In the intervening period he had served as honorary secretary and treasurer and was president of the Union in 1926–27. Having been appointed to the International Board in 1888, he continued to serve in that capacity until 1930. He never wavered in his fight against professionalism and was a steadfast opponent of campaigns to extend membership to nations other than the big four of Scotland, England, Ireland and Wales.

Aikman Smith was a product of the Royal High School and George Watson's College and a chartered accountant by profession. As a schoolboy he had attended the first international match in 1871; he had grown up with the game that he so obviously loved but which he was determined to maintain, even into the 1930s, as the game which had existed nearly half a century before.

The *bon mot* with which Aikman Smith is forever associated was delivered to King George V before that Calcutta Cup encounter in 1928. The King, who had obviously been alerted by newspaper coverage of the SRU's insistence that their players would not be numbered, asked why not. 'This, sir, is a rugby match not a cattle sale,' bristled the indefatigable Aikman Smith. And that was just the way it would remain until two years after 'Napoleon's' death. By then, presumably, Aikman Smith's colleagues considered that a suitably safe period had elapsed for his wishes to be contravened. He may well have been a martinet but he had the best interests of the game, and in particular the Scottish game, at heart. Aikman Smith was the driving force behind the early efforts to set the Union's financial house in order and it was the strength of his personality and vision which, principally, led to the SFU becoming the first Union to own its ground, at Inverleith. He was instrumental, too, in the move to Murrayfield. The stadium, even in its latest guise, represents his earthly legacy to Scottish rugby. His portrait, with its stern, bowler-hatted likeness, hangs in the library. Who knows, maybe his uncompromising spirit still stalks the corridors of power. The man who found time on his final train journey to quiz two Scotland players on rumours that they had been associating with the Northern League certainly would not be enamoured of what the game has become. For sure, James Aikman Smith will be birlin' in his grave.

NINE

The Hall of Fame

Cream of the crop

By the end of the 1997 Championship season the roll-call of individuals who have worn the blue, thistle-adorned Scotland jersey since the first turn-out against England in 1871 stood at 895. They all have their tales to tell. Some were capped once and returned rapidly to the ranks. Still, they have more caps than most.

Others have joined the legion of the immortals. From the modern era, the Hastings brothers, Gavin and Scott, captain of Scotland and the British Lions and the Scottish Cap record-holder respectively. Rob Wainwright, Gregor Townsend, Gary Armstrong and Doddie Weir – will their credentials pass the test of time? Probably. David Sole, captain of the 1990 Grand Slam side and as uncompromising a player as ever drew breath. From the same Grand Slam outfit Finlay Calder, Derek White and John Jeffrey, arguably the best back-row ever fielded by Scotland. From the 1984 Grand Slam side Colin Deans, a prince among hookers; Roy Laidlaw and John Rutherford, a half-back partnership made in heaven. Still with the 1984 Grand Slammers, Iain Milne, an immovable mountain of a man at tight-head prop, and the flanker David Leslie, fearsome, ferocious and as brave as they come. Andy Irvine, who ranks still as one of the all-time greats, but whose career was nearly at

an end by the '84 Grand Slam season and who had only a spear-carrier's role as a replacement.

This exercise of selecting the prominent players from any era is a dangerous and subjective quest. Who were the great players of the '70s? Few, surely, would argue with a selection which included Ian McLauchlan, Sandy Carmichael, Al McHarg and Gordon Brown – fire and brimstone forwards who

Brothers in arms: Gavin and Scott Hastings are the record-breaking brothers who were at the heart of Scottish success from the mid-1980s and into the '90s. Gavin, who retired from international rugby as captain after the 1995 World Cup, is Scotland's record points scorer and Scott set a new record mark of 62 caps against New Zealand in Auckland in 1996.

David Sole, 1990 Grand Slam captain, and one of the most uncompromisingly committed forwards Scotland has ever produced. Here he is in action against Western Samoa at Murrayfield during the 1991 World Cup.

Iain Milne, the Heriot's FP tight-head prop, provided the bulwark for Scotland's scrummaging effort during the 1984 Grand Slam campaign. Here, he is in action for Edinburgh District with brother Kenny and David Sole. ALAN MACDONALD

Finlay Calder sets the feathers flying during the 1990 Grand Slam season encounter against France. A Scotland back-row of Calder, John Jeffrey and Derek White represented a combination rarely, if ever, bettered in the Scottish game.

would form the core of a pack in any era. Irvine, properly, belongs in the '70s. Without hesitation, I would include among the greats, too, Jim Renwick, who possessed the wraith-like ability to ghost through gaps which barely existed; Keith Robertson, who possessed the ability to enthral and infuriate in almost equal measure; and Bruce Hay, whose pugnacious, directly confrontational preference was the very antithesis of the

75

Collectors' items: Murrayfield match programmes from the culmination of two Grand Slam campaigns.

Renwick–Irvine approach but no less effective for that.

The swinging '60s provides us with Jim Telfer, Frank Laidlaw, David Chisholm and Arthur Hastie, all from Melrose; David Rollo, a farming rock of a prop from the Howe of Fife; Derrick Grant from Hawick, who was often too brave for his own good; and Iain Laughland, the polished midfield performer from London Scottish. Ken Scotland, the Herioter who continued Dan Drysdale's Goldenacre tradition of the attacking full-back, and who rivals Tommy Docherty in the number of clubs to his name (he was capped

The Royal Bank of Scotland commissioned Ronnie Browne to produce paintings commemorating the Grand Slam triumphs of 1984 and 1990. The 1984 version, entitled The Turning Point, *captures the moment with the scoreboard showing Scotland and France tied at 12 points apiece when Jim Calder crashes through a lineout to score the winning try. All the players who took part in the four-match campaign are shown, as is SRU president Adam Robson. The players who took part in the final showdown wear the white jerseys worn on the day while the others are wearing the traditional blue.* Underdog Rampant *is the title of the 1990 painting. It depicts the Scotland captain David Sole leaving the field with the colours of the vanquished nations in his hands. The historical figures in the background include Robert the Bruce, William Wallace, Bonnie Prince Charlie and Ronnie Browne himself, barely discernible, between the Prince and Wallace. The painting shows the immediate prelude to Tony Stanger's try and Scott Hastings' try-saving tackle on Rory Underwood. Coach Ian McGeechan, SRU president Jimmy McNeil and chairman of selectors Bob Munro are also shown. Jim Telfer, assistant coach in 1990, features in both paintings.*

John Frame scores one of the fastest tries ever seen in Test match rugby at Murrayfield in 1971. The try, from the kick-off, was timed at 12 seconds after the opening whistle. The match, which Scotland won 26-6, was an extra game played to mark the centenary of the first International at Raeburn Place. SCOTTISH RUGBY UNION

The match between Scotland and Ireland at Murrayfield in 1957 was played amidst a blinding blizzard throughout. In this photograph Ken Scotland tackles Jackie Kyle and Adam Robson races through the slush in support. SCOTTISH RUGBY UNION

Arthur Smith about to score at the corner flag in this incident from the Scotland encounter with Wales at Murrayfield in 1961. SrU

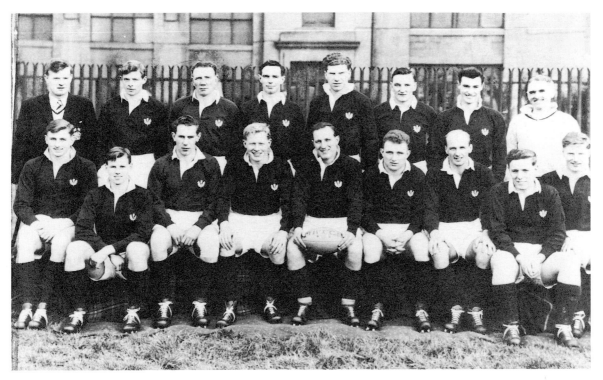

The Scotland side which broke the hoodoo of 17 consecutive defeats stretching back to 1951 with an against-the-odds victory over Wales at Murrayfield in 1955. Hugh McLeod, one of the all-time great props sits fourth from the right. SCOTTISH RUGBY UNION

out of six), débuted in 1957 and played his final Test against France in 1965, so he belongs more properly in the '60s than the '50s.

The '50s, was not a particularly happy period for Scottish rugby – at least until 1955, when victory against Wales brought an end to the four-year losing sequence of 17 games on the trot. Nevertheless, that decade, too, brought forth some star performers and top of my list is Hugh McLeod the Hawick prop who was first capped against France in 1954 and went on to play 40 consecutive Tests until his retirement eight years later – a quite exceptional achievement signifying a remarkable ability to steer clear of injury and amazing consistency of form. Douglas Elliot and Peter Kininmonth were noted back-row performers and Arthur Smith, capped 33 times out of Cambridge University, Gosforth, Ebbw Vale and Edinburgh Wanderers, scored

the Scottish try which was the overture to the 1955 victory over Wales. Tragically, he died young, at the age of 42, in 1975.

The roll-call can be as long, or as short, as we care to make it. The '40s was blighted, largely, by World War II, but from the '30s Scotland harvested two Triple Crowns, in 1933 and 1938. Jack Waters (Selkirk), Jock Beattie and Willie Welsh (both Hawick) were hard and rugged Borders forwards of the old school, and Wilson Shaw (Glasgow High School FP) was a mesmeric runner who punished England without mercy in the 1938 Triple Crown match at Twickenham when he scored two solo tries and created a third *en route* to a memorable 21–16 victory.

The 'roaring twenties' are indelibly linked with the first Grand Slam in the history of the Scottish game. The year was 1925 and the concluding victory was achieved against

Wilson Shaw touches down at Twickenham en route to the Triple Crown in 1938. Remembered fondly as 'Wilson Shaw's match' because of the pivotal role played by the Glasgow High fly-half who scored two tries and created a third. Scottish sides have travelled to English rugby's HQ in search of Triple Crown glory since but have always been sent hameward tae think again. SRU

Ian Smith, the Scotland captain seen here with the ball, led his side to a Triple Crown against Ireland in the final game of the season in 1933 when this picture was taken at Lansdowne Road. The game, played on 1 April had been postponed from February when Dublin had been hit by a ferocious blizzard. The ferry carrying the Scottish side had been unable to dock and had been forced to wait in rough seas for 16 hours in Dublin Bay. They were mighty relieved to be told that Lansdowne Road was unplayable when, eventually, they did make it ashore. The result of the re-arranged fixture was 8–6 in Scotland's favour. SRU

The Scotland side which recorded the first Grand Slam in the history of the Scottish game. The date was 21 March 1925. The opposition was England and the occasion also marked the opening of the new Murrayfield stadium. Back row: D.J. McMyn (Cambridge University), J.W. Scott (Stewart's College FP), A.C. Gillies (Watsonians and Carlisle), J.C.H. Ireland (Glasgow High School FP), R. Howie (Kirkcaldy), I.S. Smith (Oxford University). Sitting: G.G. Aitken (Oxford University), D.S. Davies (Hawick), J.M. Bannerman (Glasgow High School FP), G.P.S. Macpherson, captain, (Oxford University), D. Drysdale (Heriot's FP), A.C. Wallace (Oxford University), H. Waddell (Glasgow Academicals). In front: J.B. Nelson (Glasgow Academicals) and J.R. Paterson (Birkenhead Park). SCOTTISH RUGBY UNION

England on the day that Murrayfield Stadium was opened. Dan Drysdale was at full-back and the Oxford University threequarter line – Ian Smith, Phil Macpherson, George Aitken and Johnny Wallace – are generally reckoned to be, collectively, amongst the fleetest ever to have played for Scotland. Smith in particular – the original Flying Scot – was a real speed-merchant on the right wing and, in rugby kit and carrying a ball, was upsides with his contemporary Eric Liddell, the Olympic gold medallist immortalised in the film *Chariots of Fire*. Smith's try haul of 24 Test match touchdowns is a record which has endured for half a century. The half-backs were the Glasgow Academicals Herbert Waddell and

Jimmy Nelson and the pack was remarkably swift with five of them timed at 11 seconds or under for the 100 yards. Doug Davies was a tough-as-teak farming prop from Hawick. Jimmie Ireland at hooker was one of those sprinting forwards and on the other side of the front row was Kirkcaldy's Bob Howie. The London Scot David MacMyn and Glasgow High's John Bannerman were in the boilerhouse and the back row comprised James Scott of Stewart's FP, Alexander Gillies of Carlisle and Birkenhead Park's J.R. 'Scaley' Paterson whom Ireland, the longest surviving of the First Immortals, always reckoned was the most outstanding player of a first-class pack.

The Great War, in which so many young

Bob Howie secures lineout possession in that 1925 Grand Slam showdown against England. Murrayfield Stadium is brand new and Scotland win 14–11 but, Grand Slam or not, it would be a few years before Scottish players carried numbers on their jerseys. SRU

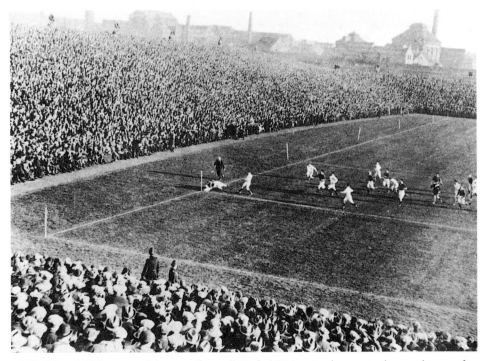

A.C. 'Johnny' Wallace, one of the magnificent all-Oxford University threequarter line, crashes over for a try in the corner during the 1925 Grand Slam decider. The densely packed terracings of the new Murrayfield stadium are clearly visible. Around 70,000 spectators watched Scotland's triumph which at that time represented a world-record attendance. SCOTTISH RUGBY UNION

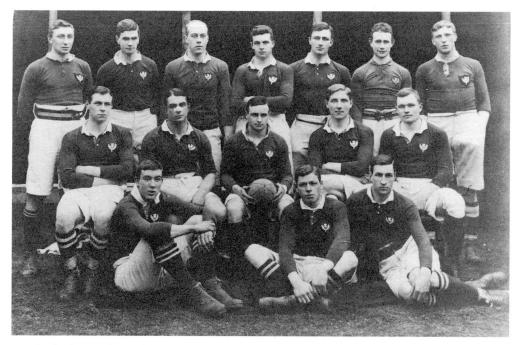

Scotland enjoyed a Triple Crown season in 1907. The side is photographed before the match against England at Blackheath. 'Darkie' Bedell-Sivright, one of the all-time-great forwards of his own or any other era, has obviously required some running repairs to an injured nose. SCOTTISH RUGBY UNION

The earliest existing photograph showing Scotland and overseas opposition. This was the occasion of the match against South Africa at Hampden Park in 1906. The Scots had played New Zealand the previous season but no photograph has survived. Scotland won the match against the South Africans, in front of a then record crowd of 32,000, by the margin of two tries to nil. SCOTTISH RUGBY UNION

Royal High School's Mark Morrison, who was one of the greatest forwards of his day, sits four-square in the midst of the side he captained to an 18–8 victory over Wales at Inverleith in 1901. Morrison went on to captain the British Lions to South Africa in 1903. Darkie Bedell-Sivright, another of Scotland's all-time greats, who was to captain the British Isles on their tour to Australasia the following year, is on the extreme left of the back row with hands in pockets. SCOTTISH RUGBY UNION

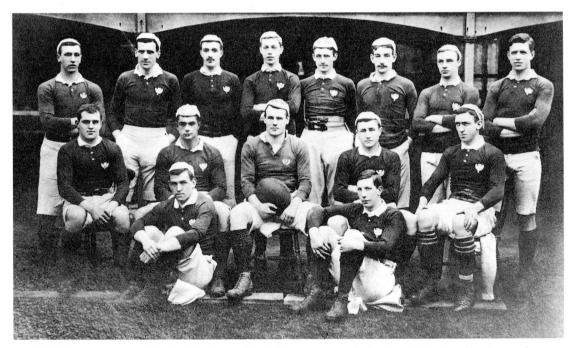

Mark Morrison captained his Scottish side to a Triple Crown against England in 1901 when this photograph was taken. The side contained six players from Edinburgh University. SCOTTISH RUGBY UNION

rugby men lost their lives, was the scourge of the second decade of the twentieth century. Some indication of the carnage which the 'war to end all wars' wreaked can be gauged from the fact that of the 30 players who took part in the Calcutta Cup match of 21 March 1914 at Inverleith 11 of them (five Englishmen and six Scots) had fallen by the time peace was declared four years later.

Prominent Scots from this period included Mark Morrison, a truly fine forward out of Royal High who was first capped as a teenager against Wales in 1896, and who would go on to win the last of his 23 caps against England in 1904. Along the way he would captain the British Lions to South Africa in 1903. A contemporary of Morrison's

was David Revell Bedell-Sivright and, to my mind, he is such a fascinating character that, of all the colourful and charismatic individuals who have pulled on that thistle-adorned jersey, he is the one who merits closer inspection. He is my first among equals and we shall return to 'Darkie' in the chapter which follows.

The first 30 years of Scottish international rugby, from the first game in 1871 to the turn of the century, also threw up more than its fair share of characters and players of genuine class. We have already looked at that 1871 game in some detail; in the decade which followed, players such as our old Edinburgh Academical friend Robert 'Bulldog' Irvine and his brother Duncan were at the forefront

The Scotland side which played Ireland at Inverleith in 1899 in what was the inaugural game at the Scottish Football Union's new ground. The Irish managed to spoil the party by winning 9–3. Back row: H.O. Smith (Watsonians), R.C. Stevenson (London Scottish), A. Mackinnon (London Scottish), W.M.C. McEwan (Edinburgh Academicals), M.C. Morrison (Royal High School FP), R.T. Neilson (West of Scotland), J.M. Reid (Edinburgh Academicals). Second row: T.L. Scott (Langholm), J.T. Mabon (Jed-Forest), J.H. Couper (West of Scotland), W.P. Donaldson, captain, (West of Scotland), G.C. Kerr (Edinburgh Wanderers and Durham), G.T. Campbell (London Scottish), L. Harvey (Greenock Wanderers). In front: D.B. Moneypenny (West of Scotland). SCOTTISH RUGBY UNION

of the game as was Ninian Finlay (Edinburgh Academicals) who was reckoned to be the longest drop-kick exponent of his day. Finlay is also the youngest player ever to have been capped by Scotland; he was aged 17 years and 36 days when he made his début, while still a schoolboy, against England in 1875 – a drawn match at Raeburn Place in which two of Finlay's brothers also played. Irvine, who had been capped in 1871 just a month short of his 18th birthday, also played in that match.

In the 1870s, the number of players in a team was cut from 20 to the current 15. In the days of 20-a-side, the forwards were the thing: the backs were there merely to defend and to return the ball if it was kicked into their realm. The Merchiston School side of the '70s for instance, played a formation of four 'goalkeepers', four 'half-backs' and a dozen 'bulldogs'. The Scottish Football Union, the precursor of the SRU, had suggested a 15-a-side format at the tail-end of 1875, but the Rugby Football Union, at that point, declined to follow suit. The suggestion was made anew the following year and, by the time that England played Ireland at the Oval in 1877, 15-a-side was the order of the day. There was no consensus however, on how teams should arrange themselves. Sometimes two full-backs were played (Scotland did not play a single full-back until the game against Ireland in 1877) and there was disagreement, too, on whether three or four three-quarters offered the optimum blend. Even in the forwards there was no uniformity of thought. When England played Wales in 1881 England used five backs and ten forwards whereas the Welshmen favoured a configuration of six backs, including two full-backs, and nine forwards.

But we digress. Another Scotsman who was capped while still at school was the Edinburgh Academical Charles Reid. He, too, was aged

17 years and 36 days when he made his début against Ireland in 1881. At a time when 12 stones, or thereabouts, was considered to be a pretty competitive poundage for a footballer Reid stood six feet three inches in his stockinged soles and tipped the scales at 15½ stones. He was an extremely competitive forward who had mastered all of the core skills. Handling came as second-nature to him and he was one of the most devastating tacklers of his day. He graduated in medicine from Edinburgh University and went on to practise as a GP in Selkirk and Swindon.

Shortly after the 1886 encounter against England at Raeburn Place, which resulted in a no-scoring draw, a contemporary account, unsigned, but probably by Irvine sings the praises of Reid to the rafters.

It is doubtful whether Charles Reid ever played a better game than he did on this occasion; and if we consider him not as a great individual player, but as a power in any team, it can be realised what Reid at his best meant to Scotland. He was the forward of his time. There was no man to compare with him in England, Scotland, Ireland or Wales. Neither was there before nor has there been since.

Besides the physical qualities which rendered him a dangerous adversary, his football at all points was perfect, and we had no specialist in our team of whom it could be said that in his own particular game he was superior to Reid. His speed was much above that of the average forward, and in many matches he made as big runs as the backs. In fact, in the international under notice, his run in the second half was the best performance of its kind of the day.

Roughness has been imputed to him, but the charge is almost groundless, and if on occasion he did use his strength, it must be remembered in extenuation that he had to put up with all manner of annoying attentions, often from aspiring individuals who would have preferred the distinction of having knocked down Charles Reid to the honour of half a dozen international caps. We have seen a shaven-headed Yorkshireman in the line-out fix on to Reid like a limpet long before the ball was thrown out of touch, and hang on until he had to be forcibly shaken off.

This is high praise indeed from Irvine, who was no mean player himself, and his defence of Reid against the charge of rough play is particularly cute. The accusation, says, Irvine is 'almost' groundless which allows much leeway for the imagination to run riot!

Another prominent player of the 1880s was Andrew Don Wauchope. He would go on to become president of the Scottish Football Union in 1889–90 but, along with his brother Philip he was a central figure in Scotland sides of the 1880s. He was a quarter-back with a distinctive, staccato stride which perfectly equipped him to make balanced, side-stepping runs through the heart of the enemy defence. A Fettesian-Lorettonian, Don Wauchope had been instrumental in the introduction of combined back-play while captain of Fettes College. He was a graduate of Cambridge University and had a spell at the Scottish Bar before becoming a stockbroker in London.

Wauchope played alongside A.G.G. Asher (Oxford University, Fettesian-Lorettonians and Edinburgh Wanderers) in a half-back role. In his 1892 offering to the Rev. F.P. Marshall's *Rugby Football* – without which generations of the game's historians would have been lost – Irvine has this to say about the Asher-Wauchope partnership, and one can infer that he was a bigger fan of Wauchope than Asher.

Asher and Don Wauchope, without doubt, constituted the best pair we have had this decade [1880s]. Asher was a very fine player who seldom showed poor form and, if he did not shine with the same brilliancy as Wauchope, he was always of immense service to his side. His running was his weak point and he was never counted a dangerous scorer. When a man does not shine as a runner, and is strong in other points, his friends at once put in a claim on his behalf as an 'all-round' player. All-round in this sense is misapplied and if a man be no runner or scorer he is not entitled to have the term bestowed upon him.

Wauchope, in the strictest sense of the word, was an all-round player as he could not only run but his kicking, tackling and general defence were very strong when he saw occasion to exert them. Asher's running was poor, and he therefore cannot justly be considered an all-round man. At the same time he was one of our most successful half-backs. He and Wauchope did splendid service for us.

Gordon Petrie (Royal High School FP) was another Scotland stalwart of the 1870s who made his mark on the game. Another strapping six-footer, who was equally adept on the athletics field and a weight-lifter and hammer-thrower of repute, he was a colossus of the international game throughout his brief career. It was a career which ended in controversy indirectly as a result of which in 1881 he was elected to the presidency of the Union. Petrie had won what turned out to be his eleventh, and final cap, against England in 1880. When the Scotland side was selected to open the international season at Ormeau, Belfast, against Ireland in February of the following year it was announced that the captaincy had passed from Robert Irvine to

Gordon Petrie, the Royal High School forward, was a colossus of the game whose career ended in controversy — and the SRU presidency. He played his last game for Scotland against England in 1880 and when he was overlooked for the captaincy the following season in favour of Jock Graham of Edinburgh Academicals, his High School team-mates were incensed. Players from the High School, Edinburgh Institution and Edinburgh University withdrew from the 1881 side to play Ireland in protest and an emergency meeting of the Union was requisitioned. At the next annual general meeting the Committee found itself under attack and Petrie was elected president.

another Edinburgh Academical J.H.S. 'Jock' Graham.

There had never been any love lost between the Academy and the Royal High School — as we have seen the Academy was born from the disenchantment of some parents with the education on offer at the High School — and the High School scholars were incensed that their man Petrie had been

passed over in favour of Graham — in spite of Graham's credentials. In his 1925 history of Scottish Rugby, R. J. Phillips refers to Graham as one of the greatest forwards the game has ever seen, a fair-haired enthusiastic schoolboy who had possessed from his earliest days the gift of leadership and who as captain of the champion school team, the champion Academical team and of the international team had gained all the honours that the game could provide.

Nevertheless, the Royal High scholars in, and around, the Scotland side of the period were incensed. One of their own, as Graham's senior, had been denied his proper place as the rightful captain of the Scottish side. Phillips, in his 1925 account, takes up the story:

> The Royal High School section blazed up in their wrath and were supported 'on principle' by the Institution and the University. The boys met in crowds at 'Daish's', the 'Albert' and the other howffs, and let loose their indignation on the Union.

> It did not require a great deal to ignite a fire. They were inflammable material, and cared less for Petrie's wrongs than they did for a good row. Representatives as far remote as Thurso and Earlston were said to have attended the indignation meetings, but it need not be assumed that the country was agitated from end to end. It was easy to procure a mandate for a local supporter who was indignant enough to deserve it.

> R.S.F. Henderson, the Edinburgh University captain, made himself very prominent in his antagonism and hostility towards the Union. As a player, he was never highly valued in Scotland. He was too stolid and too lumbering for Scottish ideas of the requirements of a forward. Later on, when he

went south, he was selected for England, although he was a Scotsman. When the storm over Petrie came to a head, it was abated by the acceptance of a compromise that in future International teams should choose their own captain.

The controversy, however, did not end there. A special general meeting of the Union was called at which a compromise which allowed the international side to select their own captain was hammered out. Nevertheless, the High School, Edinburgh Institution and Edinburgh University men withdrew from the side to play Ireland and the Irish logged their first International victory. The ill-feeling and resentment which accompanied the imbroglio simmered until the next annual general meeting of the Union when many of the sitting committee-men were summarily dismissed and Petrie was elected to the post of president.

The Irish victory, by the margin of a Scottish try to a drop-goal, had them dancing on the streets of Belfast. Jacques McCarthy, the Irish rugby writer, said this of the unconverted Scottish try by Graham and the J.C. Bagot drop-goal which occasioned Ireland's first international success:

McMullin, of Cork, making a miscatch, big Jock Graham, who was leaning against the goal post rubbing his shin, leisurely limped over and touched the ball down. Could we win? Surely we deserved it, as we had been on the Scottish line all day. The spectators became hysterical. On the line the ball was heeled out to Merry Johnstone, who, amidst vociferous profanity, missed his pick up. Campbell, darting on him, kicked the ball to touch. Before the Scotsmen had time to line up, Barney Hughes threw the ball out to Taylor, who, quicker than you could think, tossed it to Bagot, who dropped it over the Caledonian goal. Such frantic excitement as these lightning movements evoked was never seen. Men, women and children embraced each other indiscriminately.

Among other Scotland notables as the nineteenth century was drawing to a close were Harry Stevenson and Bill Maclagan, both Edinburgh Academicals, whose playing careers partially overlapped and who were among the finest backs ever to have played for Scotland.

Maclagan, who captained the invincible British Lions to South Africa in 1891 on a 'missionary' tour which was underwritten by Cecil Rhodes, played 26 times for Scotland between 1878 and 1890. He was an aggressive defender and no fool, either, with ball in hand as the Rev. Marshall's 1892 opus graphically illustrates:

Although defence was undoubtedly Maclagan's strong point, if he got the ball within a dozen yards of the line he was a most dangerous man in more ways than one, and an ordinary player might well be excused if he took second thoughts about standing up before him if he was bent on scoring.

Roughness has often been imputed to him, and there is no doubt that in his younger days he now and again gave exhibitions of his strength which were not good for the subject. More than once he has tossed a man, full pitch as the bowlers would say, on to the little paling at Raeburn Place and made the timber crack. He was one of the most powerful players we ever had, and no man on the football field could put his strength to more use than Maclagan when he cared to or when he was roused.

With his waxed moustache, Maclagan cut quite a dash in South Africa and was to play in all but one of the matches. The *Cape Times* reported: 'He has acquired the acme of perfection as a tackler, can punt with considerable ability and with either foot, and can cover the ground at a splendid pace.' The tourists were lauded wherever they went to such an extent that one of Maclagan's Scottish colleagues, Paul Clauss, was moved to observe that it had been 'champagne and travel' all the way. South African rugby was in its infancy and the colonials were no match for the British Isles side. The tourists were fêted at a rolling programme of 'smokers', dinners, a formal banquet at Government House in Cape Town and in one of his after-dinner speeches Maclagan was compelled to observe that: 'We have, indeed, enjoyed ourselves. Perhaps too thoroughly!'

Maclagan, who was one of several Scottish rugby pioneers to become a London stockbroker, was also the bearer of a gift to the Southern Hemisphere which is still in regular exhibition today. When Maclagan and his tourists set sail from Southampton aboard the *Dunottar Castle* in his luggage was a handsome silver trophy donated by Sir Donald Currie of the Union Castle shipping line. The silver cup was destined for the colonial side which performed best against the British Isles. The tourists won all of their 20 games but Griqualand West held them to only a 3–0 victory. That was deemed to have been the best performance by a South African opponent, and so the silverware went to them. More than a century later the Currie Cup is still the focus for the principal provincial competition in South Africa and the tournament takes its name from the

Scotland's Triple Crown winning side of 1895 photographed before the match against Wales at Inverleith in that year. Snow lay on the ground and the Welsh demanded that the north end of the pitch be shortened by 18 yards because, they claimed, it was unplayable. Mattha Elliot, the Hawick quarter-back whom the Mansfield Park faithful considered had been kept out of the side because he lacked an old-school-tie background, was winning his first cap and he can be seen sitting on the bear-skin rug to the right. SCOTTISH RUGBY UNION

trophy carried to the Cape by Bill Maclagan all those years ago.

Harry Stevenson was a contemporary of Maclagan's – their international careers overlapped by two seasons and five international matches. Stevenson won 15 caps between 1888 and 1893. From this distance in time Stevenson gives the impression of being a cussed individual. He stuck to his guns come what may and the following account of what was then the latest topic for heated debate in Scottish rugby circles is germane to his tale.

Around this period there was considerable debate over the optimum back-line formation and the manner in which they should play. It was the Welsh, led by Arthur Gould, who championed the then heretical doctrine of a four-strong threequarter line. The topic took up many column inches in periodicals of the day. The *Scottish Athletic Journal* devoted considerable space to this apparently arcane topic. The great and the good of Scottish rugby were among its correspondents. The new system did not even find favour with a distinguished back like Don Wauchope who declared:

I have always been a strong opponent of this new game. Beat them well forward and you have the game won. Many forwards play as if the half-backs [three-quarters we would know them as today] were the real players on the side. Consequently they never do their own share of the play. Swing the scrummage; then it is that the backs get a real chance, and then it is that the opposing backs are run over by the forwards. If our Scottish forwards will play their own good game I should not have any doubt. Forwards who are continually trying to play for their backs will invariably be beaten.

Charles Reid, too, considered that the emphasis on back-play which was what the four-man threequarter line would lead to, would do untold damage to the Scottish game:

Give me a forward team like that we had at Manchester in 1882 [Scotland defeated England by two tries to nil in the first match in which a neutral referee officiated] and I don't care how many three-quarter backs you have; we could go through them. We dribbled very close and one backed up the other so well they could not get away, and they had flyers like Bolton [W.N. Bolton, Blackheath] against us. Dribbling and tackling are the characteristics of the Scottish forwards and on them we depend to win.

The thrust of those Scotsmen who opposed the new style was that Scottish forward-play would suffer as a result. R.G. MacMillan (capped 21 times as a forward out of West of Scotland and London Scottish, 1887–97) even went as far as to suggest that the moral welfare of Scotland's finest would be put at risk if the Welsh system found favour north of the Border:

As to the influence of the Welsh system on Scottish forwards, I consider it will be deteriorating, as they will lose all their old dash. I don't say there should be no heeling out [at this period forwards more properly kicked the ball through a maul or scrummage rather than heeling it backwards so that it could be used by the backs] but as the game stands at present the attention of the forwards is entirely given up to it. The older players may be able to stick to the old genuine game which they learned at school but the younger ones will not be taught to put down their heads and shove, and will shirk and become loafers.

91

Even Watsonians, which to this day is a club which prides itself on the open and fluid style of play that is the Myreside hallmark, were not convinced as to the efficacy of this infernal Welsh invention. Admittedly their representative in the debate, H.T.O. Leggat (capped nine times between 1891 and 1894), was a forward, but the verdict from the Watsonian camp was just as damning as all the rest.

> My opinion of the four-half-back [threequarter] system generally is that it is much showier and, therefore, more attractive to the spectators. The passing is easily spoiled when the tackling is determined and vigorous. I prefer the Scottish style, undoubtedly, for this substantial reason: the Watsonians, who play essentially a Scottish game, played, under unequal conditions, the strongest Newport XV, who are acknowledged to be *facile princeps* in the four-three-quarter game, and morally beat them. I think the Scottish forwards would lose their strong points, rushes and footwork, if they adopted the Welsh system.

In actual fact, Newport won that game, played in south Wales, by the margin of a goal to a try. The Watsonians, however, considered that they had done enough – against a side containing seven full Welsh internationalists – to have put the kibosh on the four-man threequarter line. They were mistaken. The international against Wales at Raeburn Place in 1893 settled the issue once and for all. It was nip and tuck until half-time when the score stood at nil apiece. In the second half, though, the Welsh threequarter line, marshalled by Gould, swung into action and despite the impotent cry of one Scottish supporter that 'this isn't football' Scotland succumbed by the margin of a penalty goal and three tries to nil. That defeat settled it. As Phillips mournfully recounts in his 1925 history of the game:

> We joined in with the mob. Whether we were right or wrong, or whether we should have stood firm and forced our game upon the others, does not admit of more than a conjectural answer, and it is too late now to turn back the hands of the clock.
>
> The only certainty about it all is that in accepting the new game Scotland bartered her heritage, and henceforward there was nothing left in rugby that was exclusively or peculiarly Scottish. If it had been known that proficiency in the four three-quarter system entailed assiduous and intensive practice, coaching, rehearsal and training, I doubt whether it would ever have obtained a foothold in Scotland. During the years of Welsh ascendancy, when the prospects of challenge seemed hopeless, the advantages lay far more in the preparatory functions than in the formation of the teams, and the host of great Welsh players of the time owed much of their superiority to comparison with novices in the inner requirements of the Welsh game. Time has dispelled that early advantage and obliterated the distinction. Schoolboys are all now trained in the Welsh game. That they are better players, or that the straining after unity and perfection of combination has not had a deteriorating effect on the individual, even so far as self-reliance is concerned, are questions of a debatable character. To all who remember the old Scottish forward game the accuracy of the prognostications dreading deterioration of the forward play will appear remarkable.

So, Phillips, for one, mourned the passing of 'the old Scottish forward game'. Harry

Stevenson's problem was concerned not so much with the four-man threequarter system but more with his refusal to countenance the 'long-passing' game which the Union at that time wished its backs to employ. The aim was to set the wing-threequarters free with long passes from the midfield. Stevenson, at centre-half, had not been content with the dictat from on high which, as he saw it, reduced him to the role of feeder and tackler. The Union implored him to change his style for the 1891 season, but he refused. He was, though, too good a player to drop so they played him at full-back. In 1892, the Rev. Marshall's compendium of the game reported:

> Of Stevenson it has to be said that we never had a more versatile player. His defence at three-quarters in 1890 materially kept down the score and when the Union saw fit to place him at full-back in 1891 and 1892 he filled the position as adequately as any man ever we had. Centre three-quarter, however, is his true place, and in it he has never been known to play a poor game, a fitting testimony to the merit of one of the most remarkable players the country has produced and a back who will be remembered along with N.J. Finlay, W.E. Maclagan and A.R. Don Wauchope.

Stevenson played his last game for Scotland at full-back against England in 1893 after which he simply retired. He was a first-rate all-round sportsman and, as befits someone of his special stamp, at cricket he bowled an aggressive brand of underhand spin. His trademark was a frenzied dash up the wicket after letting go of his underhand delivery which prompted one of his victims to remark that it was the first time he had batted against a silly mid-on, a silly mid-off and a silly bowler!

Silly or not, Harry Stevenson ranks as one of the all-time greats and, as we have observed by his refusal to bow to Union pressure, he was not above ruffling the feathers of the high and mighty. In the same vein, when he attended the William Webb Ellis centenary celebrations in 1923 he stunned, and annoyed, his Old Rugbeian hosts by remarking that it was his earnest belief that at the Royal High School in Edinburgh they had been playing 'rugby' well before Ellis had, apparently, ignored the conventions of his day on The Close at Rugby School.

Stevenson, by this time a Writer to the Signet — a kind of top drawer Edinburgh lawyer — followed this up with a letter to *The Scotsman* in which he reiterated his contention that Rugby School's claim to have been the instigator of the carrying game was misguided. In 1937 he wrote to the newspaper as follows:

> Many years ago, when I had occasion to hunt for the origin of rugby, I discovered that the High School played a carrying game round about 1810. This fact I mentioned to some of my old English football friends and others when we gathered at Rugby in 1923 as representatives of the carrying game to help celebrate the centenary — so-called. When told that they had given the name 'Rugby' to the game, but that they certainly did not invent it as it had been played in Scotland for unknown years before 1823 and by the High School about 1810, some of them were very annoyed. I am not an old High School boy and in fact was one of her 'enemies' in the football world and only wish I could claim that my old school was as close to the origin of rugby as was the High School.

That was Harry Stevenson, a truculent

controversialist even into his old age. He is the last but one in our roll of honour; the best is saved for last. Darkie Bedell-Sivright, a powerhouse, charismatic forward with a complicated, intriguing personality whose special qualities shine still like a beacon over the years, is another – like Hely Hutchinson Almond – who deserves a chapter to himself.

TEN

First Among Equals

Darkie Bedell-Sivright

David Revell Bedell-Sivright, – Old Fettesian, son of the gentry, Scotland internationalist with 22 caps, captain of Cambridge University and of the British Lions – was one of the best read and intelligent men ever to have played for his country. He had an eye for the arts and an ear for music. He was a doctor of medicine and Scottish heavyweight boxing champion. He was also, on the testimony of all who saw him play, and those who had the misfortune to play against him, one of the most ruthlessly committed and ferocious rugby men who ever wore the thistle.

Darkie Bedell-Sivright – so-called in the politically incorrect terminology of the times because of his swarthy appearance – was born at North Cliff, North Queensferry, on 8 December, 1880. He was introduced to rugby at Fettes College, the leading Scottish public school in Edinburgh, which had been still under construction in 1871 when the inaugural international match between Scotland and England was held just a short distance away, at Raeburn Place.

After Bedell-Sivright left school he played for four clubs – Fettesian-Lorettonians, Edinburgh University, West of Scotland and

Cambridge University – and, as a hard-tackling, ball-handling, foot-rushing forward he epitomised all of the elements which turn-of-the-century Scottish packs liked to think was their special contribution to the game.

If contemporary accounts of his footballing prowess are to be believed then he probably played the game in a style which we would associate with wing-forward play today. In fact, in so many ways, in my mind's eye I see Darkie as coming very much from the same mould as David Leslie, that teak-hard flanker of 1984 Grand Slam fame.

Bedell-Sivright played 22 times for Scotland between 1900 and 1908. His pedigree was impeccable. He captained his country on one occasion, against the All Blacks at Inverleith in 1905 – a game in which the New Zealanders fielded seven backs while their forwards packed two-three-two and their controversial 'rover' proved a nuisance around the scrums – having led the British Isles to the Antipodes the previous year.

He had also toured South Africa with compatriot Mark Morrison's British Isles side in 1903 and was renowned throughout the world for the ferocity of his play. He was, in a marvellously descriptive word of the period, disregardless.

The Bedell-Sivright family had spent some time in the West Indies before setting up home on the northern shore of the Firth of Forth at North Queensferry. After school Darkie went up to Trinity College, Cambridge, and won four Blues between 1899 and 1902. He graduated with a BA from Cambridge and, after the British Lions tour to Australia and New Zealand and a short stay in Australia, returned to Edinburgh and its University where he took medicine and captained the University side between 1906 and 1909.

Bedell-Sivright led the British Lions to 14 straight wins in Australia, but then his luck deserted him. During the first game in New Zealand, against Canterbury, he broke a leg and never played again on tour; the captaincy went to Teddy Morgan of Wales. Instead of returning home, Darkie recuperated in Australia where he determined to become a stock-rearer. After 12 months, however, he decided that the life of a wild colonial boy was not for him: 'At the end of a year's jackarooing I took stock. What was I, with an average amount of brains and rather more of money, doing? Simply prostituting the one in order to increase the other. It wasn't good enough and so I chucked it and, with reluctance, came home to medicine.'

Back in his native land, Bedell-Sivright was welcomed with open arms by his old rugby cronies and soon added the captaincy of Edinburgh University to that he had already achieved at Cambridge. A contemporary remembers him thus:

My earliest recollections of Darkie Sivright are, when I was a small boy at school in Edinburgh, seeing him tearing down the football field, the terror of all school sides,

and the admiration of all the young Fettes boys. Going straight up from Fettes to Cambridge, he very quickly made his mark in the First Class rugger world, gaining his Blue in his first season.

He was always a very, very hard player and took an absolute delight in the game. To the uninitiated onlooker Darkie appeared to be a rough player but this was not so; it was only his great strength that made him a danger to the other side. I have only once seen, or heard of, him being laid out on a football field, and that was at an International match between Scotland and Ireland [Inverleith, 1907, but a Scottish victory nonetheless] when he and Basil Maclear collided; it was a case of one giant coming up against another and Darkie, probably being in a disadvantageous position, went under.

A friend of Darkie's once charged him with being an over-zealous player but he replied 'When I go on to that field I only see the ball, and wherever it goes I go too, and should someone be in the road, that is his own lookout.'

Of course during this time he gained innumerable caps for Scotland, and was for a long time one of the best forwards who ever donned a jersey. He became a player of repute, not only in this country, but also in the Colonies, touring through South Africa, Australia and New Zealand and gaining new laurels every day.

After going to Cambridge, a rumour went round Edinburgh that Darkie intended taking up the study of medicine. At the time this was treated as a huge joke, no one thinking that it was seriously meant; but in due course he duly arrived [back in Edinburgh] and immediately set at rest any doubt as to the seriousness of his studying medicine, for he forthwith commenced to settle down, and to work like the most studious bookworm. Nothing could seduce him away from his books, and at the end of the first term he passed through the class examinations with first-class honours.

His work, however, could not prevent him from being just as keen as ever on rugby football. He played for Edinburgh University, where he was always a tower of strength, and helped to keep that team one of the foremost in the country. He eventually became captain of Edinburgh University – surely a unique record for any man to have been captain of Cambridge and Edinburgh Universities. He finished his medical course with first-class honours, and took up some responsible hospital appointments.

While he was at Cambridge and Edinburgh Universities, Bedell-Sivright accumulated a massive library and spent hours each day reading. He was also an accomplished piper and pianist whose style at the keyboard was as idiosyncratic as it was on the football field. It was his peculiar foible, when tickling the ivories, to perch the music sheet on his knees instead of on the stand like ordinary mortals. There are also tales from his undergraduate days at Edinburgh which reveal that, though he was industrious and diligent as a student, he was a notable carouser as well. After one rugby victory he is said to have deposited himself on the tram rails in Princes Street and held up the traffic for an hour, no policeman being brave enough to remove him. Refreshed from his lie-down he then capped the performance with a magnificent flying tackle on an unfortunate cab horse at the West End.

On another occasion, as a newly qualified medic on duty at the Edinburgh Royal Infirmary outpatients' department, a Musselburgh fishwife was admitted to have her stomach pumped. As Bedell-Sivright was making ready with the hose, the patient changed her mind, pulled a knife from her stocking and chased Darkie along the corridor. Where scores of rugby adversaries had failed to put the wind up Bedell-Sivright, an inebriated fisherwoman had succeeded. Mind you, she was armed with a knife!

In Edinburgh, too, he developed a taste for the noble art of self-defence and became Scottish heavyweight boxing champion in 1904 during a title bout staged at Hengler's Circus in Glasgow. Darkie, and his brother James, who was capped against Wales in 1902, were regular attenders at a gymnasium run by Charlie Cotter at 84 Leith Street. Cotter was a strict disciplinarian and a trainer of high repute whose establishment was frequented by men from all classes of society. The Bedell-Sivrights rubbed shoulders, and traded punches, with miners, riveters, policemen, sailors, soldiers and stevedores from the docks at Leith. However, the Edinburgh University Athletic Club centenary history, published in 1966, recounts that the brothers were never on the best of terms and it was always Cotter's worst nightmare that they should both be in the gym at the same time. Harry Hilton Brown, an Edinburgh GP, was another who used the premises in his student days and he was enlisted by Cotter to make sure that the brothers did not meet. 'One day when Hilton Brown was training, Cotter took him aside and said, "Harry, try to get Darkie out of here as I am expecting his brother any moment now and goodness knows what will happen if they meet. I will never be able to separate those two powerful chaps if they start fighting."'

On another occasion, in 1906, Cotter was accompanying Bedell-Sivright on the train to

Glasgow where he was to make an attempt to regain his heavyweight crown.

They were travelling in the same carriage as one Whiteford, a miner from Dalkeith who was then the reigning champion. Hardly had the train passed Haymarket Station than Darkie started to shadow box in the compartment. He got more and more excited and wild as he pranced about hitting his imaginary opponent and swinging his arms about. Poor Whiteford, from the far corner of the carriage, looked on in dread with his eyes popping out of his head at this wild and powerful man. Cotter restrained him and all was well until Glasgow was reached. Unfortunately for Darkie this exhibition had given Whiteford food for thought, and when they met in the ring he was prepared for the wild rushes and flailing arms which had taken Burton [B-S's opponent when he won the championship] by surprise and proved his undoing. Whiteford avoided the wild rushes and punished Darkie unmercifully with his counter-punches. The fight went three rounds and Whiteford retained his title.

However, Darkie was never a man to take defeat lying down – literally or metaphorically – and in 1909 he regained the title. Dr C.W. Coughlan, who was also a member of that élite band which had bested Bedell-Sivright in the boxing ring – becoming Edinburgh University heavyweight champion in the process – had employed the same tactic as Whiteford. 'I made up my mind right away that, whatever else happened, I could not let Darkie lay a glove on me. If he did then it was "goodbye" to any chance I might ever have had of beating him.'

When the Great War broke out Bedell-Sivright was among the first to answer Lord Kitchener's call that his country needed him. He enlisted as a surgeon in the Royal Navy and here the tenor of our merry tale begins to take on a more sombre note.

Darkie joined the Navy on 25 January 1915, and trained at the Royal Naval Hospital, Haslar, and at the Royal Naval Division camp at Blandford before proceeding with the Royal Naval Division to the Dardanelles in April 1915. He died there, of acute septicaemia, on 5 September that same year. The circumstances of his death are as ironic as they are tragic.

He had been bitten by an insect, the wound turned septic and, in the days before antibiotics, his system was overcome by a ravaging infection. One of the roughest, toughest men ever to have played rugby for Scotland – some would say *the* roughest and toughest – was done to death by an Aegean gnat.

In the *Rugby Football Internationals' Roll of Honour* compiled by E.H.D. Sewell in 1919 as a literary and lasting monument to the British rugby internationalists who perished in the Great War, a sizeable tract is devoted to Darkie. In it, a friend provides an extract from a letter which Bedell-Sivright had written from the Gallipoli front. 'It makes me swear that I am a medico. I'd be ten times more useful with a parcel of jam-tin bombs and a few Turks in front of me, than as a sort of qualified vet.'

Another friend recounts a fateful last meeting with Darkie and hints that he might have had a premonition of his fate:

I shall never forget the last meeting I had with him. I met him in Southsea one day; he was at that time surgeon at Haslar Hospital, and arranged a little dinner party at Eastney

David Bedell-Sivright: pugilist, bibliophile, medicine man and one of the roughest, toughest individuals ever to have worn the Scottish thistle. SCOTTISH RUGBY UNION

Barracks. There were present on that occasion Darkie; Cartwright the old English captain; Maurice Dickson, the old Marlborough, Oxonian and Scottish football player; Paddy Murray and Russell-Cargill, old Edinburgh Academicals; Ronnie Fox, the old Free Forester wicket-keeper; and many other men well known in rugby, cricket and hockey circles. Darkie was strangely silent this evening and seemed quite preoccupied and not at all like his old self. I have seen a man who was with him almost to the last [at the Dardanelles]. He tells me that Darkie had returned from a long spell in the trenches at an advanced dressing-station, and came down properly fagged out. He got bitten by some kind of insect, and, being in a weak condition, poisoning set in, and he died two days after in a hospital ship, before it had weighed anchor. Darkie died fighting and thus passed away one of the finest men who ever left that famous nursery of rugby football, Fettes College.

Sewell's obituary concludes:

'Downright sheer hard play in all phases of the forward game was his forte. He was not out to excel in specialities, and did not hope or attempt to shine at hooking, or heeling, or dribbling, or tackling, or handling, or at the line-out. He just played this game for all it and he were worth, utterly heedless of all else during the 40 minutes each way. A grand

99

forward to have on your side, and beyond dispute one of the eight best of his time. Certainly one who will be remembered and spoken of as long as the rugby game is played.'

David Revell Bedell-Sivright, born 8 December 1880; died 5 September 1915. One of the greatest forwards of his, or any other, era. He was just 34 years old.

ELEVEN

Cutting the Old School Ties

The club game prospers

The inaugural international encounter with England in 1871 provided just the fillip that the game required to make the quantum leap from being a pastime enjoyed by a select band of former public schoolboys from Edinburgh and Glasgow into something approaching the nationwide game that we recognise today.

Seven clubs were represented in that Scotland XX of 1871, which gives the false impression that rugby football enjoyed widespread and popular support. In truth, virtually all of the clubs then playing in Scotland found themselves involved in that history-making match. Edinburgh Academicals (1857), Edinburgh University (1857), Merchistonians (1860), St Salvator, St Andrews (1862), West of Scotland (1865),

The Edinburgh Academical side of 1887–88 captain by Charles Reid. The captain, who was the youngest player to make his international debut with Scotland, sits at the centre of the group.

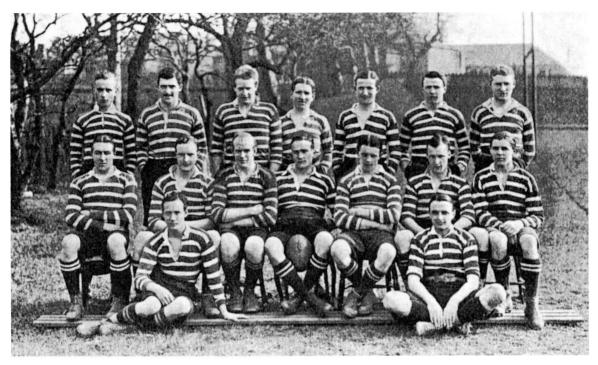

Glasgow Academicals were in virtually at the start of the Scottish game. This is their championship-winning side of 1912–13.

The Edinburgh Academical side of 1878–79. The great Ninian Finlay appears fourth from the left in the back row. Bill Maclagan, who went on to lead the British Isles side, is seated on the extreme left next to 'Bulldog' Irvine and Jock Graham.

Watsonians were another of the Edinburgh former pupil sides to make their mark on the early Scottish game. This is their championship-winning side of 1892–93.

Glasgow Academicals (1866) and Royal High School FP (1867) were the trailblazers of the Scottish game but, with the catalyst provided by the 1871 contest – and perhaps also by the handsome Scottish victory – the game was about to take off in a manner which could only have been dreamt of by the pioneers of the '50s and '60s. There were, indeed, a handful of clubs already in existence but which did not figure in the roll-call for the Raeburn Place match. For instance Edinburgh Wanderers had been operating since 1868, but the playing power of Scotland was still based to a significant degree on the recent former pupils of the handful of schools which had brought the game north of the border.

Throughout the 1870s the rugby map of Scotland began to adopt the form that is still recognisable today. Clubs sprang up in Langholm (1871), Hawick (1873), Greenock (1873), Kirkcaldy (1873), Kelso (1876), Galashiels (1875) and Melrose (1877). By the end of the decade the Watsonian club (1875) and Kelvinside Academicals (1878) had been formed and, from Wick and Lerwick (1878) in the far north to the Border country, where the game had taken hold with a vengeance, rugby union football could for the first time claim to be a truly national sport.

The most significant advance in the popularity of the game was the breaking of the shackles created by the old school tie and the foothold established in the Borders. Just why the handling game as opposed to that favoured by the Associationists should have found such favour in the Borders is a matter for conjecture. However, as we have seen, the traditional feast day games of hand ba' were already established right across the Borderland. In addition, the wool trade – spinning, dyeing and knitting – which, aside

103

from agriculture, was the principal means of livelihood in the Borders was also the industrial staple in Yorkshire, where the game of rugby was already well established. Certainly, Langholm, where tweed manufacture was the main line of commerce, had historical links with Yorkshire, and it is perhaps not surprising that it was in the Muckle Toon that rugby first surfaced in the Border country.

In fact, to Langholm belongs the distinction of being the first club of note outwith the major conurbations to prosper without a direct allegiance to the old school tie. The club was formed in 1871 when William Scott, Alfred Moses and William Lightbody – all sons of local tweed manufacturers who had been educated in England – invited the local lads to participate in this new game of rugby football. Their first get-together took place on Auld Year's Day 1871 and William Scott picked the sides from the large gathering on the Lamb Hill overlooking Milntown. The experiment must have gone well; the decision was taken a few weeks later in the Buccleuch Hotel to form a club proper. Initially, opposition from outwith the town was hard to come by and, in a variation of the medieval Uppies v Doonies encounters, the play was between the young men of the Old Town and the New Town, the boundary between the rival camps being formed by the River Esk.

William Scott, who was captain, secretary and treasurer of the newly formed club also owned the ball – which he had made by a local saddler – so he was, indeed, a supreme power in the land of Langholm rugby. Still, though, the fledgling club was experiencing difficulty in securing worthwhile opponents. Games were played against representatives from the outlying district and, perhaps naturally, because of the town's natural affinity with Carlisle, the first real game was against the lads from the Cumbrian 'capital'. There were the usual wrangles over interpretation of the rules. There was much heated debate over whether the game should be played 20 or 25-a-side. This point was settled on the basis that Langholm wanted to play 20 and, because it was their field and their ball, Carlisle could like it or lump it. Indeed, even before the game got underway at the Castleholme on 23 March 1873 the two sides had fallen out over the equally important point as to whether a goal was scored by kicking the ball over or under the bar. As we have already seen, a 'try' merely empowered the successful side to have a kick at goal, therefore this was no arcane point of law. Langholm defeated Carlisle by two goals to nil – both goals being kicked over the crossbar – and what must rank as one of the earliest cross-border club encounters was resolved in Scotland's favour when bad light stopped play and the ball was lost! Three weeks later the Langholm men travelled to 'Cairel' for the return match; on this occasion the Englishmen were victorious by the narrow margin of one dropped goal to nil.

While all of this activity was taking place in and around the Muckle Toon, the callants of Hawick were in the process of writing the first few lines in what would become the illustrious history of that famous club. On 16 October 1872 at a general meeting of the Hawick and Wilton Cricket Club in the town's Crown Hotel, two young men by the names of Ker and Michie proposed starting a football section.

Once again the game of cricket was about to spawn a footballing offshoot. It is worth noting that in the early days of the game pioneer rugby footballers followed the cricketing practice of making an 'appeal' when they considered that the laws had been broken. The captains were those empowered with the right to submit an appeal but, in reality, it appears that mass appeals were the norm. The early game was controlled by two roving umpires and it was not until some time later that the referee made his appearance as the sole arbiter of law. It was later still before he was equipped with a whistle. If an appeal was deemed to have been successful, the umpire raised his stick. If the referee allowed the appeal, the whistle was blown and the game was stopped for adjudication. If the referee considered that the appeal was unjustified then the game continued irrespective of whether or not an umpire had raised his stick. If both umpires raised their sticks, however, the referee had no option but to blow for a stoppage. The officials and the two captains were the sole arbiters of fact and law. It was not until 1896 that the practice of appealing was rendered obsolete. In view of this tortuous system of control is it any wonder that many newspaper accounts of the period reported that this, or that, game had ended in dispute?

However, let us return to events in the Crown Hotel, Hawick, on that autumn evening in 1872. It is a sign of the markedly different financial backgrounds of the Borderers and the affluent rugby pioneers in Edinburgh and Glasgow that one of the first items that had to be dealt with once the decision, in principle, had been taken to form a football club was the provision of a ball. As the jubilee history of the Hawick club, published in 1923, matter-of-factly reports: 'The young members of the club listened with considerable interest to a proposal brought forward by R. Michie and T. Ker, to open a subscription for the purpose of procuring a football as a first step towards starting the game in Hawick.'

The subscription was a success, a ball was procured and the football section was up and running. However, as Hawick's jubilee history notes, close observation of the rules of the game was not one of the chief characteristics of the fledgling footballers. Indeed, it was the football which arrived first; the rules came a poor second, some months afterwards. Eventually, Michie secured a copy of the Rugby rules and the game played in Hawick – whereby initially the only pressing requirements seem to have been that the teams be of roughly equal size and that they play in opposite directions – began to take coherent form. Around the same time a copy of the Association rules arrived in the town and in November 1873 a game was played on the Buccleuch Park under soccer rules in the first half and Rugby rules in the second.

However, the *Hawick Express* reported that Rugby had been the winner. 'As far as can be judged at present, the afternoon's play will probably result in the club adopting the Rugby Union rules as being the manlier and more congenial to the Border nature than the tamer Association game.'

Just over a fortnight later the *Express* writer's prescience was borne out when the footballers reconvened in the Crown Hotel on 8 December 1873 and a regular club was instituted. They decided, too, that the Rugby rules were those they would adopt for future play.

The formation of a club in Hawick now meant that the men of Langholm were no longer ploughing a lone furrow in the Borders. Shortly after the official formation of the club, the Hawick secretary wrote to his counterpart in the Muckle Toon suggesting that a game between the two clubs be arranged. William Scott replied saying that he thought that a very fine idea but, because the Langholm club had temporarily lost the use of its ground, the game could not be played there.

Early the following year Scott wrote again to his Hawick counterpart George Newton suggesting that the Langholm men come to Hawick and, as another indication of the state of anarchy which persisted over the laws, enclosing a copy of the rules as played in Langholm.

Langholm, 21st January 1874

Dear Sir, – At a meeting of the Football Club committee held last night it was arranged to play a match with your club at Hawick (as we have no ground here) on Saturday the 31st, if it would be convenient to you for us to come over. We play fifteen men a-side, no other rules than the enclosed, which I hope you will be able to play. We always carry a ball along with us, although we play with the ball belonging to the home club. We should like to commence play about 12 o'clock, but these particulars can be arranged at a later date. Would you please say whether you have a dressing room on your ground or not.

I am,

Yours truly,

WILL. SCOTT,

Secy., pro. tem.

PS – Please preserve the rules enclosed, as we wish to get some copies printed. If we come to Hawick I can get them then – W. S.

Scott's rules were those which he had obtained in Carlisle and were an Association-Rugby hybrid. They declared that a goal could only be scored if the ball passed under the crossbar – despite the fact that Scott had argued for over-the-bar conversions when Langholm had played Carlisle. Nevertheless, the game went ahead on 7 February 1874. The first formal football match to take place in Hawick resulted in a no-scoring draw, though a Langholm player had kicked the ball over the crossbar – or tape as it more properly was – which would have secured a victory for the visitors had they been playing to Rugby rules.

The two sides played a return match at Langholm on 21 March and although Hawick scored a 'try' the kick at goal was missed and, again, the outcome was a draw. Over the years, the Langholm spectators obtained a reputation for particularly one-eyed support for the men in scarlet. And, judging by the testimony from one Hawick player who took part in that second match, it was a reputation won early. The Hawick forwards had been mauling the Langholm men back to their line in double-quick time when, suddenly, the maul stopped and started moving just as rapidly in the opposite direction. The Hawick backs alleged that when the home spectators saw their side getting the worst of it, they had joined in at the rear of the maul and marched the Hawick men back upfield.

Hawick – or, as an off-shoot of the cricket club, Hawick and Wilton as they should more properly have been termed – were not at this stage the famous Greens. From 1878 the club uniform consisted of navy-blue jersey, knickers and hose with a blue and white striped belt. The original colours had been blue and white striped jerseys and the famous green jerseys did not make their appearance until 1885 by which time the relationship between the cricketers and their footballing off-spring had come to an acrimonious end. The rugby men wanted some autonomy from their erstwhile cricketing allies, but the cricketers would have none of it and, because they held right of tenure on Buccleuch Park, the footballers were forced to move to the next-door field on the Volunteer Park where the Hawick junior sides Trades and Linden still play. The parting of the ways was acrimonious in the extreme with the Hawick and Wilton element disputing the breakaway contingent's right to call themselves Hawick FC. The cricketing footballers even disputed the breakaway club's right to claim 1872 as their year of formation or to list the names of captains from that year. Nevertheless, in its new guise the Hawick club soldiered on regardless and to future glory, while Hawick and Wilton fell by the wayside as a football club but exists still in cricketing guise.

The game as played in the Borders by the mill hands and agricultural workers was altogether of a ruder and generally more robust nature than that enjoyed by the professional men in the cities. In fact, one city referee who had charge of an early Border derby match remarked, after a particularly torrid afternoon when he had been the butt of much ribald comment from the touchlines, that it was not a referee these people needed but a missionary.

Perhaps the Rev. Dr James Barclay, the Canonbie minister who had introduced the game to his parishioners, was thinking along the same lines when he was reported in the *Eskdale and Liddesdale Advertiser* as having done so to 'retard the drinking habits of the Canonbie colliers'. The following week the local paper was fizzing with letters from indignant parishioners. The editor brushed aside the allegation that his paper and the good reverend had libelled an entire community by declaring that he had copied the report from the *Hawick Advertiser*.

With the game now firmly established in Langholm and Hawick – other sides had also blossomed in the two towns, most notably Hawick St Cuthbert's – the new-fangled game obtained an even more secure foothold when teams were set up in Kelso, Galashiels and Melrose with Jedburgh following somewhat later in 1884.

The circumstances surrounding the formation of the Gala and Melrose clubs are particularly noteworthy; they also provide stark evidence of the strong rivalries which have sustained the town-based teams of the Borders, who would tear lumps out of each other on the football field but closed ranks

The Gala side of 1887–88.

when the common enemy was from outwith the Borderlands. This self-protection mechanism – in light of a game dominated throughout its formative years by a hierarchy bound together by the old school tie – would assume shape and form with the establishment of the Border League, which is still the world's most venerable rugby competition.

The Gala club, founded in 1875, contained a good sprinkling of players with public school backgrounds and a couple of Yorkshiremen, one of whom, W.H. Hudson, was elected captain for the 1876-77 season. Hudson and a number of his team-mates lived in Melrose and, although we cannot be certain now of the minutiae which surrounded the acrimonious debate which ensued, it seems that the Melrose contingent wished to move the headquarters of the club to the Abbey town. Lo and behold, one dark night in 1877 the Gala goalposts disappeared and mysteriously sprouted the following day at The Greenyards. Gone, too, were the Gala minute books, their black and yellow striped uniforms and the ball. They have long memories in the Borders and the ultra-competitive nature of rugby throughout Scottish rugby's southernmost outpost was born of incidents like the strange case of the disappearing goalposts.

For a region which has never been able to boast of many more than 100,000 souls, the Borders, and the clubs which emanated from its principal towns, has bequeathed a remarkable legacy to the game in Scotland. Border clubs have always been there or thereabouts when championship honours were being distributed and, since the advent of the official championship stakes in 1973-74, only Heriot's FP, Boroughmuir and Stirling County have, at the time of writing, encroached upon the Border clubs' monopoly of the championship crown. The conveyor belt which used to supply Border players for the national side – after a sticky start early on when Borderers complained that the area was not getting the recognition it deserved – has slowed down of late but the 1970s achievements of Hawick and Gala, who each supplied half a dozen players to the Scotland XV, is unlikely ever to be repeated in the modern era. For the record, Gala supplied Arthur Brown, John Frame, Jock Turner, Duncan Paterson, and Nairn McEwan to the side, captained by Peter Brown, which defeated England 16–15 at Twickenham in 1971; the same players turned out when Scotland defeated England 26–6 a week later at Murrayfield in a special game to mark the centenary of the first international. Hawick's sextet appeared during the 1978 Championship season when Jim Renwick, Alastair Cranston, Colin Deans, Norman Pender, Alan Tomes and Brian Hegarty were the chosen ones. Rabid 'Robbie Dyes' could stretch a point and claim that they went one better than their arch-rivals Gala during the match against Wales that season when Graham Hogg, a son of Hawick but playing out of Boroughmuir, came on as a replacement. But that would, indeed, be gilding the lily.

The south of Scotland has always maintained a love–hate relationship with officialdom as represented by the Scottish Rugby Union and its predecessor the Scottish Football Union. For instance, the Union was wont to become much exercised by the gifts on offer for the victors at the Border seven-a-sides. Numerous official missives winged their way from Edinburgh to offending clubs whose spectators had proved to be too boisterous for effete city ears and the Border League itself – established in 1901–02 by Langholm, Hawick, Gala, Melrose, Selkirk and Jed-Forest, to be played on a home and away

The Edinburgh University side, containing eight Internationalists, which won the Unofficial Championship in 1900–01. The side was captained by A.B. Flett.

basis with, horror of horrors so far as the Union was concerned, a trophy for the victors – went ahead despite the teeth-sucking disapproval of the powers that were.

There are even recorded instances of the full wrath of the Union descending upon Border clubs, which found themselves banned as a result. Two instances will suffice to give a snapshot of the relationship which existed between the Union and its brethren in the deep south. Gala were playing Watsonians at Mossilee in November 1894. The Gala players, led by their captain Tom Murdison, took great umbrage at what they considered to be the less than satisfactory nature of the refereeing. The spectators, too, let the referee know in no uncertain terms that they did not consider him to be having the best of games.

The referee submitted a report to the SFU and the committee backed the referee. Official sanction was about to descend on Murdison and the club when they intimated that they intended seeking redress through the courts. A law suit was raised but it soon fell by

the wayside for lack of funds. The challenge to the authority of the Union was something quite unheard of. The Union decided to make an example of Murdison, those who had supported him, and the club by a blanket ban. Murdison, and his financial backers, were banned *sine die* and the club was suspended until March the following year.

Then, in 1910, it was the turn of Hawick to be up before the SFU. The referee in the Hawick v Gala local derby in March of that year had reported Hawick to the Union for the mayhem which enveloped him at the end of the game. Unruly spectators, incensed at some of his decisions, had invaded the pitch. Scenes of great disorder erupted with missiles being thrown at the unfortunate individual. Only by the combined efforts of the players, police and Hawick officials was the referee able to reach a safe haven. The Scottish Football Union investigated and the verdict transmitted to Hawick declared that: 'While satisfied that no blame attaches to the officials or players of the Hawick Football Club, the

Edinburgh Institution, later to become Melville College FP. This is their championship-winning side of 1880–81.

Committee have resolved, after careful consideration, that the club play no more matches during the remainder of this season at Mansfield Park, or within a radius of ten miles thereof.' However, the club was able to stage its seven-a-side tournament in April of that year and the general consensus was that the club had escaped lightly.

While the Border clubs were making their sometimes stormy way along the road to acceptance in the Scottish game, the whip-hand still rested with the blue-chip clubs which had been in at the start. There was, of course, no official club championship in the beginning, but Edinburgh Academicals, from their formation until 1871–72 were the leading club in the land. In that 1871–72 season Glasgow Academicals and Edinburgh University shared the 'championship'.

Thereafter, the Academicals of Glasgow and Edinburgh vied with each other on an almost seasonal basis for the honour of becoming the leading club. As the century drew to a close Edinburgh Institution FP (which was to evolve via Melville College FP to the Stewart's-Melville FP of today), Royal High, West of Scotland, Watsonians, Clydesdale, Jed-Forest and Hawick each found their names up in lights – in the case of Hawick this had been literally true.

What became known as the Electric Light Match took place on the cricket field in Hawick on the evening of Monday, 24 February 1879. Electricity was, of course, at that time still a great novelty and the Hawick committee, hearing that a football match had been played in Sheffield under the electric light, determined to bring the

The Royal High School FP side dubbed Nat Watt's Lambs because of their robust style of play.
Nat Watt is seated fourth from the left.

wonder of the age to the Borders.

Melrose were invited to participate in the match, which would be illuminated by two Siemens dynamos each providing 1600 candlepower and driven by steam engines. The Hawick committee displayed entrepreneurial nous way ahead of their time by forming a limited liability company to protect the club's finances if the enterprise turned out to be a damp squib. Posters advertising the match were displayed throughout the Borders – a copy still exists in the Melrose clubrooms – and special trains were laid on frae a' the airts. The club had agreed to underwrite the cost of excursion trains from Melrose, Galashiels, Selkirk and St Boswells. The enterprise proved such a draw, however, that the influx of spectators from

Selkirk alone more than squared the £10 bond.

Nevertheless, the committee spent an anxious 24 hours before kick-off when the town was hit by a torrential storm which left snow lying six inches deep on the pitch. An army of unemployed workers was hired to clear the snow and, because they had not been instructed which part of the field to clear first, they began with the spectator enclosures. Soon after work had begun, and with a thaw underway, a snap frost descended on the cricket field. The areas which had been cleared began to resemble 'a field of ice with little ridges of scythe-like formations (being the outside of the shovel marks) running cross ways and length ways all over the surface, and giving the ground the appearance of a huge

111

A side no longer with us. The great Fettesian-Lorettonian side of 1885. A.R. Don Wauchope, who went on to become a stalwart of the Scotland side, is seated in the centre of the photograph.

carrot grater. Had the field itself been subjected to similar treatment the game would have been altogether impossible,' reports Hawick's jubilee history.

Throughout the afternoon huge crowds milled around the ground, each individual determined to catch a sight of these miraculous new machines. As the time of kick-off approached there were thousands of spectators, from all over the Borders, pushing and straining to get into the ground. The admission charge had been set at sixpence – one shilling for the reserved areas – and the takings amounted to £63. This equates to well over 2,000 spectators paying at the gate, but such was the crush and so overwhelmed was the poor committee-man sitting at a kitchen table equipped with an oil lamp and porcelain bowl for the takings that the same number again gained admission for nothing. Three or four times the heftier members of

the club had to employ all of their mauling skills to force shut the gates and prevent the multitude outside from rushing in *en masse* without paying.

For the first few minutes after the gate was opened the people came in a steady stream, occasioning the gatekeeper little trouble save keeping him busy, but as they arrived far faster than they could be admitted, the crowd outside gradually increased to huge dimensions and, as all were eager to get inside, quickly became impatient. The gate, which was an iron railing one, opened in two halves, and one half was opened and the other closed. The pressure of the crowd against the gate became heavier as the crowd increased, until the closed half of the gate was suddenly burst open, and the human avalanche – irresistible and triumphant, and it may be added, free, gratis and for nothing

Stewart's College F.P. This photograph dates from 1888.

— swept in, casting on one side the gatekeeper, table, chair, lamp and bowl in one confused heap. A few members of the club were quickly collected, and together, they succeeded after considerable difficulty, in forcibly closing the half of the gate again, and the gatekeeper was once more established at the receipt of custom.

The match itself was played out under the eerie and spasmodic light provided by the two generators – eerie and spasmodic because the crowd was so taken by the novelty that, time and again, individuals would rush in front of the lamps to see their huge shadows dance across the snow-covered grass. The players themselves would lose the ball in pools of darkness and many fine dribbling runs were cut off in their prime when the participants simply lost sight of the ball. For once, though, the game wasn't the thing. Hawick won by a

goal to nil; but the thousands who had braved the cold and who had come from all over the Borders and further afield had done so not so much for the fitba' but, in the manner of a revivalist crusade, to see the light.

Although the game had taken off in a huge way in the Borders, it would be almost the turn of the century before a club outwith the Edinburgh-Glasgow axis made its mark by winning the unofficial championship; that club was Hawick in 1895–96. The following season Jed-Forest shared the championship with Clydesdale and Watsonians but, despite spasmodic successes, the twentieth century would be almost half gone before Border clubs began to lay regular claim to championship honours. The manner in which the Scottish club game developed from its origins in the schools is one which has, on the one hand, proved providential but on the other has meant that – in the cities certainly –

The Hawick side of 1929–30 which won the Border League eight times in a row. The president, J.R. Morgan is flanked on his right by Willie Welsh and, on his left, by Jock Beattie. Doug Davies, who stands third left in the middle row, completed a trio of forwards who were among the most formidable of their day.

it was for too long confined to a minority, middle-class ghetto with no real chance of making the breakthrough into the population at large where Association Football held sway as the People's Game. Nevertheless, just as Scottish rugby as a whole owes a tremendous debt to the town-based Border clubs, which owed no allegiance to the old school tie, the groundwork done by the rugby-playing schools – mainly but not exclusively in the fee-paying sector – has served the Scottish game well for almost all of its existence.

Imagine how the map of Scottish rugby, and the game itself, would have turned out had the model established in England and Wales – with town-based sides like those in the Borders emerging as the leading clubs – been established in Scotland. Such conjecture became merely academic when the FP clubs abandoned their 'closed' status and began recruiting from outwith the schools which had spawned them. Nonetheless, it is probably true to say that Scottish rugby would have presented a completely different face to the world had it marched, from the outset, to the beat of a different and more egalitarian drum.

The focus of the Scottish club game is now the SRU championship which arrived – away ahead of its time and as a template for other nations to follow – in season 1973-74. Up until then clubs had organised their own fixtures, generally on the basis of long-standing tradition, and it was difficult if not downright impossible for relative latecomers on the scene to break into the self-perpetuating hierarchy of top clubs. There was, too, an 'unofficial' championship inspired and administered by the Scottish newspapers

Heriot's FP, were in the vanguard of the campaign to inaugurate an official club championship in Scotland. This is their unofficial championship-winning XV of 1919–20.

as a means of bringing some coherence and bite to the club season. Ultimately, some 33 clubs were involved in this deeply flawed entity which depended for its outcome very much on the strength of opposition faced by individual clubs. Nevertheless, in the absence of an alternative from the governing body, it was the only game in town and conducted without the Murrayfield stamp of approval.

Towards the end of the 1960s it had become generally recognised that ambitious, new clubs – and in this context 'new' could mean a stripling like Boroughmuir, founded in 1919, which won the 'unofficial' Championship at its first time of trying in 1955, the year of its admittance to the élite – were having their development stifled. Additionally, it was widely accepted that, for the sake of the national side, officially

sanctioned competitive rugby would have to be introduced. Push turned to shove, eventually, when Heriot's FP, backed by Glasgow High School FP, proposed a motion, couched in guarded terms, to the 1969 AGM of the SRU: 'That the committee of the Scottish Rugby Union should investigate the introduction of a system of competitive club rugby in Scotland, such system to be introduced at the earliest possible date.'

The investigation proved that the notion was worthwhile and, despite the administrative headaches that national leagues posed, the championship was up and running by the start of the 1973–74 season. It was an immediate success and nowhere more so than at Mansfield Park where Hawick held a stranglehold on the Scottish title for the first five seasons.

A unique occasion at The Greenyards in 1977. Hawick and Gala had tied for the official club championship that had come in three years beforehand and a play-off, won by Hawick, drew one of the largest ever crowds seen at the Melrose ground. Here, Peter Dods (Gala) is in receipt of the ball with Hawick's Kenny McCartney and Jim Renwick moving across in defence. SOUTHERN REPORTER

Hawick's fourth Scottish crown was won in a play-off against Gala at The Greenyards after the two clubs had finished the season inseparable. Thereafter, Heriot's FP – who had a proprietorial interests in the championship in that, officially at any rate, it had been their idea – took the trophy back to Goldenacre in 1979. Gala won the next two championships, followed by Hawick, then Gala again. Between 1984 and 1987 Hawick won four on the trot at which point Kelso enjoyed two seasons as the champion club. As the 1980s drew to a close, Melrose were emerging as a real force in the land and their championship in 1990 was but an early warning of the dominant force that they were to become. Boroughmuir won the championship the following season; but there then followed three back-to-back championships from Melrose, which were followed, in season 1994–95, by a real rags to riches victory by Stirling County. The

Bridgehaugh side had clawed its way through six divisions within as many seasons to achieve first-division status in 1989. Within six years they had won the championship, a remarkable achievement indeed.

Since then, though, Melrose have confirmed their status as the leading club in Scotland. Where Hawick left off in the 80s Melrose have taken over with real aplomb. Championships in 1996 and 1997, both achieved at the start of the professional era wherein, arguably, competition has never been more fierce, have – at the time of writing – underlined the Greenyards' club as the foremost in the land.

The official championship was the making of the club game in Scotland and where Scotland led other Home Nations have followed. The championship spawned another novelty for the Scottish game when it was the recipient of commercial backing from the soft

Hawick captain Norman Suddon is borne aloft by Colin Deans and Alan Tomes in celebration of the Mansfield Park side winning the first official Scottish championship in 1973–74. SOUTHERN REPORTER

Gala won three Scottish championships in 1979–80, 1980–81 and 1982–83. This is the Netherdale club's 1983 championship-winning side captained by David Leslie. SOUTHERN REPORTER

Hawick established themselves as Scotland's top club with five consecutive championships between 1974 and 1978. The champagne flows after the play-off victory against Gala in 1977. SOUTHERN REPORTER

Hawick were to the forefront again with another four consecutive championships between 1984 and 1987. This is the side, captained by Colin Deans, which was successful in 1985. Hugh McLeod, the president that year, was Hawick's double British Lion who had earlier played a central role in the success of the club by introducing new training methods learnt on his Lions' crusades. SOUTHERN REPORTER

Heriot's FP, captained by Andy Irvine, ended Hawick's monopoly of the championship in season 1978–79.
JACK FISHER/HERIOT'S FP

Another year, another trophy. The Hawick side which lifted the title in 1986. SOUTHERN REPORTER

Kelso enjoyed a two-season spell as champions of Scotland in 1987–88 and 1988–89. This is the side which lifted the championship trophy in 1988. SOUTHERN REPORTER

Boroughmuir became only the second side from outwith the Borders to win the Scottish championship when they powered their way to the title in 1990–91. The Meggetland club had won the old Unofficial Championship at the first time of trying in 1955.

The season 1989–90 heralded the appearance of Melrose as Scotland's top club of the 1990s. Between 1990 and 1997 the Greenyards club won no fewer than six Scottish titles. This is 1990-vintage Melrose with 'Gel' Tait and Keith Robertson held aloft. SOUTHERN REPORTER

Stirling County posted a unique achievement with their Scottish championship in 1994-95. The Bridgehaugh club had battled its way through every division to wear the crown in 1995. WHYLER PHOTOS

Melrose were virtually unassailable, with only Watsonians coming close, en route to the title in 1997. Captain Bryan Redpath is the man with the silverware. SOUTHERN REPORTER

Hawick, who had won Scotland's first Official League Championship, record a unique double by winning the first Scottish Cup. The Cup final, played at Murrayfield against Watsonians in 1996, was an occasion long overdue in the Scottish game. Hawick captain Brian Renwick reaches out for the SRU–Tennents Cup. SOUTHERN REPORTER

Scottish rugby's first Cup competition culminated in three finals at Murrayfield on Saturday 11 May 1996.

drinks company Schweppes in 1977. This was an association which was to last for nine years until McEwan's took over the sponsorship in 1986. Rival brewers Tennent-Caledonian replaced McEwan's at the start of the 1995–96 season and with them came yet another innovation. The first truly national cup competition, which had been one of the disregarded aims of the founding fathers of the Union in 1873, finally came to fruition when Hawick – first to have their name inscribed on the League trophy – came from behind to beat Watsonians in the Murrayfield final and repeat the feat with the SRU-Tennents Cup.

In its second season, Melrose crowned a season of outstanding achievement with victory over Boroughmuir in the final at Murrayfield. Melrose achieved the first League and Cup double in the history of the Scottish game. In 1997, too, they had won the Border League and their own seven-a-side

119

Melrose clinched the League and Cup double with victory over Boroughmuir in the 1997 SRU–Tennents Cup Final at Murrayfield. They had already that season won the Border League and their own seven-a-side tournament. It was a remarkable achievement. Here the victors enjoy the spoils of victory in their Murrayfield dressing-room.

Captain Bryan Redpath accepts the trophy from SRU president Fred McLeod.

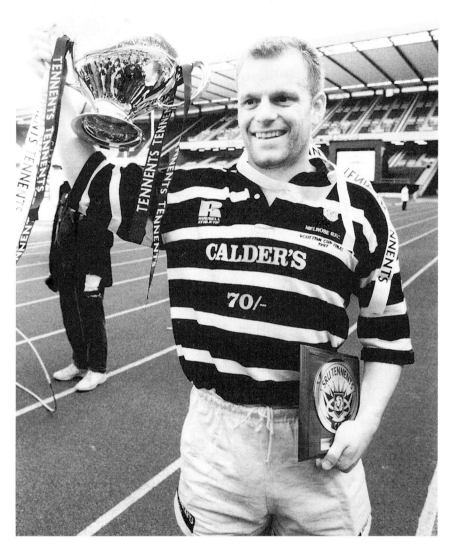

Rowen Shepherd was named man of the match for his personal contribution of 26 points to the 31–23 victory which included a hat-trick of tries.

tournament. It was a domestic Grand Slam and one unlikely ever to be repeated. That Melrose side, led by the international scrum-half Bryan Redpath, has truly earned itself a place in the annals as one of the best club combinations ever seen in Scotland. The Melrose club has not, yet, matched the championship-winning prowess of the Hawick sides of the '70s and '80s but it has prospered, arguably, at a time when the across-the-board competition has been fiercer and more sustained. The '90s belong to Melrose, who look like being the club for the new millennium.

121

TWELVE

A Home to Call Their Own

Scotland's International grounds

The circle was squared in the autumn of 1996 when the Scottish Rugby Union unveiled the final stage of its £44 million redevelopment of Murrayfield Stadium. The occasion was the hanselling of 16 new hospitality suites; in naming these latest additions to the Murrayfield complex, the Union acknowledged a link with the past and paid homage to one of Scotland's greatest ever sides.

There is a clue in the names bestowed upon each of the new suites – Drysdale, Smith, Macpherson, Aitken, Wallace, Waddell, Nelson, Davies, Ireland, Howie, MacMyn, Bannerman, Scott, Gillies, Paterson and McKenzie. They are, of course, members of that 1925 side which defeated England on the very day that the original Murrayfield Stadium was opened to a world-record crowd destined to witness Scottish rugby's first Grand Slam. Sir R.C. McKenzie, you might not know. He was the Glasgow Academical who had the great good fortune to be president as Phil Macpherson and his men played their way into rugby folklore, becoming along the way, Scottish rugby's first immortals. McKenzie was a former international player himself. He made his début against Ireland in 1877 and promptly celebrated with a hat-trick of tries and two

dropped goals. The opening ceremony was performed by Jimmie Ireland, the last surviving member of Macpherson's side, and the seamless link spanning 71 years of occupancy on the meadowlands by the Water of Leith was complete.

Scottish rugby's latest home, with seating accommodation for 67,500, hospitality suites catering for over 2,000, and new offices and comprehensive library facilities for the SRU, transform Murrayfield into one of the biggest and most modern sporting venues in Europe. Plans have been drawn up for a new and extensive museum which, it is hoped, can be built before the turn of the century. This latest transfiguration of Murrayfield Stadium may be the most radical yet but, in reality, it is just the latest stage in a process of evolution which stretches back to the 1920s, when the Union reacted to the growing popularity of the game and abandoned its first permanent home at Inverleith for the Edinburgh Polo Club's wide-open spaces down by the riverside.

The new Murrayfield was officially opened by the SRU Patron, HRH the Princess Royal, on Saturday, 19 November 1994, when South Africa, then recently returned from international exile, defeated Gavin Hastings' Scotland side 34–10.

Scottish rugby's long association with Murrayfield began in the early 1920s as the game outgrew Inverleith. And although the land was actually purchased from the Polo Club in 1922, it was not until three years later that the then state-of-the-art stadium rose from the riverside meadows. The new stadium's introduction to the rugby public could not have taken place under more auspicious circumstances. The date was 25 March 1925 and G.P.S. Macpherson's Scotsmen secured the first Grand Slam in Scottish rugby history. They did so with an epic 14–11 win over England.

The tale of Scottish rugby's quest for a home to call its own begins not at Murrayfield and not in the twentieth century at all. It begins in the year 1871 and across the city, five miles to the north-east of Murrayfield.

Raeburn Place, in the Edinburgh suburb of Stockbridge, was where it all began. Here, as we have seen, in the former village which even by 1871 was becoming very much a part of the city, a Scottish XX played an English XX in the world's first rugby union international. Scotland won by a goal and a try to a solitary try from England. The *Glasgow Herald* of Tuesday, 28 March 1871, reported that the game had been played 'with a most gratifying result for Scotland' and before a 'very large turn-out of spectators', each of whom had paid a shilling for the privilege of being 'in' at the start of something big.

The venue of Scotland's next home game in 1873 was the West of Scotland Cricket Ground at Hamilton Crescent; the fact that Glasgow, or more properly Partick, was considered a suitable venue indicated that the handling code, even then, had influential devotees in the west of Scotland.

For the next 22 years, with the exception of three further visits to Hamilton Crescent,

Raeburn Place, the home of Edinburgh Academical FC, was recognised as the cradle of Scottish rugby from 1871 until the move to Inverleith in 1899. Here, we see the kick-off in the game between Scotland and England at Raeburn Place in 1892. The conical mound, with flag-staff at the summit, provided a vantage point for spectators who could not gain entry to the specially erected stands. SCOTTISH RUGBY UNION

The painting, by W.H. Overend and L.P. Smythe depicts the Calcutta Cup match at Raeburn Place in 1886. The Scottish forward in the foreground racing back in support is Charles Reid, who was first capped while still an Edinburgh Academy schoolboy. The Calcutta Cup, which was first played for in 1879, was fashioned from the silver rupees withdrawn from the bank when the Calcutta Rugby Club went into abeyance. EDINBURGH ACADEMICAL FC

Powderhall in Edinburgh was used as an International venue while the new ground at Inverleith was being made ready. This is the match against Ireland in 1897. SCOTTISH RUGBY UNION

the Edinburgh Academical cricket ground continued to find favour as the first-choice international venue. However, as the very first game had gone there only after a split vote on the cricket club committee, it became apparent that the SFU would have to find a venue of its own on which to stage its international matches. With a splendid disregard for the international events which were taking place on its doorstep, the Academy refused to be overawed and continued to insist on its pupils making use of the playing field on the morning of international matches.

The SFU decided that the situation could not continue and stepped up its quest to find a permanent location for its international matches. An unsuccessful approach was made to Fettes College, whose governors declined to lease a plot of land where Broughton High School and the Lothians and Borders Police HQ now stand.

By 1895 the relationship between the Union and the Academical Club had come to an end, the Academicals declaring that, regretfully, Raeburn Place would not be available for lease in future. For the next four years, while the Union continued its efforts to secure a playing field of its own, international matches maintained a nomadic existence with Old Hampden Park and Powderhall in Edinburgh being pressed into service.

But, in the meantime, the Union had secured land at Inverleith just a mile or so north of Raeburn Place and, for the princely sum of £3,800 (to be paid for then, as now, with debentures), the SFU became the world's first rugby union authority to enjoy the benefits of its own ground. The moving force behind the purchase was the SFU's legendary honorary secretary and treasurer James Aikman Smith. A stickler for the laws and an arch-opponent of professionalism (or anything which smacked of it), Aikman Smith exerted a stern yet benign influence over

Inverleith, now the base of Stewart's–Melville FP, was Scotland's International ground between 1899 and 1925. This is the match between Scotland and Wales in 1907. The palatial press box in the background is, of course, no longer there.

Scottish rugby for the next three decades and more.

The Inverleith ground, now the home of Stewart's-Melville FP, and incorporating the Daniel Stewart's and Melville College playing fields, was made ready for international use by the reconstruction of an impressive stand. The ground was ready in time for the Welsh match of January 1899 but the wintry weather caused the match to be postponed, and the official opening did not take place until the game against Ireland a month later.

Sadly for the Scots, the Irish – no doubt apologetic in the extreme – managed to spoil the party by recording a 9–3 win. However, honour was restored a fortnight later in the rescheduled game against Wales when Mark Morrison's Scottish XV scored an emphatic 21–10 victory over the Welshmen. The SFU's new home, which from the outset attracted huge crowds, proved to be a major success with players and viewing public alike.

Inverleith continued in service for a quarter of a century until, by 1925, it had been outgrown. The SFU had attempted to purchase an additional plot of land to the east of the ground on which it had intended to construct a second stand, but negotiations fell through and the decision was taken to begin looking, once again, for a suitable plot of real estate.

And, once again, the man doing the looking was Aikman Smith. By 1922 he was reporting to the SFU committee that the ideal site might have been found. The area in question was the 19 acres owned by the Edinburgh Polo Club at Murrayfield. The go-ahead was given and, with yet another issue of debentures, the ground was purchased and work began on building the stand and raising the three embankments which for the next six decades would be such a feature of the Old Murrayfield.

But why Murrayfield? Who was the Murray who has given his name to a sporting stadium known the world over? The answer appears in a housing transaction concluded over 250 years ago when Archibald Murray, second son of Archibald Murray of Cringletie, near Peebles, built himself a mansion on the policies of Nisbet Park, which at the time was open countryside. The house,

The decision to move to the Edinburgh Polo Club's grounds at Murrayfield would, by the time the new facility was opened for the Grand Slam decider against England in 1925, provide Scottish rugby with the world's most lavishly appointed stadium. These hitherto unpublished photographs show the embankments being raised with the stickyard in the foreground. The foundations for the massive West Stand are made ready and, girder by girder, the stand begins to rise from the ground. The finished article is seen from the air. The two wings extensions to the main stand were added in 1936. SCOTTISH RUGBY UNION

completed in 1735, still stands at the head of Murrayfield Avenue and, much added to, is now a residential home for the elderly.

However, by 1925 the SRU's new Murrayfield stadium was ready for use. The final game at Inverleith was played against the French in January of that year (a 25–4 win) and with subsequent victories over Wales (24–14) and Ireland (14–8), the stage was set for a fairytale Grand Slam baptism of fire for the new stadium.

Workmen toiled until the last moment putting the finishing touches to the stadium which was to host the biggest rugby union crowd the world had ever seen. As the late Doug Davies, the rugged Hawick forward and a member of the victorious Scotland pack, observed: 'They were still working on the place when we got there. The smell of freshness was everywhere and there were still bits and pieces to be finished off.'

At Inverleith the maximum attendance had been 30,000 but on 21 March 1925 over 70,000 spectators thronged the wonderful new ground for the Grand Slam showdown with England. They were expecting something special and were not disappointed.

Fortunes ebbed this way and that as the lead changed hands three times and the participants played themselves almost to a standstill in the bright spring sunshine. Scotland trailed 5–8 at the interval, England having taken the lead with a Luddington penalty goal. Scotland snatched it back with a try by Nelson converted by Drysdale, and then England moved back into the driving seat with a Hamilton–Wickes try, converted by Luddington.

After half-time, England forged further ahead with a try by Wakefield, but Scotland fought back with a Wallace try converted by Gillies. Then, with just five minutes left, Herbert Waddell ('showing commendable coolness in a nerve-trying situation', said the *Glasgow Herald* match report) dropped a goal from the 25-yard line. The ball sailed between the uprights and the partisan crowd cheered with delight. England threw everything but the kitchen sink at the Scots in the closing five minutes and at one point it seemed as though L.J. Corbett was certain to score and deny the Scots their first Grand Slam. The Bristol centre-threequarter was in the clear with the line at his mercy but, again in the words of the *Herald* scribe, he 'fell through sheer exhaustion when another yard would have carried him over'. Scotland continued to defend as if their lives depended upon it and, with virtually the final kick of the game, England played their last shot when T.E. Holliday, the Asparita full-back, sent an attempted drop-kick wide of the uprights. That was it. The new Murrayfield had been the setting for one of the most exciting games of rugby ever seen and Scotland had won the historic first Grand Slam.

The massive crowd was ecstatic and the *Glasgow Herald*'s man in the press box wrote in understated prose: 'There was a wonderful scene at the finish, many of the crowd swarming on to the field so that the players had to make their way to the dressing-rooms through a delighted and cheering crowd.'

In the ensuing years the face of Murrayfield continued to change in an effort to keep pace with the demands of the game and the exigencies of the time. Then, as now, the demand for stand tickets was insatiable. In 1936 two wing extensions were added to the already cavernous stand and seating capacity was raised to 15,228. The clock tower, for so many years a feature of the south terracing but now relocated behind the East stand, was presented to the Union in 1929 and in the following year Aikman Smith presented the first score-box.

Another innovation took place in 1959 when Dr C.A. Hepburn provided funds to pay for the installation of undersoil heating. Thereafter, the Murrayfield pitch became immune to the vagaries of the often disruptive weather.

With the SRU offices transferred from Coates Crescent to Murrayfield in 1964, the stadium was now, more than ever, the proper HQ of the game in Scotland, and still Murrayfield continued to develop and attempted to keep pace with the rapidly expanding popularity of the game.

The Union had been considering covered enclosures or a new stand to replace the East terracing but, at the time, these concepts were laid aside on the grounds of cost. Like most sporting venues, Murrayfield continued to operate a 'come one, come all' policy of admission at the turnstiles. But in 1975, when a then world-record crowd of 104,000 (with many thousands more turned away) jammed in to see Scotland defeat Wales 12–10, the decision was taken on safety grounds to introduce a ticket-only policy with an upper limit of 70,000.

In the early 1980s, with safety considerations on the massive East terracing in mind, and with the continuously rising demand for seated accommodation, the radical decision was taken to demolish the East terraces and to construct a new stand. The £3.15 million plan was financed in large measure by a Scottish Sports Council grant and the issuing of 5,000 interest-free, 20-year loans of £400, for which the lender was awarded the right to purchase one ticket for each home international. The stand was in use for the games against Ireland and Wales in 1983 but officially opened by the SRU's enthusiastic patron at a special Barbarians fixture in March of that year.

The timing was a year out. Just 12 months later and the East stand would have stood silent witness to a Grand Slam, just as the new stadium had done 59 years before.

This time it was Jim Aitken's men who played out the final act of their Grand Slam drama before the Murrayfield faithful. The visitors this time were the French. The final scoreline of 21–12 does not tell the entire story. The Scots were sorely harried by Jean-Pierre Rives's Frenchmen whose discipline finally deserted them after the Scots, showing great character and courage, had weathered the French storm and through the boot of Peter Dods had reaped the whirlwind of penalties which the Welsh referee Winston Jones awarded against the Tricolors.

For the Scots the turning point came with Jim Calder's try from a lineout on the French line. It was immortalised as *The Turning Point* in the Royal Bank-commissioned painting by Ronnie Browne. Scotland had won her second Grand Slam and, once again, Murrayfield had provided the backdrop to the action.

It was always intended that the new East stand would be just the starting point for a comprehensive facelift. Initial proposals were for a 65,000 capacity stadium with two-tier stands on the end terracings, the upper deck providing seating accommodation while the lower tiers would provide covered terracings for those who still preferred to watch their rugby from a standing position.

But the Hillsborough soccer stadium disaster meant that the plan had to be re-evaluated. Lord Justice Taylor's inquiry and subsequent report recommended in 1990 that all stadia which came within the remit of the Safety of Sports Ground Act 1975 should be all seated by the start of the 1995 season. As the Act made no distinction between football and rugby, the SRU was left with no alternative but to comply. Murrayfield would have to become an all-seater super stadium.

The design team began work in 1990, but not before Murrayfield had hosted its third Grand Slam. From the moment David Sole led his side out with that slow, almost menacing, gladiatorial march until the final seconds when the Scots defended like lions to maintain their 13–7 lead, it had become obvious to all 55,000 present that here was a game in a million.

It was a day of high passion, courageous commitment and almost unbearable excitement. It was a day when 'The Flower of Scotland' came of age as the Murrayfield anthem and it was a day, too, when all of the great prizes were on offer to the side which could best hold its nerve. The Grand Slam, the Championship, the Triple Crown and the Calcutta Cup: they were all there for the taking, and they would go to the side which

wanted them most. They went to Scotland. It was Murrayfield's third Grand Slam and, surely, it had been the most compelling.

Behind the scenes, though, the redevelopment plans were at an advanced stage. A three-phase plan was approved in 1991. The first phase called for the redevelopment of the terraces to provide continuity with the East stand and the provision of two-tiered seated accommodation for 26,000 spectators along with hospitality provision for around 1,000.

Work began on the new North and South stands at the conclusion of the 1992 Championship season and was completed at the end of December in the same year. The stands, to the marvel of many, were in use by the start of the 1993 season and for the World Cup Sevens tournament in late spring of the same year.

The new Murrayfield under construction to provide a new stadium fit for the millennium.

The new stadium complex, with seating for 67,500, corporate hospitality facilities for 2000, offices, library and a new museum promised before the year 2000, in all of its glory.

And the Sevens circus had hardly vacated the premises before the builders moved in again and demolition work began on the grand old West stand. Originally, it had been intended to retain the structure but with the addition of a second tier. However, due mainly to the success of the new Murrayfield debenture scheme, the Union decided to broaden the scope of the plan by opting for complete demolition which would mean 2,500 extra seats and a total ground capacity of 67,500.

As the wreckers moved in it was, for many, like watching the departure of a dear old friend. From the dust, though, rose the final piece in the new Murrayfield jigsaw. The arena was complete and, just as in 1925 when workmen laboured through the night to make ready the Old Murrayfield, the new stadium was made ready for public inspection on the day of the 1994 Calcutta Cup match only after much burning of midnight oil by a small army of dedicated workers.

The game itself (if not the result, which was a 15–14 defeat for Scotland) was a more than fitting introduction to the new Murrayfield.

Sixty-nine years beforehand 70,000 spectators had marvelled at the new home of Scottish rugby. On 5 February 1994 some 49,500 of their latter-day counterparts did the same. At that game only the central section of the new West stand was in operation. Throughout the summer, work continued on the wing sections and the project was complete in time for the Springboks match and the official opening ceremony.

Which is where we came in. Scottish rugby has a stadium more than fit for the twenty-first century but the pukka, pony-riding gents of the Edinburgh Polo Club certainly wouldn't recognise the old paddock now.

By the turn of the century Murrayfield's last remaining links with the 1925 stadium will have gone. Even the single remaining and most obvious association with the original amphitheatre which was the wonder of its age, is set to go. The pitch and its sub-soil was laid down three-quarters of a century ago. The Scottish Rugby Union plans to relay the hallowed turf before the new millennium begins. The whispering grass. If it could talk what tales it could tell.

THIRTEEN

Spanning the Twentieth Century

Jimmie Ireland

There is no substitute for the first-hand account, the testimony of the eyewitness, the individual who was actually there. Jimmie Ireland, the last surviving member of Scotland's Grand Slam team of 1925, is a man who can provide a player's account of the first Grand Slam in the history of the Scottish game and, in many ways even more invaluably, someone whose experience spanned the twentieth century during which rugby underwent a myriad of changes to become the game we know today.

Scottish internationalist and a Barbarian – Glasgow High School FP's first – international referee, president of the Scottish Rugby Union and chairman of the International Rugby Football Board – Jimmie Ireland, born on 10 December 1903 in the second city of Empire, and educated at Garnotbank Primary and the High School of Glasgow, provides a unique insight into the game that was and the game that is.

When we spoke we did so in his flat in Polmont – a flat he and his wife had moved to on their return from London after Jimmie had retired from the senior position he held in the brewing trade. Originally, they had intended the modest Polmont flat to be a pied-à-terre in Scotland, to be used as a base from which

they could look for the preferred retirement location on the Clyde in Argyll. But they never got around to it, and Polmont it was.

When we spoke Jimmie was well into his nineties but still the upright gent that he had been in his playing days. His mind was as sharp as a tack and he had total recall of a lifetime spent in the game. He made no bones about it. He didn't like what had happened to the game which had been his lifelong love and considered that he and his contemporaries had enjoyed the best of it by a long chalk.

The 1925 Grand Slam, which hanselled the new Murrayfield Stadium in spectacular style, was the highlight of Ireland's playing career but, as we shall see, 'Grand Slam' was a term never used at the time. Then, as now, victory over England was the principal motivating force in any season. It just so happened that the 14–11 win over the Auld Enemy on 21 March, 1925, was the final instalment in a winning sequence which read France (25–4), Wales (24–14) and Ireland (14–8). The Welsh and the Irish had been accounted for in Swansea and Dublin. The Tricolors had been defeated in the final international match at Inverleith and the denouement was played out in the pristine and, ready just in time, Murrayfield.

Jimmie Ireland, the longest surviving member of Scotland's 1925 Grand Slam side. Ireland's experience as player, referee and administrator provided him with a unique overview of the development of the game throughout the twentieth century. FALKIRK HERALD

Ireland, a hooker whose initials, J.C.H., gave rise to the teasing epithet Jimmie Cannae Hook, played in all but the opening game of that season against France. He won his third cap in the game against the Auld Enemy and played eight more times for his country before retiring from the international arena in 1927. 'I continued playing club rugby with Glasgow High until 1931 and then retired from the game as a player. Later, I refereed the five internationals before World War II. To be honest it wasn't something that I particularly enjoyed. It was just one of those things that you did to put something back into the game.'

Ireland's first contacts with the game before the Great War and his sporting experiences at the High School in Glasgow provided him,

through his schoolmasters, with a direct link to those who had moulded the late nineteenth century game into what it has become today.

'I went to Garnotbank Primary School and then on to the High School of Glasgow in 1916. That was when I made my first efforts in rugby. I had watched games before that because both my brothers played for the High School. It was very much a rugby household but nobody was allowed to talk rugby at home in case they got swollen-headed. I got my schools cap when I was 14, which was pretty early. I was a hooker then and was a hooker throughout my career.

'Schoolmasters had a terrific influence. They were the be-all and end-all of the game. They sacrificed a lot of their time. On Tuesday afternoons, Thursday afternoons and Saturday mornings the same three masters were to be found at Anniesland. They were great chaps. They gave us all the coaching that we ever had. That was when the basics of the game were drummed into you and, in actual fact, it was the only coaching we ever had. Even when you went on to play international rugby you brought with you everything you had learned at school. There were no coaches in the senior game in those days. The captain and the senior players would decide what the tactics were going to be but everyone who played the game then had learnt the basics at school.

'These masters at the High School would be in their thirties or thereabouts and they had links going right back to the beginnings of the game. The rugby part of the school was absolutely super. It was a great thing to be involved in. The school was in Elmbank Street in those days and we used to go through to Edinburgh to play the likes of George Heriot's and Watson's College. We went through by train. We paid our own fare too. It was a bit of an adventure and great fun.'

Ireland maintains that the game as played in the early years of the twentieth century, both at school and club level, bore little resemblance to the game of today.

'The standard of rugby was very high. It was a very open style we played then. We had none of this nonsense with the ball getting stuck with the forwards. The ball was nearly always in the open – with the backs – except when the forwards were dribbling. Nowadays when the ball gets stuck in a loose scrummage the ball in those days would be on the ground and we would form a scrummage and take it away with the feet. Immediately you had got the advantage the scrum-half, or anybody really, would get the ball away and open the game up.

'The art of dribbling is worth talking about. And it really was an art. You would dribble the ball away from a loose scrummage, but the real, proper time to think about dribbling was when you wheeled away from a set scrum. The scrum would wheel and the second rows would take the ball on with their feet. We would be packing down in a three-two-three formation and the second rows would break away and charge upfield with the ball at their feet. Breaking off at the knuckle it was called when the forwards generated a footrush at a set scrummage.

'It was a grand feeling to be involved in a dribble. It took an awful lot of stopping. If you had three or four chaps bearing down on you with the ball at their feet then you really did have to think twice about trying to stop it. You would have the poor full-back waiting to throw himself at the feet. It was quite a thought. A quick dribbler could run like the wind. We did a lot of practice. It was a recognised part of the game. We would dribble from one end of the field to the other.'

The lost art of dribbling, of course, was what gave rise to the forgotten Scottish battle-cry of 'Feet, Scotland, Feet'. There were few more awe-inspiring sights in the game than that of a Scottish pack in full cry, bearing down on the opposition with the ball at their feet.

'It was a controlled thing. You didn't just kick and chase the ball. You controlled it with the feet just as they used to do in soccer and, strangely enough, a lot of our chaps were very good soccer players. We had a scrum room at Anniesland and we used to do all of our dribbling training playing soccer with a rugby ball. A good dribbler had the ability to control the ball just as a soccer player would and there was also inter-passing between the forwards. John Bannerman was a super dribbler but he couldn't pass the ball whereas Ludovic Stewart who was in the same side with me at High School, had perfected the art so much that he could sweep the ball from one foot to the other – cross-dribbling it was called.

'In those days, too, we had the famous Rugby Rovers' game against Queen's Park FC. In fact the only newspaper cutting that I ever kept was one from that game in which it was written that J.C.H. Ireland had scored a brilliant goal. I was terribly proud of that. We were allowed 13 men against their 11. We had such men as J.M. Bannerman, the Dykes brothers, Herbert Waddell and Roy Kinnear the Herioter who actually played for Queen's Park and went on to play professional rugby with the Northern Union. The Rovers' games were played at Hampden Park. It was a big occasion, huge crowds. It was always something to be picked for the Rugby Rovers. We would have a dinner afterwards at Reid's of Gordon Street. Great days.'

Jimmie is now well into his stride and the reminiscences are flowing thick and fast – the people and the places remembered from a

Ireland, who played out of Glasgow High School, was that club's first Barbarian and went on to become president of the Scottish Rugby Union and chairman of the International Board. He would not trade his playing days for the lot of the modern professional.

lifetime in the game. But mainly the people.

'I had a great pal in Hawick, Doug Davies. He was a lifelong friend due, I think, to the fact that the very first international I played in, somebody belted me and Doug who was a very old hand said 'leave the laddie alane' and when Doug said that you tended to do as you were told. Later on, when I was president of the SRU, another great Hawick player, Willie Welsh, had turned pro and I was seen to have shaken hands with him. That didn't go down well in some quarters. Different times, indeed.'

And soon, Ireland is returning to his theme that the game just isn't what it was. It would be easy to dismiss his memories as those of an old man hankering after lost days of youth when the summers were longer and, of course, warmer and the rugby was altogether of a rosier hue, too. But he was there. As a boy, he played the game as the German Kaiser waged war on the battlefields of France. He was the last of his generation, the last of the 1925 Grand Slam heroes. If he says it was so,

then he is, at the very least, deserving of a serious hearing.

'The game was much more open, much more of a sporting and athletic spectacle than it seems to be nowadays. The real bug-bear in terms of what has happened to the game was that the International Board set out to make it something which was of much more interest to the spectator. But, in my opinion, they got it all wrong. They just closed the game down and made it less interesting for the onlooker. You see, in the very early days, with people like H.H. Almond the headmaster of Loretto, the thinking was that rugby was a game for players and it didn't really matter a hoot what the spectators thought.'

In the late autumn of 1996 Jimmie was back at Murrayfield to perform the opening ceremony at a block of new SRU hospitality suites each named after a member of the 1925 Grand Slam side and that season's president Sir R.C. McKenzie of Glasgow Academicals. Until very late on in his life Jimmy was a habitual and welcome guest of the Union at home internationals in the stadium – unrecognisable from 1925 – where he had experienced his 80 minutes of rugby glory.

He was much too much of a gentleman ever to have said so during those latter day outings to Murrayfield but he confided, not for the first time, over coffee and biscuits in Polmont that latterly the sport had not enthused him in the way that it once had.

'I don't fancy the game much nowadays. The brutality of it and the importance of it. I'm still very interested in the game, and the fellows who play nowadays seem to enjoy it, so it is up to them, and if they like the way the game is played now, then that is nothing to do with me. But I do think that we have ruined the game by trying to please the spectator. In the mid-fifties we stopped playing the ball with the foot after a tackle and that has led to an awful lot of difficulties. The forwards get together and start tearing the ball out of each other's hands and the next thing is they are tearing lumps out of each other. I don't like that.

'In my day there wasn't what I would call rough play in the way there is today. The laws when I played didn't aid rough play, if I can put it that way. For instance, in my refereeing days, even when I was refereeing internationals, we had about five things to bother about – putting the ball unfairly into the scrum, the knock-on and so on; but now the referee has a host of things to look out for. Frankly, it is beyond them and it has bred a feeling that the referee is too much to blame for anything that goes wrong.

'The size of players taking part in international rugby these days is quite remarkable. When I was playing for Scotland I was just under six feet and weighed twelve stone eight pounds. The likes of Scaly Paterson – J.R. Paterson – a magnificent

wing-forward would be no more than five foot eight inches or thereabouts and not a very heavy fellow at that. Now you have wing-forwards who stand six foot four inches and who weigh in at 18 stone. In addition, no self-respecting international hooker these days would want to be weighing less than 15 stone. Even allowing for the fact that people generally are bigger than they were half a century ago, the size of rugby players now is absolutely remarkable.'

Jimmie got his 1925 call-up to the colours after serving as a reserve in the opening championship game against France.

'It was John Bannerman who told me. He was a clubmate, of course, and he phoned me up after the French match and told me that I would be in the side to play Wales. Then there was a postcard from the union confirming my selection.'

Later on that season there was also a little local difficulty with his employers, Singer's of Clydebank, when he asked for the Saturday off to go through to Edinburgh to play against England.

'This story has been told often enough but it was true. I was working in the accounts department for Singer's of Clydebank and when I asked for the Saturday off to play for Scotland they asked me if I was sure that I needed the whole day. It was a wee chap in the accountancy office who wondered if I would be okay with just a half day. He hadn't the power to say that I could take the whole day off and he had to put it to his boss. Eventually, they said it was all right but they weren't impressed at all that I was playing rugby for Scotland. Singer's was a soccer place.'

Despite the fact that he had been an official reserve for the match against France at Inverleith – the last occasion on which what is now the Stewart's-Melville FP ground was used for an international – Ireland had played no part in the proceedings.

'There were no replacements in those days. You were a reserve but once the team had got to the ground and they were all fit and well then your part in the exercise was over. I recall that after it had been confirmed that I wasn't required, I sat in the enclosure with Margaret McLean, the girl I was to marry, and her mother and father. Her brother Robbie was the Scottish sprint champion who ran seven times second to Eric Liddell in the 100 and 200 yards. Eventually, though, he got one championship after all these years of chasing Eric.'

Eric Liddell, of course, is the double internationalist – rugby and athletics – immortalised in the Oscar-winning film *Chariots of Fire* who would not participate in sport on the Sabbath because of his Christian beliefs. He became a missionary in China, where he had been born of missionary parents, and died in the Japanese internment camp at Weifeng in 1945 at the age of 43.

Liddell was probably the greatest athlete Scotland has ever produced. At the 1924 Olympic Games in Paris he declined to run in the 100 metres heats because they were scheduled for a Sunday. Instead, he triumphed in the 400 metres to win Olympic gold. He was capped seven times out of Edinburgh University on the wing for Scotland in 1922 and 1923 and, despite the fact that their international careers did not overlap, Ireland knew him well.

'On his last visit to Scotland he stayed the night with us in Glasgow. He was a delightful fellow. He wasn't at all a Holy Willie. He was just a nice, good man. He wouldn't play on the Sabbath but he didn't make a great deal of it. That was just the way he was and everybody respected him for it.'

The regime surrounding international

Eric Liddell, the international wing who refused to compete on the Sabbath because of his Christian faith, winning his Olympic gold medal at the 1924 Games in Paris. Liddell, who died in a Japanese internment camp during the Second World War was, says Ireland, a nice, good man and not at all a Holy Willie. He stayed with the Irelands during his last night in Scotland. EDINBURGH UNIVERSITY ATHLETIC CLUB

weekends in the 1920s was as nonchalant as it is super-heated and intense in these days of professionalism and interminable squad sessions. Ireland recalls the routine leading up to that 1925 Grand Slam showdown with England. It was no different to all the others.

'On the morning of the international the Glasgow chaps got the 11 o'clock train from Queen Street to Waverley Station. We would arrive in Edinburgh about 12 o'clock and have lunch in the North British Hotel. The team would have lunch together and then go to the ground. For the game against England the dressing-rooms at Murrayfield weren't ready and so we togged in the hotel and went to the ground by bus. After the game we came back to the hotel still in our playing kit to get changed and have a bath in our rooms. No, actually, we didn't have a bath in our rooms. The Union wouldn't pay for en-suite bathrooms and we had our bath in the bathrooms down the corridor.

'It was always a great thrill to play for Scotland but, even more than that, it was great fun meeting your team-mates again. We were all very pally. Compared to nowadays it all seems so low-key but on the morning of an international match there was the same excitement in the air that there is nowadays. There was no coaching, though, or squad sessions or anything of that sort.

'Basically, what happened was that John Bannerman would tell you what to do although John wouldn't really go into the specifics. John wasn't much of a tactician. But somebody like Dan Drysdale might point out that the opposition full-back was a bit dicey and that we were going to try him out with a few high kicks early on. He might say the left centre was reckoned to be a bit weak in defence. Let's have a go at him. But no more than that. Other than that there was no detailed game-plan as to what you should do and so on.

'There was no detailed talk about who would tackle the first man round the scrummage or who was going to tackle the full-back or the wing if the need arose. You had just been brought up at school to know what to do. It was common sense. The tactics were very much unstructured. There was no distinct route that a fellow had to take. But, in my opinion, international matches in those

days were very much more entertaining than they are now. Nowadays if so and so gets the ball he is told what to do. In my day you did what the hell you liked with it . . . what was best. I don't think we lost anything at all from not being coached.'

The new stadium at Murrayfield, where a then world-record crowd of 70,000 turned out to watch the game against England, was the miracle of the age. It was the most modern and among the first, genuine arena-type rugby stadia in the world.

'After that match against France at Inverleith the international game in Scotland was bound for Murrayfield. I had seen it passing in the train but none of us, certainly none of us from Glasgow, had been at the ground before we turned up to play England. It had been well written up in the papers and so we knew what it was going to be like. There was just the one stand there, the West stand, and the all-round terraces, but even so it was a magnificent place.

'I always remember that for the bus ride from the North British to Murrayfield we got a police outrider escort. That was very impressive, I thought. Murrayfield itself was the last word. It was a huge modern stadium. But our preparation was still all very low-key. For instance, there was nothing like David Sole's slow march out onto the pitch in 1990. I must say, I didn't agree with that. I thought it showed a wee bit of arrogance. I don't want to take anything away from David or the chaps who played for Scotland that day but I didn't like it. But I'm a right old die-hard and I daresay I'm out of step with the times.'

The match itself was one of the all-time great encounters of the rugby world. The Scots eventually won 14–11, but the lead changed hands three times with England, led by Wavell Wakefield, hammering away at the Scottish line, to the point of exhaustion, in an unsuccessful effort to turn the game their way. Ireland remembers well his first sight of the new stadium on match day.

'When we came out on to the pitch we saw one of the biggest crowds that had ever been at a rugby match. There were 70,000 or thereabouts in the ground. I got a real thrill about that. From the pitch all you could see were acres of faces but I remember picking out Margaret sitting in the stand. You know, we didn't know a thing then about playing for something called the Grand Slam. To beat England. That was the thing. The Grand Slam was just something that somebody invented later – I suppose it was the Press. The great thing, always, was to beat England. I was lucky. I played them three times and we won three times.

'The game seemed to go on for ages. It was a real struggle. I would say that even by the standards of today we were pretty fit. You know, five of the Scottish forwards who played that day could do the 100 yards in just over 11 seconds. That was dashed good going. It was a pack which could really get about the field and the backs were of a different class too.

'But, no matter how fit we were, nearly everybody was almost out on his feet by the time the final whistle went. John Bannerman's greatest pleasure, though, was to see that no matter how tired we were, there were half a dozen Englishmen lying down on the ground out for the count. That pleased him more than winning the game. He said we had played the Englishmen into the ground.'

Phil Macpherson, one of the great all-Oxford University threequarter line (the others were I.S. Smith, G.G. Aitken and A.C. Wallace), captained the side that day, but John Bannerman was the undisputed leader of the pack.

'Phil was simply a wonderful captain. He was a super chap and a marvellous player. So full of friendship and full of life. Of course, politically, John started off as a Nationalist, then he became factor to the Duke of Montrose, who was a staunch Liberal, and John became a Liberal and he ended up a Liberal peer. So far as his playing was concerned, and I don't mean to do him a disservice, I don't think he was a brilliant player but, my goodness, he was consistent. He was capped 37 times for his country and, so far as I was concerned, it was a joy to play with him. He was so full of enthusiasm. Most of our chaps, and more so the England players, were desperately tired after the game but I don't recall me personally being completely done for. The crowd ran on to the pitch at the end and we had a struggle to get back to the stand.

'At the dinner in the Freemasons' Hall in George Street, John Bannerman myself and two of the English players – R.R.F. MacLennan and another whose name I can't remember – sat and sang Gaelic songs. MacLennan had an estate in Scotland and he had been taught by a Gaelic nurse and, even then, John was something of an authority on Gaelic culture. After the dinner we went dancing, so we couldn't have been that tired.'

That 1925 match was, of course, the highlight of Ireland's international career. He continued to play for Scotland until 1927 and, as he has said, experienced two further victories over the Auld Enemy. In 1926 at Twickenham, Ireland exchanged jerseys with the England prop 'Marine' Webb of Northampton and learnt at first-hand the thrifty nature of the Union in those days.

'I received a bill from the Edinburgh outfitters Aitken and Niven for 12s 6d. When, years later, I joined the Marines I met 'Marine' Webb again in Plymouth and was able to tell him that he had cost me the princely sum of 12s 6d.

'When my international career came to an end I knew that I would be dropped. I was completely off form with the High School as well. Nobody said anything. The letter from the Union just didn't arrive. I fancied myself as a scrum-half or a threequarter and, at Anniesland, if somebody was off I would be shoved into one of these positions and, looking back, it didn't do my rugby any good. I was quite fast, I could do the 100 in just over 11 secs but it didn't do my rugby any good. People used to say that I didn't want to be a forward any longer. It wasn't true, but that was the perception and I was out of the side.'

Once his playing career came to an end in the early 1930s Ireland took up refereeing. He was an international touch-judge too.

'I ran the line at the 1938 Triple Crown game at Twickenham. That was a thriller – Wilson Shaw's game. At one point Wilson dashed for the line and scored and I asked him why the hell he hadn't run around the posts, but he said he didn't dare because the last time he had done that the ball had been knocked out of his hands. He was a very special player indeed.'

Ireland's playing career spanned the period when allegiance to the Old School Tie held true in Edinburgh and Glasgow while the game in the Borders was still the province of the artisan. However, he never experienced any sense of élitism in the 1920s game.

'No, there just wasn't any of that. Maybe that was more of an Edinburgh thing. Certainly at Glasgow High School we always got on terribly well with the Borderers, particularly the Hawick players. They were the tops. The Borderers probably went in for more forward play. In the forwards you were dealing, in the main, with fellows who were doing physical jobs every day of the week and

a bang in the face probably wasn't going to make the same impression on them as forwards from the cities who were mainly office people.

'Hawick's Doug Davies just epitomised the hard Border farming forward of those days. Whenever our two clubs were playing against each other I used to put him down and say: "You'll have been round the hill this morning Doug" and he would say "aye."

'As I've said, he looked after me in that first international against Wales in Swansea. I think I was probably getting the better of the Welsh hooker in the scrums, and they thought they would try and even things up a bit. He was a tough, tough player but someone who became a friend for life.'

From the vantage point of someone whose life has spanned the best part of a century, Jimmie Ireland is ideally placed to identify the players who made the most impression on him – the best players that he had ever seen or encountered on the field of play.

'That's a very difficult question because we are talking about so many different players from different eras, but England's Wavell Wakefield was a very fine forward. He must be one of the best ever. John Jeffrey also ranks high in my mind. He was always on the ball and seemed to be tireless. Another very fine fellow was Colin Deans the Hawick hooker – a very good player and a good captain as well.

'If I was pressed to name the best backs I ever saw, I would probably have to go for the Oxford threequarter line en masse – Smith, Aitken, Wallace and MacPherson; but Ken Scotland was another very fine footballer. I don't think he ever got the recognition he deserved.

'Both the 1984 and 1990 Scottish Grand Slam teams contained some fine footballers. David Sole was a very fine player indeed, but I've already said that I didn't like that walk out on to the pitch and I didn't like him cutting the sleeve off his jersey either. He did it so that his opposite number couldn't grab hold of it in the scrum, but he was also making a statement that the referee didn't know what he was doing. I didn't like that.

'I would have to say that I don't like professionalism. There's too much money in the game now. John Bannerman once said that when the game became a matter of personalities it would be on its downward path and I think that is quite right. People are becoming more important than the game. The game is the thing, even more than the team. Schools are so important. That's where the groundwork has to be done to ensure that young people playing the game know what it's all about. The game, at all levels, should be about camaraderie. If we lose that then we will have lost the one thing which set rugby union apart from all other international sports. And what a great loss that would be.'

Ireland's critical views on the professional turn that the game has taken are a lament for the lost values and attitudes of a bygone era. They are none the less valid for that. But in the realm of the true Corinthian, the arch opponent of the corrosive effects of filthy lucre, Ireland was but a beginner compared to James Aikman Smith, the leading apostle of amateurism who as honorary secretary, committee-man and president, steered the Scottish Football Union and then the Scottish Rugby Union down the straight and narrow path of militant amateurism from the turn of the century and into the 1930s.

Jimmie Ireland as a young internationalist was somewhat in awe of the seemingly authoritarian Aikman Smith.

'I knew him as well as anybody could. Napoleon he was called. He was Mr Rugby. In Scotland and even on the International Board his word was law. I was one of his favourites. I don't know why. When I was retiring as a player he said to me: "Look here my boy. I hear that you're going to referee. Remember, a referee is a painful bloody neccessity. Never forget that."

'He would have been an old man by that time but, somehow, you never thought of Aikman Smith as an old man. He was very good. He did have a reputation as being a bit of a martinet and, probably, it was well deserved but, in terms of the period he was operating in, he was a very fair man. Everything was well considered. Frankly, I think most of the chaps on the SRU were frightened of him but the players got on with him very well.

'He was undoubtedly very hard on professionalism. He had nothing against professionals on an individual basis. It was the concept of professionalism that he was set against. Roy Kinnear from Heriot's FP, who was capped thrice for Scotland in 1926 and who was the father of the comedian of the same name, went to Northern Union as a professional.

'Aikman Smith was obviously sorry to see him go. But what I am about to tell you is a side of Aikman Smith that nobody knew much about. When Kinnear had finally made up his mind to go Aikman Smith said to him that he should bring in his agreement. Aikman Smith studied the contract and told Kinnear that he was getting a good deal and that he couldn't do any better than that. That was the other side of the famous Aikman Smith who was so hot on professionalism.

'The point was that he abhorred the thought of professionalism within rugby union but he had nothing against the Northern Union game and, one assumes because he was willing to help Kinnear, he had nothing against chaps who decided that they wanted to go.'

Ireland himself moved into the administrative side of the game soon after his retirement as a player. In tandem with his refereeing duties he became an SRU representative for Glasgow in 1936. He was president of the Union in 1950–51 and for five years in the '50s was a Scottish representative on the International Board.

'I was actually chairman of the International Board when we admitted the Dominions of Australia, New Zealand and South Africa into full membership of the Board. Until then it had only been the Home Unions, Scotland, England, Ireland and Wales who were in full membership. That was a historic day for the world game.'

Ireland left Singers for Mackay's, the whisky merchants and then went to the brewers William Younger's where he remained for 34 years until his retirement, the final 15 years being spent in London where he was responsible for the company's affairs in the south of England.

In 1964 Ireland was made an honorary vice-president of the South African Rugby Football Board. The award recognised the work which he had done on behalf of the Dominions during the campaign to have them admitted to full membership of the IB but also, on a personal level, his friendship with Danie Craven who, it seemed, almost singlehandedly oversaw the affairs of Springbok rugby for much of the twentieth century. The two of them had a lot in common.

CHAPTER FOURTEEN

Best Team of Seven Men

Melrose legacy to the world

The best ideas are often born of adversity and it was a temporary pecuniary embarrassment that spawned the seven–a–side game which is now played all over the rugby world. The concept of an abbreviated game of rugby was the brainchild of the Melrose quarter-back and apprentice butcher Adam 'Ned' Haig. The year was 1883 and, some say, because of a cash shortfall which had resulted from that season's encounter with near neighbours and traditional rivals Gala, the Melrose club was in sore need of a quick financial fix.

Folklore has it that when the two clubs, which as we have seen began as one, were due to meet in the 1882-83 season, the Greenyards' committee-men decided to increase the entrance fee from threepence to sixpence. This did not go down well in Galashiels where the Braw Lads and Lasses determined that they would go to the game but, if the price increase was insisted upon, then they would watch the match from the other side of the fence. The Melrose committee, realising that the Gala spectators were determined to remain outside, quickly took stock. On the basis that half a loaf was better than no bread, it was decided that the entrance fee would, indeed, be the customary

threepence. By this time, however, the Gala masses had stormed the gate and most of them gained entry for nothing. The upshot was that the Melrose club were left with a gaping hole in the bank balance. All minds were set to work on how the shortfall could be made up.

Ned Haig was born in Jedburgh on 7 December 1858. He was a teenager when he upped sticks and settled in Melrose, where he was taken on as an apprentice butcher by Davie Sanderson. Their association transcended an alliance forged in trade and they formed an alliance at quarter-back for the Melrose club. Haig was 22 when he made his début at The Greenyards – so called after the 'green yairds' employed as a source of horticultural produce by the monks from the nearby Cistercian abbey – after he had his appetite for the game whetted in the local Fastern's E'en Ba' game. That was in 1880. Three years later the club was undergoing its financial crisis and it was the young quarter-back who came up with the idea of staging a sports day with place- and drop-kicking competitions, dribbling races, foot races and a football tournament. Many years later Haig explained the rationale behind the concept which, no doubt, had been discussed and

Adam 'Ned' Haig, originator of the seven-a-side game. Want of money, said Haig, made the Melrose club rack its brains in an effort to come up with a money-spinning idea which would keep the club afloat. The first Melrose Sevens were staged in 1883. The rest is history. SOUTHERN REPORTER

debated with his playing partner in the back shop of their butcher's emporium in Melrose:

Want of money made us rack our brains as to what was to be done to prevent the club from going to the wall. The idea struck us that a football tournament might prove attractive but as it was hopeless to think of having several games in one afternoon with 15 players on each side, the teams were reduced to seven men.

With the passing of the years the ancillary events have, largely, fallen by the wayside, leaving the football tournament as the principal attraction. The original format, however, is recalled in the still current title of 'The Sports' endowed upon the numerous seven-a-side tournaments which sprang up in the Borders in the wake of that initial success

at The Greenyards on 28 April 1883.

And success it was. The ladies of Melrose had provided a handsome silver trophy 'for the best team of seven men in any Border football club' and, glory be, it went to Melrose. The Melrose victory, however, was accompanied by not a little controversy as this splendidly partisan account of the first Sports, published in the Galashiels-based *Border Advertiser* on 2 May 1883, so vividly describes:

Under the auspices of the above [Melrose] club the Sports were held in the Greenyards field on Saturday. The event began at 12.30 and concluded at 7.30. The day was not very favourable being very cold during the forepart and wet long before the close.

By the time the competition had started an enormous crowd of spectators had gathered, special trains having been run from Galashiels and Hawick and about 1600 tickets being taken at Melrose during the day. From the former place alone there were 862 persons booked, of whom 509 came by special train and the other 353 by ordinary train. Despite the crowd and open character of the field, there was no attempt on this occasion to force entry without payment, the ground being kept by a large staff of County Police under Mr Porter. As football has been the popular game of the season in the district, perhaps its nature corresponds with the spirit of the hardy Borderers. The competition has been looked forward to with great interest as most of the clubs of the district were expected to compete for the prize – a silver cup presented by the ladies of Melrose.

The excitement during the game was thus great and that portion of the spectators belonging to the various townships did all it could to encourage its club. Specially was this the case on the part of the Galashiels people who leaped the barrier on several occasions at critical points of play by their club and mixed among the players. To their credit be it said, yet, no portion of spectators, however warm their feelings, interfered with any of the clubs. The competition was played under rugby rules – 15 minutes' play being allowed to each heat, and seven members of each club competing. The regulations were that in the first heat, should two clubs tie, they would both be allowed to play in the second, should two clubs tie in the second round of the competition, they shall play on until one scores, when that one shall be declared the winner of the heat.

Melrose and Gala were left to decide the result of the final. The ground by this time was soft and slippery owing to the rain and the Gala team were pretty well knocked–up after a tough contest with St Cuthberts. After a short interval, however, they were forced to begin again or run the risk of being disqualified. The Melrose team had a long rest and the two clubs they had played previously were both light and they were therefore much fresher than their opponents. The interest of the spectators in the proceedings were now increased and the

The Melrose Seven which won the world's first seven-a-side tournament, held at The Greenyards on 28 April 1883. The afternoon ended in some controversy as Melrose scored the winning try in extra-time and immediately left the pitch to collect the Ladies Cup. Thus was born the seven-a-side concept of sudden-death. Haig is photographed in the back-row second from the left and his quarter-back partner Davie Sanderson is seated at the front. MELROSE RFC

result was contemplated with considerable curiosity, as it was known that keen rivalry existed between the two clubs, both having denied defeat in the last match played between them.

They played for 15 minutes, a fast and rough game but, as nothing was scored, it

Pace, power, possession and vision are the attributes which combine to create a seven capable of beating all-comers. In the early '70s this Gala outfit captained by Peter Brown had them all and, in the mid-'80s, the mantle of Kings of the seven-a-side circuit had passed to Kelso photographed here after winning the 1986 Melrose final.

145

The Hawick Seven of 1926–27 which won the Border circuit 'Grand Slam' with trophies from Gala, Melrose, Hawick, Jed-Forest and Langholm sevens. Back row: W.A. Mactaggart, A.C. Pinder, A. Bowie, R.N.R. Storrie. Front: J. Fraser, G.R. Cairns, D. Patterson (president), D.S. Davies, W.B. Welsh.

Perhaps the greatest club seven of them all. The Hawick players who contributed to their club's ten-in-a-row record between 1966 and 1967. They won all of the spring and autumn tournaments in 1966 as well as the Gala and Melrose tournaments in 1967. Back row: Robbie Welsh, John Auckinleck, Alex Graham, Rob Brydon, Jim Hay, Brian Patterson, Douglas Jackson. Front row: Colin Telfer, Peter Robertson, Hugh Laidlaw (president), Norman Suddon and Harry Whitaker.

was agreed by the captains to play another quarter of an hour. After ten minutes' play, Melrose obtained a try and left the field without either trying to kick their goal or finishing the game, claiming the cup; but their title to do so was challenged by Gala on the grounds that the game had not been finished. The proceedings were then brought to an abrupt conclusion and the spectators left the ground amid much noise and confusion. It is said the referee decided the tie in favour of Melrose but that they should have played the quarter of an hour before they were entitled to claim the cup. The Galashiels supporters were warm in their declaration that their townsmen had hardly got justice, and the opinion generally expressed was that the final should have been postponed to another day, in order to give both clubs fair play.

Melrose – J. Simson, D. Sanderson, N. Haig, J. Riddell, T. Riddell, G. Mercer and J. Tacket.
Gala – A.J. Sanderson, J. Hewat, W. Rae, W. Wear, T. Oliver, J. Ward and T. Smith.

First round: Gala 1 goal 1 try, 2 touches-down, Selkirk 0; St Cuthbert's–Hawick 1 goal 3 tries, Earlston 0; Melrose 1 goal 3 tries, St Ronan's–Innerleithen 0; Gala Forest v Kelso (Gala Forest walkover).
Semi-finals: Melrose 1 goal 2 tries, Gala Forest 0; Gala 1 try 2 touches-down, St Cuthbert's-Hawick 0.
Final: Melrose 1 try, Gala 0.

That contentious, extra-time try, which by happenstance gave rise to the sudden-death seven-a-side denouement, was scored by Haig's partner and captain Davie Sanderson. The controversial manner in which the Melrose men had secured the Ladies cup did not prevent other Border clubs from latching onto what had turned out to be a money-spinning event which more than lived up to its billing of 'five hours' entertainment for sixpence'; in short order, Gala, Hawick, Jed-Forest and Langholm followed suit. It was an idea whose time had definitely arrived. Selkirk and Kelso decided to stage their own tournaments in the autumn and soon city clubs were getting in on the act too.

Edinburgh Institution, Newington and St George's were organising tournaments in the first decade of the twentieth century and, because the Tynedale and Carlisle clubs had been early participants in the Border sevens, tournaments began to spring up in the north of England. The concept took a little longer to arrive in London and it was a Scot, Dr J.A. Russell Cargill, who was the driving force behind the Middlesex tournament at Twickenham, which was staged for the first time on 24 April 1926.

The seven-a-side concept has now been adopted all over the world. It was given a huge nudge along the way to world status by the SRU centenary sevens, which took place at Murrayfield in 1973. Hong Kong, where the first tournament was staged in 1976, has assumed the mantle of the premier event on the world stage, where national sides now strut their stuff in the magnificent HK Stadium gifted by the Royal Hong Kong Jockey Club. But in a club context – and the more so since Melrose took the decision to invite overseas guests – a gold winners' medal from The Greenyards is still a treasured and hard-won possession for any rugby player, anywhere in the world.

Ned Haig's brainchild received the stamp of approval from those who run the world game with the decision to stage a Rugby World Cup Sevens tournament every four years from 1993. The inaugural tournament, won by Andrew Harriman's England side, was

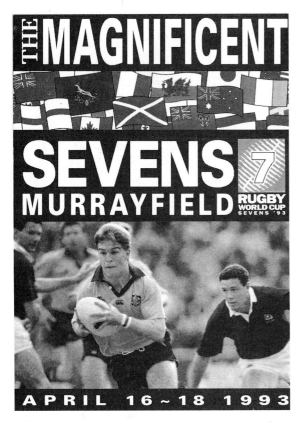

The Hong Kong Sevens gave the abbreviated game a place on the global stage but to Murrayfield in Scotland, the home of the game, went the honour of staging the first Rugby World Cup tournament.

England were the victors at the inaugural RWC Sevens at Murrayfield. Andy Harriman's men fought off a stiff challenge from the Southern Hemisphere and South Pacific maestros of the game, who were incapacitated by the dreadfully inclement weather which accompanied the event.

staged at Murrayfield over a bleak and wintry three days in April of that year. The ambience of the event was not helped, either, by the fact that Murrayfield stadium was in the throes of reconstruction. But a Caledonian link with the past was forged when the Scottish Rugby Union provided the RWC trophy to be competed for in perpetuity.

The nine-carat gold goblet which stands ten inches high is a scaled-up replica of the original Ladies Cup from The Greenyards. The SRU commissioned the Edinburgh jewellers Hamilton and Inches to carry out the work and the Melrose Cup was born. The walnut plinth is encircled by a gold band on to which are engraved the names of the winning nations. The name of England is there from 1993. In 1997, in Hong Kong, Fiji won the tournament under their captain Waisale Serevi who is, without doubt, the best seven-a-side player the world has ever seen.

No better indication can be obtained of just how Haig's 1883 inspiration has grabbed the imagination of the rugby world than by casting an eye over the list of nations who competed in the three qualifying tournaments for the RWC Sevens in Hong Kong. In Lisbon, Uruguay and Dubai 64 nations played for the honour of being among the final 24 in Hong Kong. All of the major league nations were there – South Africa, New Zealand, Australia, Scotland, England, Ireland, Wales and France. The sevens specialists from the Pacific – Fiji, Western Samoa and Tonga – were always among the favourites. But there, too, were representatives from nations as diverse as Korea, Namibia, USA, Luxembourg, Tunisia, Latvia and the Netherlands. Probably, only a few of them knew of the debt they owed to Ned Haig and to the Melrose club. Haig, who died on 28 March 1939 at the age of 80, has bequeathed a legacy to the game which few, if any, can match or master.

The RWC Sevens trophy, named the Melrose Cup in honour of the club which gave the abbreviated game to the world, was commissioned by the Scottish Rugby Union for perpetual competition by the world's top sides. It is modelled on the original Ladies Cup first competed for at The Greenyards in 1883.

His headstone – 'Erected by the Border rugby clubs in memory of the originator of seven-a-side rugby' as the inscription details – marks his final resting place within sight of the Eildon Hills. But his real memorial is to be found all over the world wherever sevens are played – Ned Haig, a member of the original magnificent seven.

FIFTEEN

Gentlemen and Players

The path to professionalism

The amateur ethic, that Corinthian concept of play-up and play the game for love not money, had been the leitmotif of rugby since the days of the gentlemen pioneers; they had blazed a trail which withstood the encroachment of commercial pressure for a century and more. But amateurism, like virginity, is a state of being which, once lost, can never be recovered. There is no such thing as a semi-virgin. Throughout the 1980s the game's administrators comforted themselves with the delusion that they were governing a semi-professional game which at heart was still imbued with the all-encompassing amateur ethos handed down like a holy grail by the founding fathers.

However, by the time the first World Cup was staged in New Zealand and Australia – with only lukewarm support from the Northern Hemisphere unions – the Big Lie, which was what amateurism had become, was fast being exposed in all of its tawdry livery. That 1987 World Cup was the catalyst of the professional revolution that would sweep away the barricades of amateurism within a decade. For the first time the cream of the world's players were gathered together, and the stars from Scotland, England, Ireland and

Wales had a chance to see how the other half lived. They were amazed and angered by what they saw. There on television in New Zealand, was the All Blacks captain Andy Dalton starring in an advertisement extolling the virtues of a farmyard buggy. Officially, he was on screen as Andy the farmer, not as Dalton the All Blacks captain. But he was cashing in, with the blessing of the NZRFU, on the reflected glory of his All Black status – and this at a time when the amateurism regulations in the Northern Hemisphere were still being administered with an iron fist. Only seven years earlier the Scotland captain Ian McLauchlan had been banned *sine die* for daring to publish an autobiography. The Southern Hemisphere administrators' approach in turning a blind eye to Dalton's entrepreneurism was 'shamateurism' personified.

The final stage towards professionalism began with episodes like Dalton's buggy. It started as a steady trickle and ended in a rushing torrent discharging from the Ambassador Hotel on the Boulevard Haussman in Paris on Sunday, 27 August 1995. Mark the date well. It was one of the most momentous days in the history of the game. It was the day when the game's

French revolution: Over 100 years of amateurism were consigned to history at an International Board meeting in Paris on 27 August 1995. Fred McLeod (left) and Allan Hosie of the Scottish Rugby Union outside the Ambassador Hotel where the epoch-ending decision to declare the game 'open' was taken. JAMES GALLOWAY

supreme body, the International Rugby Football Board, conceded publicly, and for the first time, that the amateur centre would no longer hold. Within a month the Paris decision to declare the game 'open' – reached by a special meeting of the IB council – had been rubber-stamped at a full Board meeting in Tokyo, and more than a century of tradition had been consigned to history.

But this was no sudden, Pauline conversion on the road to rugby's Damascus. Before the 20-strong council – with representatives from Scotland, England, Ireland, Wales, Australia, New Zealand, South Africa, France, Argentina, Canada, Italy and Japan – reached its epochal decision, it had been wrestling with commercial forces over which it had no control. These agents of Mammon had the game by the throat and, against a backdrop of feverish commercial activity, the International Board was fighting to retain control over the game it administered. A last stand against

The IB council in session at the Ambassador Hotel. McLeod and Hosie are in the centre of the facing table. Here, in the Salon Molière, the game's administrators decided that if they could not regulate an amateur game, then there was no point in putting these regulations in place. IRFB

151

professionalism in Paris would have met with a similar fate as befell General Custer at the Little Big Horn. But the Board members who had met in closed session over three days in the Salon Molière at the Ambassador Hotel, knew full well that the days of the amateur game were numbered.

Tales of breaches of the amateurism regulations were legion. The Southern Hemisphere nations – New Zealand, Australia and South Africa – were rumoured to have been paying their players in one way or another for years. In France the wage structure – win bonuses and all – was alleged to have been lifted holus-bolus from rugby league. Italy had for years been a lucrative winter haven for Antipodean players, who were not there for their love of pasta.

The word was that English clubs were paying inflated expenses and in Wales the tales of 'boot money' and carpark takings being earmarked for the players were arising with monotonous regularity. Rugby had become a laughing-stock. Shamateurism was rife and the eternal cry of the administrators was along the lines of bring us the evidence and we will take action.

Then, in 1994, and in the face of mounting evidence that the regulations were being flaunted on a worldwide basis, the International Board decided belatedly to take action. A four-man Working Party, chaired by the Welsh Queen's Counsel Vernon Pugh and comprising Fred McLeod of Scotland, Rob Fisher of New Zealand and the IB chairman, Bernard Lapasset of France, was set the task of sorting the wheat from the chaff. How true were these rumours about systematic abuse of the amateurism regulations?

By early 1995 the Working Party had produced its report. It made sorry reading for the declining band of die-hards who clung to the notion that rugby was still an amateur sport. Pugh's summary, couched in the understated prose of the trained lawyer, concluded that the status quo was no longer an option:

All recognised that the breaches of the current regulations are so wholesale and often representative of a considered assessment of that which is believed to be right for the game, that they are essentially incapable of consistent and effective disciplinary action. All agreed that the pressures on and within the game were such that, like it or not, the game would inevitably become fully professional if it were not better regulated. All agreed that the present situation brought considerable and sometimes deserved criticism of our administrators of the game and all agreed that the commercial pressures were now such that, important as indeed is the amateur principle, the major threat to the game is its potential takeover by those commercial interests. This makes it all the more important that we get right the solution to the amateur debate.

The Working Party report, in its 19 closely-typed foolscap pages, presented a picture of widespread abuse. The amateurism regulations, which in 1990 had been amended in a too-little, too-late series of concessions, were being thwarted throughout the world. Those 1990 amendments provided for reimbursement of legitimate expenses, a so-called personal and communication allowance, payment as the beneficiary of a trust fund and, most nonsensically of all, payment for product endorsement so long as that product – such as playing kit – was not directly related to the game. This particular amendment threw up the ludicrous situation whereby some Scotland players were allowed to endorse leisurewear by means of a photograph in a Murrayfield international programme while their English counterparts, punting the same product, were denied that right at Twickenham. With masterly understatement the Working Party concluded:

> The nature and extent of the breaches of the current regulations has been found to be most concerning. It is, perhaps, not representative of the game world-wide to summarise the current position in a few lines. However, although the truth may be unpalatable to some involved in the administration of the game within the major Unions the facts are that many, and in some countries most, of the senior club coaches are paid. Sometimes the payment is disguised by reference to a misleading job description, sometimes it is the so-called 'sponsors' or 'friends of the club' that pay. The practice is more often than not accepted and tolerated by clubs and Unions and sometimes encouraged.
>
> Many involved in the game have employment with organisations, including governments, that enable them to spend all their time and effort on rugby playing matters. These may be coaches or organisers of the national team or persons engaged at a lower level within the game.
>
> Players, to a greater or lesser extent, receive payment for playing in many countries. These are usually relatively modest sums, and often reflect the success or otherwise on the field. In France, for example, a participant is entitled by law to be called an amateur as long as his remuneration from the game does not exceed a certain defined amount. Apart from France, who are but an example, few if any of the major Unions are free of some form or other of payment to players and coaches.

Many within the game believe that payment for involvement is justified. It is a myth that players do not wish to be paid. Many do. Very few, however, would expect or believe that rugby could be their sole or major source of income.

The report acknowledged that, in many ways, it was the administrators themselves, with increased demands on players, who had created the climate in which Test stars were now demanding fair recompense for their endeavours. And, in an anonymous reference to the Southern Hemisphere nations, it noted that several Unions were greatly concerned at the likely continuing drain on their players to rugby league if it continued to be impermissible to provide material reward for their players. Finally, the summary of how the then extant regulations were being put into practice concluded: 'The public perception cannot be ignored. In general the attitude of the Unions is regarded as anachronistic and potentially unfair on those who have great talent or on whom great demands are made.'

The Working Party report was presented to the International Board in March 1995. The IB accepted that disregard of the amateurism regulations and their spirit, and the unwillingness or failure to enforce them, was bringing the administration of the game into continuing disrepute, but despite Pugh's assertion that time was not on their side, it decided to meet again after that year's World Cup in South Africa.

Before the Board met again that August in Paris, the goalposts were moved by the media magnate Rupert Murdoch and by a larger than life former Wallaby Test prop and lawyer by the name of Ross Turnbull.

Maybe the International Board would have reached its epochal decision in August 1995 under its own steam. Maybe the 'open' game

– which is the IB's euphemism for professionalism – would have evolved naturally as a result of Pugh's Working Party report. We will never know. There is no doubt, though, that when high rollers like Murdoch and Turnbull – who had Murdoch's arch rival Kerry Packer on side – arrived at the poker table, the stakes were raised to a level which scared the living daylights out of the Board. Board members will dispute the veracity of this claim. But it is difficult to escape the conclusion that they had to sanction an 'open' game in Paris if they were to retain any semblance of control; the game had already turned pro as a result of an extraordinary announcement in Johannesburg just 24 hours before the World Cup final between South Africa and New Zealand at the Ellis Park stadium.

The world's media were already in town for the great showdown between the Springboks and the All Blacks. For them, as for the players, it was the end of a gruelling five-week trek around the rugby citadels of Nelson Mandela's new 'rainbow nation'. The South African Rugby Football Union's chief executive Ed Griffiths had called a news conference for first thing in the morning on Friday, 23 June, in the trophy room at Ellis Park.

For most of the media people it was a distraction they could well have done without. There were previews to be filed for the next day's final and that was more than enough to be getting on with. However, Dr Louis Luyt, the autocratic chairman of South African rugby, invariably made for good 'copy' so there was a full-house of writers, photographers and camera crews when Luyt, unexpectedly accompanied by his Australian and New Zealand counterparts Leo Williams and Richie Guy, entered the packed room.

The announcement, when it came, sent shockwaves through the world game. The three Southern Hemisphere nations had sold the broadcasting rights to all of their top-level rugby to Murdoch's News Corporation for £370 million. The ten-year deal would encompass a new Tri-Nations Test series and a Super 12 provincial tournament involving composite sides from New Zealand, South Africa and Australia. Luyt, Williams and Guy steadfastly denied that, armed with the war-chest which the Murdoch cash provided, the Southern Hemisphere game had, to all intents and purposes, gone professional and that the Test stars could now be handsomely rewarded. Luyt said the new-found riches would be used for 'rugby development'. Nobody believed him.

But Murdoch's totally unexpected coup had not been the only game in town. In fact, although it was not known at the time, the Newscorp *tour de force* represented a classic counter-attack on the blind-side manoeuvre being masterminded by Ross Turnbull. His World Rugby Corporation concept was a direct descendant of a 'rebel' plan for a global rugby network dreamt up by another Australian, David Lord, in 1983. Lord's brainchild never really got going. Turnbull, by comparison, came very, very close to changing the face of world rugby for ever. Maybe he did, at that, but not in the manner which he had hoped.

Ironically, the World Rugby Corporation owed its existence to Murdoch's foray into the world of Australian rugby league with his Super League concept. Extra cash and TV exposure was attracting Australia's rugby league stars away from the official Australian Rugby League camp and into the Super League fold.

Kerry Packer's media empire in Australia stood to lose out in a big way if ARL fell by the wayside in face of the threat from the

Murdoch-inspired Super League. Super League also represented a major new threat to rugby union. It would only be a matter of time before union Test players would be lured to Super League because of the Murdoch cash which was now on the table. That was a possibility, or a probability, which particularly worried the New Zealand RFU.

The World Rugby Corporation plan was as simple as it was audacious. Without the players there could be no game and WRC set about signing up the top 1,000 players in the world. Kerry Packer, taking on his old rival Murdoch, was involved from an early stage and rugby union had became a chip in a global showdown between two of the world's most powerful media magnates.

Turnbull and his associates came within an ace of pulling it off. Most of the world's Test stars were interested; 18 of the 25 Scottish players who had participated in the World Cup tournament signed on the dotted line. The recently retired Scotland captain, Gavin Hastings, acted as WRC's recruiting sergeant in Scotland. The great fear among the playing élite was that they might be left on the shelf if the concept proved to be a winner. The plan for a global network of franchises – which could, if necessary, be sold back to the existing Unions, who would continue to administer the sport began to unravel in South Africa. The Springboks' World Cup-winning captain Francois Pienaar obtained signed contracts for WRC from virtually every member of South Africa's world championship squad. But he never handed them over. The affair ended in court and, by a combination of cash and threat, carrot and stick, SARFU managed to get their players back on-side. When the top players in Australia and New Zealand saw that the Springboks had jumped ship, they, too, began to abandon WRC and Turnbull. The great adventure was over. It had, though,

served as yet another reminder to the International Board that the game was now a serious and global commercial commodity. There were major corporations ready and willing to pump massive sums of money into an amateur sport. That was the super-heated atmosphere in which the supreme council of the International Board – with Fred McLeod and Allan Hosie representing Scotland – met in Paris in August 1995.

The council had met for three days before the results of their deliberations were announced to the world on Sunday, 27 August. The timing of the announcement was sublimely symbolic or catastrophically ironic, depending on your point of view.

On 29 August 1895, in the George Hotel, Huddersfield, 11 clubs of the Yorkshire Union had broken away from the amateur game to form the Northern Union or, as it became, the Rugby League. They were joined almost immediately by other clubs from Lancashire and Cheshire and the great rift which separated the two codes of rugby was born. The parting of the ways had been over money. The North of England clubs, which drew their players from the ranks of the working-classes, wanted to compensate their members for wages lost through playing rugby. They called it broken-time money. The south of England clubs – bastions of the professional middle-classes – whose members were not losing money through playing their sport, considered rugby to be a recreation which would become tainted if the players were paid.

In Paris, just two days short of rugby league's centenary, Rugby Union abandoned its efforts to keep Mammon at bay. The official announcement was made, in French, by IB chairman Bernard Lapasset, who declared that this was, indeed, a momentous day on which Rugby Union had recognised

International Board chairman Bernard Lapasset of France, flanked by IB secretary Keith Rowlands and Marcel Martin of France breaks the news: the days of amateurism are gone forever. IRFB

that the constraints of the modern game did not permit full maintenance of the amateur principles. Pugh's Working Party, he intoned with a facial expression which suggested that he was officiating at a funeral, was to be congratulated on bringing Rugby Union to those historic decisions which would enable the game to continue its spectacular growth and popularity.

Pugh, so much the architect of the bridge between amateurism and professionalism, declared that the game was about to enter a very different world. It would change for all concerned – administrators and players alike. The challenge, now, was to retain the special character which had made rugby the game it was.

At the heart of the IB council decision was their recognition of the fact that there was no point in legislating for an amateur game if that legislation could not be properly policed. It

was acceptance of the inevitable. The regulations relating to amateurism would be repealed at the interim meeting of the council in Tokyo the following month. The official statement, which pronounced the death sentence on amateurism, declared: 'Subsequent to the repeal of the amateur regulations, rugby will become an open game, and there will be no prohibition on payment or the provision of other material benefit to any person involved in the game. Payment may be made at any level of participation. There should be no pay ceiling. Payment for result is not prohibited.'

At the time of writing we are almost two years into the new 'open' game and it has been a period of unprecedented turmoil. In Scotland, the Scottish Rugby Union – which, against historical precedent, was one of the first Northern Hemisphere administrations to embrace the challenges of professionalism –

Vernon Pugh, the Welsh Queen's Counsel, who took over the reins of the International Board during the months of turmoil and dispute which followed the decision to usher in an 'open' game. IRFB

has found itself under fire for its governance of the game. Within six months of the Paris meeting it fought off a special general meeting challenge to its policy of setting up a professional structure based on the four domestic Districts – Edinburgh, Glasgow, North and Midlands, and South of Scotland. Ostensibly, the debate was about whether the four District sides should compete in two new European competitions. In reality, it was about some of the senior clubs' drive for a greater degree of self-determination.

As a result of that victory the SRU set in place a scheme to pay up to 100 players on a three-tier salary scale ranging from £20,000 – £50,000 a year. The former Scotland prop Alan Watt became the first player to be paid by the Scottish Rugby Union. Subsequently, and in the face of outright hostility by a few of the leading clubs, who feared that

empowerment of the Districts would be to their detriment, the Union consolidated its position by offering a degree of self-determination to those Districts with professional coaching and administrative staff.

Then, in early 1997, the Union – spurning calls from among others the assistant national coach David Johnston that it should undergo an external review so that it might be better placed to administer the professional game – carried out its own review of its management structure. Senior figures from the worlds of business and commerce were drafted on to new executive boards. This did not, however, satisfy the leading dissidents, who found themselves a quartet of champions in the form of the former Scotland captains David Sole, Jim Aitken, Finlay Calder and Gavin Hastings. The Famous Four, as they were soon dubbed, took their crusade against empowerment of the Districts and for an independent review of the Murrayfield structure around the country. These campaigns, unsuccessful though they were, have taken place too recently to determine whether or not they are of lasting significance or, indeed, whether they deserve a place in a history of the game. However, even with the passage of time and the 20-20 vision that the long-view will provide, it will surely be considered significant that four such luminaries of the Scottish game took it upon themselves to challenge the fitness of the Scottish Rugby Union to govern.

If professionalism in Scotland was accompanied by some of the most difficult times the game had ever experienced, then in England it often seemed as though World War III had broken out. Millionaire businessmen, following the lead given by Sir John Hall at Newcastle, bought into leading clubs and the stage was set for a no-holds-barred showdown between the senior clubs and the Rugby

The Famous Four: The Scottish Rugby Union faced an unprecedented challenge to its stewardship of the game from four distinguished former Scotland captains. Gavin Hastings, Jim Aitken, David Sole and Finlay Calder maintained that the Union's empowerment of District rugby was sounding the death-knell of the club game and they called, too, for a high-powered independent review of the SRU's management structure. STAN HUNTER

Football Union; just as in Scotland but more so, the issue was one of self-determination. As Hall so succinctly put it, the professional game had to be run by professionals.

While the RFU mandarins at Twickenham were waging war with their clubs, they opened up a second front with their Five Nations partners. For much of 1996 England were excluded from the Five Nations championship after having negotiated a unilateral £87.5 million broadcasting deal with Rupert Murdoch's BSkyB satellite station for all Twickenham Test matches. The Celtic partners on the Five Nations committee – who stuck to their guns over the principle that the TV rights to the Five Nations tournament were the property of all the participants – faced down the RFU. Only after a compromise deal,

whereby cash from the Five Nations matches at Twickenham would be disbursed to all of the participants, was England readmitted to the tournament. The Scottish Rugby Union's Fred McLeod was a leading player in the challenge to the RFU's position and one of the most adamant that principles were not for sale, whatever the price.

These were the low-lights of the transition from amateurism – or shamateurism – to full-blown professionalism. As indicated earlier, it is too soon to pass judgement on how the game has coped, but an interim adjudication might well conclude that, even allowing for the fact that almost everyone involved was stumbling along in uncharted territory, the transition could have been handled a lot better.

Vernon Pugh, by now the first elected chairman of the International Board, sought to place that transitionary period in perspective when he gave a 'state of the union' interview to the IB's official publication *The Oval World* in the spring of 1997. First of all, he addressed the speed of change to professionalism and considered whether or not he had any regrets.

Not the speed of change, but the lack of competence in its management. I very much regret that in the Northern Hemisphere we reacted so badly. This is particularly so, in approaching the difficult task, that we failed to maintain the relationships that had cemented us together for so many years. There was a failure to understand that to accommodate a totally new game we simply had to work together, to define our common objectives, set our goals and implement them in a spirit of determined consistency and harmony.

I have to say that the events that occurred and the damage to that relationship was not something I or most of my colleagues foresaw when professionalism was proclaimed. It has made it much more difficult to achieve a smooth transition – a transition we always knew would take two to three years, even in the best and most ordered of organisations.

The breakdown in relations between the RFU and the other northern unions led to fundamental disagreement between the unions and, in turn, between unions and clubs. It afforded those who do not have a traditional background and feeling for the game, or the interests of the game at heart, the opportunity to achieve positions of great prominence and influence within it. I am pleased that we seem to have recovered much of that lost ground but, in the interim,

some of the positions we have been forced into are not those that any sensible person would have planned. In effect we've taken two steps back and one step forward rather than the three steps forward we should have taken.

I am not alone in being deeply disappointed in the lack of mature judgement, and the failure to recognise that we had to build on the long-established and proven structures of the Home Unions, Five Nations and the IRFB. Hopefully, that is now past us in Europe as we come to terms with some very important substantive problems such as player movement, union–club relations, the potential devaluation of Test rugby and the equitable distribution and use of the new money in rugby.

Pugh does not consider that the ill-will and bad blood which has characterised so much of the metamorphoses to a professional game is insurmountable. The damage, he says, is not irreparable.

The greater damage that has been done is to leave an element of mistrust between the national unions themselves and also between some clubs and their respective unions. Such attitudes are quite foreign to the game historically and it has, in reality, been quite unnecessary. We now need to stabilise relations. The IB has an important part to play, but certain principles are very important. Primary among those is the recognition that the pinnacle of rugby within any union is its national team. At the same time there has to be the recognition that a strong national team can only be achieved with a strong provincial or club structure and that the best for rugby is only achieved by working together. Also, it is important that we take a long-term view. The whole nature of the game has been changed very quickly and if we emerge from that change after three years or so in a healthy state that will be a great achievement. If we do, and I am confident, we will have succeeded in a short space of time to do that which has taken other sports generations of evolution.

Evolution, not revolution, was the International Board's aim when the game was declared professional in Paris. In which case the choice of that city which sits bestride the Seine – where they know more about revolution than most – was a singularly inappropriate setting in which to usher in the evolution. No matter. For nigh on 150 years rugby union football has survived and prospered as a gracious pastime played and administered by decent, affable people. It prides itself on a code of conduct, chivalric almost, which makes it virtually unique among its peers and rivals. The challenge for the next 150 years is to ensure that the game can withstand the corrosive effect which money has had on other sports and to maintain that special ethos which, we like to think, sets rugby apart. I, for one, believe that it will. Here's to the next 150.

Appendices

Appendix I

Scotland v England, 1873

The following account of the Scotland v England match at Hamilton Crescent, Glasgow, on Monday, 3 March 1873, was penned by the Rev. P. Anton (St Andrews University) who was a member of the Scotland side which played in the no-scoring draw. His first-hand account of the game was written for *Scottish Sport* on the eve of the 1896 encounter with the Auld Enemy. The 'St Andrews man' referred to in the text is Anton himself. The 1873 game was notable because immediately afterwards a meeting took place in the Glasgow Academy building at Elmbank Street during which the decision was taken to establish a Scottish Football Union.

The air is full of commotion of the coming Rugby International to be played at Glasgow tomorrow afternoon. 'Are we to have all the play and none of the luck, as usual?' The formerly high-mettled racer has become a grocery hack now, and moves in very prosaic ways, but he confesses that these sounds stir his old blood, and bring back the old days when he was elected more than once to do battle for his country against the prowess and heroism of England.

What a proud man he was that day three-and-twenty years ago, when, along with nineteen others, he marched out of the little Scottish pavilion at Hamilton Crescent Park through a dense and greatly admiring and cheering crowd, and 'lined up' in front of the English! Did he not understand then the feeling of his sires at Bannockburn? In the first half it was our part to defend the eastern goal.

The English made a splendid appearance as they defiled into the arena. All that training could do had been done. The previous year we had committed a preposterous and silly blunder. We sent to the Oval swift, light forwards, and we were terribly punished for our mistake, and still more terribly laughed at. The heaviest player was with us, also the lightest. Our man had a workman-like look, but the general appearance was irregular. We missed greatly 'Affy' Ross, the St Andrews crack, who had shone out at the first International at Raeburn Place, and as fine an all-round rugby player as ever dropped, punted, or dribbled. Wanting both 'Affy' and Munro, we had still men whose names were household words. There were Irvine and Mein, M'Farlane and Chalmers, Moncrieff the Hon., and St Clair Grant. Neither the Finlays nor Neilson played that year.

I do not know how they select their 'Internationals' now, but I can tell you how we did then. In judging merit we took into consideration the athletic record. It was a point in Irvine's favour that he was more than fairly good with the hammer. Again, M'Farlane's claim for place was helped because he was the best quarter-mile runner in the north. His dash and stride were alike magnificent. At mid 'quarter' it was a sight to see him rising in his stirrups and cutting to pieces the men about him. At the inter-varsity sports he won the silver medal with a broad jump of 22 ft. Professor Christison, who was standing beside me at the time, said it was 'like the bound of a panther'. I remember I wondered if a panther could do it, but kept a stiff upper lip, not wishing to damp the growing enthusiasm of my venerable interlocutor. These considerations made good M'Farlane's claim to quarter-back.

Thus our team was made up, and we never had a difference. When the names were published everybody was pleased. There was not a murmur, and, barring the chances of the game, not a fear. Glasgow as the field of operations was also a happy hit. It was felt all that was needed was a hot, rattling game played in the midst of the Glasgow people to develop the football ardour that then lay slumbering.

Be it known that at that time, with the exception of St Andrews University, there was not a single rugby club north of the Forth, and south of it to the Tweed only four other clubs of notable pretensions. The Association game was hardly yet above the horizon.

It was a transition time in many ways. Hacking and tripping had just been abolished. The Union had also passed a law that the ball could only be seized on the bound. These reforms had greatly popularised the game. But little did we think, that wet, sunshiny afternoon, we were playing in the dawn of such a resplendent football day as was then about to break over Scotland!

The game was not without its humours. If a dispute should arise, it was suggested that Joe Arthur, the Glasgow Academical captain, should champion the Scottish side. Joe had an irresistible 'talking over' way with him, and seeing he was not in the team, it was thought some recognition should be made of his special powers! Again, seeing the ground was to be sloppy, the English team went into a cobbler's to get leather bars fixed to the soles of their boots. I presume the cobbler was nothing worse than a 'Scots-wha-hae' patriot. At any rate, when the job was done, the boots and feet could not be got to correspond. There were two or three more of the latter than the former. Some of the English wanted 'lefts' and some wanted 'rights'. What was to be done? The hour of onset was near. The missing boots not being found, the players put on dress boots on the bootless feet. The Englishmen were late in arriving, but little did we know the most extraordinary, the most ludicrous, circumstance which had detained them. Goldsmith put down the cobbler who repaired his boots as a philosopher. I am not aware, however, that this was the view the English internationalists of 1873 took of the Glasgow shoemaker.

The sun shone, but there had been rain the previous night, and the ground had a hard bottom and a muddy surface. The fight, from first to last, was of the most determined character. Several notable things took place in the course of the match. With the wind and the sun both against us, we pressed the English in the first half. During the next half, when, having them with us, we thought we would certainly score, the English pressed us. Then the mauls presented a strange spectacle. Owing to the nature of the atmosphere, so soon as the packs were formed, a great column of steam rose right up from the scrummage, and bent eastward with the wind.

These were two characteristics of the match, but there were others two still. In the first half of the game Freeman got hold of the ball between the English '25' and the centre, and dropped the most magnificent kick ever seen. Its fame is historical. The ball went high in the air, and dropped far behind the Scottish goal-line. There was a cry of 'goal', succeeded by a dead silence. The ball was so high up it was difficult to say how it had gone. The umpire settled matters by declaring a 'poster', and the game again went on.

When the sides were changed the Englishmen abandoned their long shots, and determined to lower the Scottish flag by industrious efforts, bringing about a touchdown behind. The pressure they brought to bear on us was of the strongest. The English forwards, stimulated by the example of Stokes, the Blackheath man and captain, worked with desperate resolution. And they were within an ace of succeeding. They compelled us to form a maul within three yards of our goal-line and some eight yards from our goalpost. It was evident the game had reached a crisis, and the excitement was wound up to the highest pitch. Almost by instinct the Scotsmen allowed their St Andrews representative to take the centre of the scrummage.

When he gave 'down ball', the maul, which has become as historical as Freeman's 'drop', then began. The steam rose in a dense cloud. For some time there was not a single movement either way. The pressure was tremendous. The English then pressed the Scotsmen a foot or two to the rear. Goaded to their utmost, and putting the edge of their boots in their 'goal rut', they stopped their backward movement, and after a space we found ourselves gaining. Inch by inch we pressed them back, till finally we clove their ranks in two, and the St Andrews man, who to prevent heeling had kept the ball between his boots the whole time, was able to snatch it up, and make a very creditable run, and so ended in 'a draw' as hard, if not as fast, an 'International' as has ever been played. And for these three things will it remain memorable by players and spectators alike – the great steam, the great drop-kick, and the great scrummage.

Appendix II

The following account, by Hely Hutchinson Almond, headmaster of Loretto School and one of the founding fathers of the game in Scotland, appeared in *Football: The Rugby Union Game*, **edited by the Rev. F.P. Marshall and published in 1892.**

RUGBY FOOTBALL IN SCOTTISH SCHOOLS

by H.H. Almond, MA, LLD, Headmaster of Loretto School

Scotch public school cricket could hardly claim a chapter in a book on cricket. Even for the size of the schools it is seldom good except in respect of fielding, which is usually excellent. But Scotch school football is a very different thing. The only two schools which send up a fair proportion of their sixth form to the universities have within the last twelve years obtained between them thirty-five 'blues', whilst the two English schools which have been most successful in this respect have only obtained twenty-nine. And yet these two Scotch schools between them number only about 330. Rugby football has, in fact, fitted in with the national genius, though it was utterly unknown in Scotland forty years ago. Not that there was no football. At school we used to play a game which we enjoyed very much: two walls, the whole breadth of them,

were the 'hails'. It was said that the ball had once been kicked right across. Two good drop-kicks might have amused themselves by clearing both walls from the outside. At Glasgow College we had wider scope. The 'hails' were about 400 yards apart. It was not a bad game we had there; the great beauty of it was that there were no rules.

So far as I know, Rugby football was introduced into Scotland in 1855 by a small knot of men connected with the Edinburgh Academy. Mr Alexander Crombie, of Thornton Castle, may fairly be said to be the father of the game in Scotland, for he was the chairman and organiser of the club. The hon. secretary was Mr William Blackwood, the well-known publisher. The former learnt to play at Durham Grammar School.

Very slowly the game spread. There was a kind of mongrel 'Rugby' at Merchiston in 1858. Some of the rules were very funny. 'Off-side' was voted 'rot'; but if a player lay on the ground with the ball, no one might touch him till he chose to move. A closer conformity to the game was, however, enforced by an approaching match with the Edinburgh Academy; but so little did any of us, masters or boys, then know about it, that I remember how, when Lyall ran with the ball behind the Merchiston goal, the resulting try was appealed against on the ground that no player might cross the line whilst holding the ball. The previous rule at Merchiston had been that he must let go of the ball and kick it over before he touched down. It must be said in excuse for this and other similar sins of ignorance, that the only available rules were those printed for the use of Rugby School. They were very incomplete, and presupposed a practical knowledge of the game.

Gradually, however, the game approached, with local variations and resulting disputes, to that then played at Rugby. Clubs were formed in the West of Scotland, at the Scotch universities, and at various schools, but for a long time, in fact until well on in the 'seventies, the only schools able to play each other on even terms were the Edinburgh Academy and Merchiston, and occasionally the Royal High School.

So far as I am aware, the first attempt anywhere made at concerted action was the meeting of a committee of three schools in Edinburgh to codify the rules. The 'Green Book', which was the result of our deliberations, was assented to by the other then existing Scotch clubs. A committee on a somewhat similar basis challenged England in 1870, and, to our utter astonishment, the first national match was won by Scotland at Raeburn Place in 1871. And here let me make a personal confession. I was umpire, and I do not know to this day whether the decision which gave Scotland the try from which the winning goal was kicked was correct in fact. The ball had certainly been scrummaged over the line by Scotland, and touched down first by a Scotchman. The try was, however,

vociferously disputed by the English team, but upon what ground I was then unable to discover. Had the good rule of the 'Green Book' been kept, viz., that no one except the captains should speak in any dispute unless appealed to, I should have understood that the point raised was that the ball had never been fairly grounded in the scrummage, but had got mixed up among Scottish feet or legs. This I only learned afterwards, and my fellow umpire was at a distance from the scene of action. Indeed, when the game was played 20-a-side, the ball, at the beginning of a scrummage, was quite invisible to anyone outside, nor do I know how I could have decided the point had I known what it was. I must say, however, that when an umpire is in doubt, I think he is justified in deciding against the side which makes most noise. They are probably in the wrong.

At the end of the same year the English Rugby Union was formed; and soon after this the committee which had hitherto done all the work was hurriedly and unceremoniously displaced by the formation of the Scottish Rugby Union. This step was doubtless due to a misunderstanding as to the intentions of the committee, which was supposed to be too exclusive, although it was only taking time for the consideration of a rule about the admission of new clubs and the formation of a working executive. It was unfortunate, however, that the committee was superseded at that particular time, because it had arranged for a conference with England about the rules of the two countries, which differed in several respects – notably, about the important question of picking up. The new Union adopted the English rules and any changes in them subsequently made by England in bulk, and hence afforded a precedent for the claim on the part of England of a sole right to legislate, which caused such a stir some years afterwards. But a still greater evil was the exclusion of the schools from all share in legislation.

The schools are the nurseries of the game; it began with them; it is perhaps, under all modern circumstances, their best instrument of 'education', in the true and wide sense of that word, for I cannot conceive of any school making a good stand-up fight against the soft and self-indulgent ways of living in which town boys, at all events of the richer classes, are usually brought up, in which football is not a flourishing institution; nor is the Association game a possible refuge for Scotch schools. We are all Rugby, and rugby, I hope, we shall remain; for the defect of the association game is that it gives no exercise for the upper limbs, and thereby does not tend to the strengthening of the lungs, and the equal development of both sides of the person, as the Rugby game does, so that we are at the mercy of the club. And I am afraid that in their legislation they have not sufficiently in view of what is really the great end of the game – viz., to produce a race of robust men, with active habits, brisk circulations, manly sympathies, and exuberant spirits. I don't think I am overstating my charge when I say that they regard it far too much as a means of attracting spectators. This is in itself an evil. When a man is past playing football, which is ten years sooner by the modern game than by the old one, he ought, as a rule, to be taking hard exercise in some form himself whenever he gets the chance, and not spending his Saturday afternoons as a stationary and shivering spectator. But putting aside this aspect of the question, I have no doubt that the tendency of recent legislation has injured football as a school game. By increasing the pace it has also increased its most serious danger, which is not to the limbs, but to the heart. Boys with even slightly weak hearts

ought not to play the modern game, though they might safely play the old game. And all who know anything about schools are aware what a serious evil it is that many boys should be excluded from the chief school games. Further, the old game could be advantageously played at least four days weekly. I am convinced that the modern game should never be played, at least by big side, two days in succession, and certainly not within three days of a 'big match'. And, lastly, the discouragement of dropping would have been impossible had the voice of the schools been heard in the Unions. Dropping is one of our very best outdoor occupations for odd times, and it is quite impossible to get boys to practise with the same keenness when a dropped goal, by an infatuation which I cannot understand, has been made to count less than a goal from a try. Let me hope that at least this monstrous innovation on the essential spirit of rugby football may soon be repealed, not only in the interest of schools, but in that of the beauty and science of the game. My own belief is that some day legislation will retrace its steps still further. There is great danger in the practice of dropping on the ball to save, and already many serious accidents have happened from a player being kicked when falling on the ball. Schools will not be able to resist the outcry which will be caused by one boy killing another in this way, by mere accident or from momentary loss of temper. My own belief is, and always has been, that the worst change ever made in the game was the abolition by the English Union in 1872 (endorsed with all other English legislation by the then infant Scottish Union) of the old rule that the ball might not be taken into the hands except in the case of a free catch or when fairly bounding.

Holding, however, as I do, that recent legislation has both injured the game and made its position precarious, I believe that Rugby football, even as it is, is the best instrument which we possess for the development of manly character. In one point at least it is superior to the old game. The development of passing and of combined play generally has fostered unselfishness. A player used to play chiefly for his own hand; now, if he is worth playing, he plays for his side. Passing was, however, quite as consistent with the old rules as with the present. I tried to introduce long passing for years without much effect. I was told that it would 'look like funking', etc. To the best of my belief its efficacy was first proved in the Fettes and Loretto match in November 1880, and its introduction at Oxford by the old boys of the two schools was the chief cause of the football supremacy of Oxford a few years afterwards. But a still more important point even than passing appears to me to be combined play among forwards. In the art, one school – viz., Merchiston – has usually enjoyed an unquestioned pre-eminence. I have no hesitation in saying that in recent years I believe the best football in the world has been played at Merchiston. Few of its boys go to English universities, and they commonly leave school younger than is the case at Loretto and Fettes. Still, with only about one hundred and thirty boys in all, it has held its own in Scotch School championships against the far superior numbers and greater age of Fettes, and has completely distanced Loretto. Since 1880, when the three schools first began to play each other regularly, Merchiston has won the championship six times, Fettes thrice, and Loretto twice, the remaining year being a tie between Merchiston and Fettes.

It is a pity that the Scotch schools have no opportunity of measuring their strength against the great English schools. Rugby once invited Loretto to play them at Manchester at the beginning of the Christmas holidays, but there was an epidemic at Loretto which made it impossible. And I may add that I think all matches between schools ought to be played in term time and on the school grounds. Such intercourse between schools, to a limited extent, is well worth the time and money. The headmasters of the great English schools have, however, generally a great aversion to football matches between schools. I believe they are afraid of rough play. If so, their fears are groundless. No keener matches can possibly be played than those for the Scotch School championship. And they are usually played with the utmost fairness, and in a good-humoured, sportsmanlike spirit. In fact, I believe that house matches at schools are often played in far worse temper than any matches between well-disciplined schools are likely to be. I have seen the Fettes and Loretto teams standing by in silence, while some point was being discussed between captains and umpires about a disputed goal on which a match depended.

The facts as to 'blues', however, given at the beginning of this chapter, when coupled with the fact that Merchiston scarcely enters into this competition, prove indirectly the great excellence of Scotch School football. This arises from several causes.

1. I think that North-countrymen in general are bigger-boned and more muscular than southerners are. Also, possibly, children are more hardily brought up in Scotland before they come to school than they are in England, though the extent to which modern softness of living vitiates family and nursery life everywhere is lamentable.

2. Our constantly playing against each other creates a great enthusiasm for the game. Besides the matches mentioned above, an Edinburgh Day School championship and an entirely Day School match between

Edinburgh and Glasgow are merely samples of what is going on in secondary schools in Scotland generally. There are also matches for 2nd and 3rd fifteens, played on the same days, twice each season, as the Fifteen matches. To get into one of the teams at once gives a boy a certain degree of school position. There are also matches for boys 'under fifteen' which are as keenly fought as those for their seniors.

3. It has come to be understood, even by the smallest boys, that a place in any of the teams cannot usually be gained without a good deal of trouble and self-denial. Small schools also become aware that they cannot hope for football eminence unless they bring not only a select few but the whole mass of their boys into the fittest possible condition. The desire to do this therefore gives rise to sanitary rules of various kinds. Regular exercise in all weathers is insisted upon; boys are encouraged to sleep with open windows, and schoolrooms are kept fresh and airy. And perhaps, above all, the importance of a proper dietary becomes evident; and the detestable and loathsome habit of 'grubbing' all sorts of unwholesomes, even between meals, becomes warred against not only by masters, but by prefects and by public opinion. Why so many public schoolmasters permit unlimited 'grubbing', and yet regard the less injurious vice of smoking as one of the gravest of school offences, is more than I can comprehend. I think also that it is becoming evident to the more far-sighted men in my own profession, that attention to matters of this kind produces benefits of a higher order than any football excellence. And this very fact serves to strengthen and perpetuate the foundations on which really good school football rests. On the indirect bearing of all this upon school morality I need scarcely enlarge to all who know anything about schools.

I subjoin the special system of training carried out at Merchiston during the football season. The particulars have been kindly supplied to me by Mr Burgess, to whom Merchiston football has been so largely indebted for its vigour and excellence.

Boys are called at 7, when they turn out in flannels, and have a run or smart walk of about three-quarters of a mile, then a cold bath and rub down. Breakfast at 8; school from 9 to 12.

Monday, 12.30 to 1.30 – Big side (as often as possible a team of masters and old boys play the Fifteen on Monday).

Tuesday, 12.30 to 1 – The Fifteen look after the lower teams and make them play up. From 1 to 1.30 they practise drop and place kicking, and the halves and quarters practise passing.

Wednesday, 2.30 to 5 – Football match, or if before a school match, a cross-country run of from seven to ten miles, usually over the Pentland Hills.

Thursday, 12.30 to 1.30 – Big side.

Friday, 12 to 1 – Cadet corps drill; 1 to 1.30, kicking in field as on Tuesday.

From 3 to 6 – There are four periods, three of work and one of gymnastics, so that every boy gets about forty minutes gymnastics every day.

On Friday night they have in addition fencing and boxing. The Fifteen have also half an hour of this every night after preparation.

Every boy in the school must play football, unless exempted by the school medical officer.

All boys are accurately weighed and measured twice a term.

The bearing of the last particulars on football may not be obvious. But nothing makes a boy believe in a good physical system so soon as the increase of his measurements. They are the tangible outcome of the system under which he is being trained. And when you have once got his belief and will on your side, he is on the high road to becoming both a more vigorous football player and a better man. The system pursued at other leading Scotch schools does not differ materially from that of Merchiston. We, at Loretto, have rather less gymnastics. But 'fives' are more prominent with us, and 'shinty', or 'hockey', as well as, occasionally, Association sides, are both a pleasing variety, and also, I think, an excellent and not too violent training. All training, however, should be carefully watched and studied. There is a great deal still to learn about general principles, and these ought to be applied with discrimination to particular cases by any schoolmaster who knows his business. Training which would be too severe for the rapidly grown or anaemic boy is the best possible discipline for the flabby, lazy, greedy boy, or for the boy who prefers sitting over the fire with a book to the free air of heaven. But by training I do not mean special rules of life adopted for a short season and then suddenly dropped. The greatest obligations I owe to any instructor are due to a certain Mr Harrison, who was a medical student when I was a master at Merchiston. He fully persuaded me that training, in its true sense, was that wholesome and vigorous condition in which we ought to try to live always, and that boys or men who habitually, in this sense, live in 'training' are not only on the right road towards usefulness and happiness in life, but that they need no change, or, at most, a very slight change, in diet or exercise, to make them most fit for athletic games of any kind.

A word or two ought to be said as to the organisation of football in a school. As it is obvious that the available players are not likely to be an exact multiple of thirty, there ought to be considerable elasticity, on the lower sides at least, as to the number playing on a side.

The best practical plan for ordinary sides, as distinct from school matches, is to divide the number of available players into a number of nearly equal sides, 'big side' being the smallest and having about thirty-four on its list. Two boys should be made heads of each side, and great care should be taken in their selection – knowledge of the game, and power of enforcing order and obedience being the most necessary qualities. They should have printed school lists, with the boys on their sides ticked off, and either the medical officer or some competent master should look through these lists to see that no boy is placed on a side for which he is too small or too delicate. It is easy for the captains to arrange exchanges, or to let boys who can be spared off to play fives or take some other exercise. The head boy of the school, or of the house, should of course be bound to see that those who for any cause are off football or other school games do not 'slack', but have other sufficient exercise. A certain number of 'crocks' or 'slackers' are a necessary evil; but if not looked after they constitute a great source of danger. They are far more liable than football players to take any epidemic, and they are apt to get into lounging, lethargic habits, which are also a most infectious malady, if the 'crock' or 'loafer' is unfortunately a boy of any influence.

Great care should be taken that no favouritism is shown in choosing the school teams. My experience is that it is easy to show boys what a dishonest thing it is to use any public office, such as that of captain of a team, for private purposes; and surely any headmaster or school chaplain who gives his boys anything worth calling religious teaching, will speak often and strongly about the right use of responsibility of any kind. Certainly, to take the lowest ground, the excellence of school football greatly hinges on the certainty felt by every boy that he will get absolutely fair play, and that any mistake made about him will be one of judgement. One cannot aim at too high a standard of school morality in such matters. Another very important point is that of referees at sides. Masters who know the game will of course help in this way, and where the cricket professional resides refereeing should be part of his duties. Members of the Fifteen also, who are temporarily 'crocked', should, if capable, be sent to referee, and at the same time to coach lower sides.

Much more, however, may be done to prevent 'crocking' than is usually supposed. The most common cause of it is that a boy gets a slight sprain or twist about the knee or ankle, hobbles home with it, and thinks little more about it till the next morning, when the joint has swollen and water probably set in. He should have been carried home, and then immediately had the place fomented with water rather hotter than he can bear; he should then lay up until seen by the medical officer. About two-thirds of the ordinary sprains will be arrested at once if treated in this way. Boys should, of course, be frequently spoken to about these and kindred matters. They are a most important, but too often neglected, part of their education.

Lastly, no idle spectators should be allowed to stand looking on at school sides. The very sight of loungers takes the spirit out of players, and the loungers should be doing something else if they are too feeble for football. 'Spectating' generally is, in fact, the greatest of all football dangers. When boys are allowed to look on at a big match they should all be sent a run of a couple of miles afterwards to quicken their circulations and to prevent that deadliest of dangers, 'a chill'.

The Fettesian–Lorettonian Club

The history of Rugby football in Scotland, dating from 1871, when the first International match between Scotland and England was played, is very closely associated with the history of the teams of old boys of one or other of the great Scottish schools. In the Scottish team of 1871 a very large proportion of the players was drawn from the Edinburgh and Glasgow Academical clubs, and throughout the 'seventies in a very marked degree, and during the 'eighties up to the present decade in a lesser degree, these clubs have been represented in the Scottish national matches. Scotland has owed much of her success in the field to such men as Hon. F.I. Moncrieff (the captain of the first Scottish team), R.W. Irvine, N.J. Finlay, J.H.S. Grahame, W.E. Maclagan, Charles Reid, and H.J. Stevenson, of the Edinburgh Academicals; and T. Chalmers, Malcolm Cross, D.Y. Cassels, W.A. Walls, and J.B. Brown, of the Glasgow Academicals. Merchiston Castle School was the training ground of at least three of those whose names are given – selected from giants of football.

About the year 1881 the prominence of old Lorettonians and old Fettesians in the International teams became noticeable, and up to the present time it is clear that players from Loretto School and Fettes College have assumed the lead over the other schools in the number of representatives in the Scottish teams. Many have also found places in the chosen teams of England. But not only in the national teams, but, in more pronounced fashion, in the University fifteens of Oxford and Cambridge have they been very prominent. During the unbroken record for three years held by Oxford, Loretto had always served 'blues', while at Cambridge Fettes has always had a noteworthy representation. The two schools have had eleven captains of Oxford and Cambridge in eleven years, but a record was reached in 1889–90, when exactly one-third of the two University teams was Fettesian-Lorettonians. The origin of the club was, however, on this wise. In the summers of 1880 and 1881, cricket teams of OLs and OFs went tours in Yorkshire and were very successful; and as a result the idea of the formation of a club took definite shape at an informal meeting at Lasswade in the autumn of the latter year. The original circular, signed by A.R. Paterson, a well-known Lorettonian and Oxonian, and by A.R. Don Wauchope, an equally well-known Fettesian and Cantab, called a meeting at which the club was duly formed; at first, chiefly as a football club, but during the eleven years of its existence it has developed several other branches of athletics.

The performances of the club in football are perhaps worthy of a brief sketch. During the season of 1881–2 five matches were played; the first three against the strongest clubs in Scotland, viz., West of Scotland, Edinburgh Wanderers, and University, and each match was lost by narrow majorities. But the visit to the North of England to play Manchester and Huddersfield can only be described as having created a sensation in the football world. Both matches were won easily, the first by three goals to a try, and the second by one goal and three tries to nil. The team in England comprised six Oxford and two Cambridge 'Blues' as well as four Scottish and one English International players. The current issue of the *Athletic News* remarked; 'Those persons who saw the doings of the Fettes-Loretto boys in Huddersfield and Manchester are willing to swear that a better team never existed, and a general wish has been expressed that Don Wauchope should bring his grand team into the North of England once more.'

These successes set the club on its legs, although they were nothing to what was to follow, for from that time, December 1881 until January 1888, the club won every match except three, which were drawn, viz. those against the Edinburgh Academicals in 1884, and Bradford in 1886 and 1888. The last three successive seasons have each seen the club narrowly defeated by the Bradford club; in 1889–90 by a dropped goal to nil; in 1890–91 by a try to nil; in 1891–2 by a goal to nil, each match being productive of a splendid struggle.

Perhaps the most strikingly successful season of the club was during 1883–4, when eight matches were played, seven being won and the other drawn. The team that year was as follows:

H.B. Tristram (Oxford University and England) (back); D.J. MacFarlan (London Scottish and Scotland), G.C. Lindsay (Oxford University and Scotland), E. Storey (Cambridge University) (three-quarter backs); A.R. Don Wauchope (Cambridge University and Scotland), A.G.G. Asher (Oxford University and Scotland) (half-backs); A. Walker (West of Scotland and Scotland), J.G. Walker (Oxford University and Scotland), A.R. Paterson (Oxford University), C.J.B. Milne (Cambridge University), R.S.F. Henderson (Blackheath and England), W.M. Macleod (Cambridge University and Scotland), H.F. Caldwell (Edinburgh Wanderers), F.J.C. Mackenzie (Oxford University), C.W. Berry (Oxford University and Scotland).

E. Storey was the only player behind who did not secure his national cap. He would probably have gained it but for an accident which stopped his football altogether.

Of all the first-class men who have played for the F-L's there is no one who stands out so prominently as A.R. Don Wauchope. His brilliant and consistent form through all those years, from 1881 to 1888, for his country, university and club, dwarfs the performances of almost any other player one could name. Can any person forget the overwhelming excitement and even delight of the Yorkshire and Lancashire crowds when their favourite, 'the great Don', got the ball: the shouts and cries from thousands of throats resounding round and round the enclosure as each opponent tried to tackle him and was left lying on the ground, until at last the ball was safely carried over the line? One of A.R. Don Wauchope's greatest triumphs happened in 1885 at Bradford, when he ran in behind twice – the only scoring in the game. In 1883 at Huddersfield his play was quite phenomenal; he ran and re-ran the whole of the opposing side time after time, to what might be called 'a dead standstill', to the infinite delight of a huge crowd of genuine Tykes, who yelled in desperation, 'Why, 'e's like a bloomin' eel; they can't 'old 'im nohow!' The great feature of his play was, of course, his running and dodging powers, but there was not a single point in half-back play in which he did not excel. Dropping at goal was perhaps a weak point – he always preferred to run – and it was in this particular that A.G.G. Asher, his companion half-back in many a struggle, was so strikingly good. H.B. Tristram in his best days has hardly been equalled as a full-back. He seemed to be able to get the ball away to a greater distance than any other back, and when he got the chance he did 'down' his man. At threequarters one must refer to such distinguished players as D.J. MacFarlan, G.C. Lindsay, M.F. Reid, P.H. Morrison and P.R. Clauss. The first-named was the most consistent player of the lot, but Lindsay, Morrison and Clauss were all brilliant at times, while Reid, if an unreliable player, used to drop a goal in the most unexpected way, just when badly wanted. He is one of the few who obtained his national cap when a schoolboy. In later days C.E. Orr and W. Wotherspoon have been among the most noticeable players in the club. It is difficult to discuss the form of all the better-known forwards who have played for the F-L's, but it can be safely asserted that, speaking widely, the forward teams of the last few years have not been of the same class as formerly. The preponderance of light men amongst them has enabled opponents to 'shove them' in the scrummages; this has been specially marked in the late matches and defeats at Bradford. After all, however, the club will always hold, under existing circumstances, the same high position among Rugby football clubs of the United Kingdom. The members have all undergone the same vigorous training, at schools remarkable throughout the land by means of their intellectual and physical success. The best reason one can give for the uninterrupted prosperity of the Fettesian-Lorettonian club, is that teams who are chosen to represent it have considered it good enough to train for the tours and keep in good condition when away; in fact, there is a rule of the club which prevents the acceptance of invitations to football dinners. It is unnecessary to add more to this sketch, except perhaps to express the hope that the club, unique in many ways, may continue in the future as it has done in the past to play an honourable part in Rugby football, and be as often on the winning side.

Appendix III

This account of the pioneering days of the Scottish game was penned by the Scotland captain Robert 'Bulldog' Irvine in the 1892 edition of *Football: The Rugby Union Game.*

INTERNATIONAL FOOTBALL: SCOTLAND

by R. W. Irvine

While the Scotch maintain, and no doubt with truth, that football is a national game, and has existed in Scotland in some form or other since the time when the Caledonian savages first took to wearing boots, nevertheless Rugby football as at present played is, it cannot be denied, a game adopted from across the border. Its very name implies this, and when he considers how important a part the great English school, Rugby, played in developing and fostering the game, in establishing the present laws of the game, and in popularising it throughout the country, no Scotsman, however patriotic, will grudge that the name Rugby should be for ever associated with the game, even though he may be the last to admit that either Rugby or the country in which it lies has any present pre-eminence over his own country in that sport. Football seems to be a game peculiarly congenial to the '*perfervidum ingenium Scotorum*'. Not only is

it played well and enthusiastically in the schools, but it is also astonishing how kindly grown men who never saw a Rugby ball till nearly twenty, and to whom, when they begin, the meaning of 'off-side' is one of the mysteries, take to the sport, and how soon they become, at least in the scrummage, first-rate players.

Scotch Rugby football may be said to have sprung up from boyhood into robust manhood with the first International match in 1871. In saying this there is no disparagement to the earlier players. Far from it, '*Vixere fortes ante Agamemmona multi*'. Many of us can recall to mind Rugby players, heroes of our boyhood, who flourished before International matches were dreamed of, and the idea of a football Union had not yet taken shape, players who would have made many of our cracks of the present day look small. The Rugby game was played, and played well, by school and club thirty years ago and more; but in those days inter-scholastic matches were very local and comparatively few, while inter-club matches were even fewer. Except in Edinburgh and Glasgow there were very few properly organised Rugby clubs in Scotland. There was one, and a good one – St Andrews – a club whose prowess was known far and wide, and which made up for the paucity of its matches by the fervour with which it entered into those it did play. Provincial Rugby football hardly existed. There is no evidence of any provincial Rugby club out of Edinburgh (and district), Glasgow (and district), St Andrews and Aberdeen University, playing regularly as a club, before 1870. For some years prior to that, however, signs of greater activity and enterprise were becoming visible in the Scotch Rugby world. Edinburgh and Glasgow clubs were playing more matches among themselves, and journeying more frequently to each other. But what gave the great impetus to the game had to do with our neighbours across the border. For some years previous to 1871 an annual match had been played in London – an International match it was called – it was played according to the laws of the dribbling game. England usually won, but the Scotch made a good fight always. This match at first attracted only a sort of curiosity in Scotland, and a languid sort of interest. But in course of time, as the Scotch were beaten time after time, and it was quite an accepted truth that Scotland was in football, as in cricket, wonderfully good for its opportunities, but far behind England, the souls of certain Scotch past and present players stirred within them. The idea dawned upon them, 'If there is to be an International match, let it be a real one, and don't let the relative merits of England and Scotland in football matters be decided purely by Association football, let us ask them to send a Rugby team north and play us on our native heath.' The Scotch leaders felt that they could not be so very far behind their opponents, and at all events, better to know the truth than to be set down as inferior, as it were, by proxy. At

last, after much consultation, and in some trepidation, but not at all in despair, the missive was despatched. Scotland did not undertake to play only Scotsmen residing in Scotland. She reserved to herself the right to get them from wherever she found them, and it was to be a really representative team; and she would admit that if it was beaten. There was no Scottish Rugby Union then, except the rough-and-ready Union, in connection with which Scottish Rugby players should always hold in venerable remembrance F. Moncrieff the first Scotch captain, H.H. Almond, J.W. Arthur, Dr Chiene, B. Hall Blythe, and Angus Buchanan. A team was selected without wrangle and without jealousy, and invitations were sent to the team to play in a great match, and responded to with alacrity.

The first Scotch team was selected from Edinburgh Academicals, Edinburgh University, Royal High School FP (which was supposed to mean former pupils), St Andrews, Merchistonians, Glasgow Academicals, and West of Scotland. The men were requested to get into training, and did it. It was twenty-a-side, and the Scotch forwards were heavy and fast. We were ignorant what team England would bring, of what sort of players they had, and of how they would play; and though assured by Colville, a London Merchistonian – and a rare good forward, too – that we would find their size, strength, and weight not very materially different from our own, many of us entered that match with a sort of vague fear that some entirely new kind of play would be shown by our opponents, and that they would out-manoeuvre us entirely. The day of the match soon settled that uncertainty. The English twenty were big and heavy – probably bigger and heavier than ours, but not overpoweringly so. Before we had played ten minutes we were on good terms with each other. Each side had made a discovery – we that our opponents were flesh and blood like ourselves, and could be mauled back and tackled and knocked about just like other men; they that in this far north land Rugby players existed who could maul, tackle, and play-up with the best of them. There was one critical time during the match. Feeling was pretty highly strung. It was among the first no-hacking matches for many of the players on both sides. Now, hacking becomes an instinctive action to one trained to it; you hack at a man running past out of reach as surely as you blink when a man puts his finger in your eye. There were a good many hacks-over going on, and, as blood got up, it began to be muttered, 'Hang it! why not have hacking allowed?' 'It can't be prevented – far better have it.' The question hung in the balance. The teams seemed nothing loth. The captains (Moncrieff and F. Stokes) both looked as if they ought to say 'no' and would rather like to say 'yes', and were irresolute, when Almond, who was umpire, vowed he would throw up his job if it were agreed on, so it was forbidden, and hackers were ordered to be more cautious. The match was won by Scotland by a goal and a try to a try – the Scotch goal placed by Cross (not Malcolm, but his big brother) from a very difficult kick – and though many matches have been played since then between the countries, there has not been one better fought or more exciting than this, the first one. The Scotsmen were exultant, and the winning ball hung for many a day in the shop of Johnnie Bowton, at the Stock Bridge, adorned with ribbons like the tail of a Clydesdale stallion at a horse show. With this match and victory the life of Rugby football as a national institution fairly commenced. It was the end of the season, and the last match played; but by the beginning of another year enthusiasm was fairly taking

possession of the Scotch Rugbeians. The winter of 1871–72 saw an activity in rugby football that it had never known before. Not merely was this so in Scotland, England, too, was waking up and girding her loins. Her defeat had nettled her. The Rugby Union was formed – the 'Rugby Footby Union', as it was once styled by a hilarious and bibulous Scotch forward. The leading Scotch clubs joined it, and in 1873 the Scotch Football Union was formed, the original clubs forming it being the same that had originated the International match – viz. the Universities of Edinburgh, St Andrews and Glasgow, the Academicals of Edinburgh and Glasgow, the Royal High School, the West of Scotland, and the Merchistonians, with power to add to their number. The original object of the Union was stated in three propositions, which still hold good: (1) To encourage football in Scotland; (2) to co-operate with the Rugby Union; (3) to select the International teams.

The spring of that year saw the second International match played at Kennington Oval. Much deliberation was bestowed on the selection of the Scottish team. Trial matches were played; London was appealed to to supply some good Scots, and on February 5th, 1872, the Scottish twenty turned out full of hope on Kennington Oval. The match was peculiar. Almost immediately after kick-off the Scotch forwards carried a scrummage, followed up well, and in a trice Cathcart had dropped a goal. England looked dubious. One of them remarked, 'We have no chance against your pace.' The result showed how far off his reckoning was. The rest of the match was one continual penning of the Scotsmen, the only flash of luck they had being when Chalmers once made his mark near the centre of the field, and L.M. Balfour, an Academy boy of sixteen, very nearly placed a goal from it. Scotland was beaten by two goals and two tries to a goal. The English team was a grand one; forward it was the heaviest football twenty that ever played together. Back, very little was required, but Freeman and Finney could have done all that was required behind by themselves. The licking did Scotland good. Their previous victory had made then very cocky. They thought that because they had beaten England in 1871, that, therefore, they had nothing to learn from them. They now saw that in the proper arrangement of their men, and in the proper selection of men for the back places, they were a century behind England. They also found out that touch is something more than merely the boundary of the field of play, and that half the game of back six played across the touchline. They also found that light fast forwards were no good against heavy fast forwards in a twenty-a-side match. Like wise men they took the lesson to heart. They formed their own Union in the next year, and they instituted the inter-city matches between Edinburgh and Glasgow.

The inauguration of the inter-city match was a great hit. It has become between Edinburgh and Glasgow what the International is between England and Scotland, and has given the same impetus to the game in the respective cities. Edinburgh won both matches, a team was chosen, and the third International match was played in Glasgow at Partick. The ground was a quagmire, and the match ended in a draw, after a game which while stubbornly fought out by the players, must have been monotonous to a degree to the onlookers, and must have had a great deal to do with depopularising the Rugby game in Glasgow. It was one succession of weary mauls, broken by an occasional rush, but at this interval of time the impression left was that of a muddy, wet, struggling 100 minutes of steamy mauls, and standing out in bold relief, Freeman, the

English three-quarter back, making his mark, and having such an appalling drop at goal as one seldom sees in a football lifetime.

The next season saw the International played in London, and won by England by a goal (dropped by the demon Freeman) to a try and a disputed try. In this match Scotland had, admittedly on all hands, the pull all through. She was superior for the first tie behind the scrummage. Kidston, St Clair-Grant and A.K. Stewart shone brilliantly, and the forwards had rather the pull of their opponents. Still the luck was against Scotia, and she had to pocket another defeat. How lucky the southerners thought themselves was well seen in the fervour with which their skipper, in a speech at the dinner of the match, thanked God that Jupiter Pluvius had come to the rescue, and made the ground so slimy as to take the heels from the fleet Scotch backs.

1875–76 saw much the same state of matters. The inter-city matches continued to be toughly and grimly fought, but the metropolis always kept the whip-hand. The International of 1875 was played in Edinburgh, and was a draw – as usual, Scotland fully holding its own forward, but being lamentably weak behind. The number of shaves the Scotch goal had from the dropping of Pearson and Mitchell that day no Scotsman playing will ever forget. Another draw in favour of England.

1876 saw the fight again removed to London; and on the Oval, for the third time in succession, the Thistle was nowhere. Scotland had the pull forward, but behind were far inferior. She had one half-back who weighed somewhere about nine stone, and the other dislocated his thumb early in the game, and R. Birkett and Collins ran over them as they pleased, while Hutchinson had a run for England, which will live in football history, nearly the whole length of the ground, and the try was consummated by Lee. England had a goal and a try to the good, and two matches to the good on the whole.

1877 saw a change. An agreement had at last been come to regarding the fifteen-a-side, and it was to be tried this time. Scotland had previously routed Ireland in a match remarkable for the number of goals gained – six goals to nil – played at Belfast. In this match Ireland showed much good material, but it was raw. Much good Hibernian breath was expended in shouting which would have done more good to the distressed country if spent in shoving. 'Oireland, Oireland, get behind yourselves,' a despairing son of Erin was heard to cry, as the Scotch forwards were wedging through the Irish with the ball before them, and the Irish did not seem to know where it was, and were not coming round. But if Scotland had the best of it on the field, and if Ireland was raw at the game that day, Scotland was certainly boiled next morning. Flushed with this victory, Scotland met England full of confidence a fortnight after in Edinburgh. The teams were well matched. Scotland was in good form behind and fully held its own; the match was fast and furious to a degree never before seen in an International, and when within five minutes of 'No side', Grahame got the ball and chucked to Malcolm Cross, and Cross, quick as lightning, dropped at goal, the excitement beggared description. The match was won by Scotland by this dropped goal – and we felt that our long struggle for fifteen-a-side had not been in vain. The verdict of players and public was hearty and unanimous, and the twenty-a-side International was from that date a thing of the past. In that year, too, the first attempt was made to have a more true trial match for the selection of the team than had hitherto been accomplished – and the East v West match was the remedy proposed and adopted. Whether it has been a success or not is a question, but it has ever since been the substitute of the second inter-city, and now there is an inter-city before New Year in one city, and the East v West after New Year in the other.

1878 saw Scotland's fifteen again on the Oval; again saw a splendid fast match, and at last saw the spell of Scotch ill-luck on the Oval broken, for not only was she not beaten, she very nearly won – in fact, many of the team thought she had won – but it was only a draw; no score either side. The Scotch had there probably the best forward, and indeed, all-round team, they ever put on a field. Their backs, too, were good – had much improved on their three years before form – but had not yet acquired anything like the finish and easy certainty in catching and dropping the ball that we saw in Stokes and Pearson and used to see in Freeman. They could drop as far, and Finlay, probably, was the longest drop in Britain, Stokes not excepted. They could tackle – I would rather fall into the hands of any back in the three kingdoms than into those of W.E. Maclagan when roused. They could utilise touch – none neater at taking a little punt or drop at a nice angle into touch at a critical moment than Malcolm Cross. But with all that they wanted the freedom, dash, and style altogether which characterised the play of the English. Their play, compared with that of the Englishmen, was like the play of clever ponies, or big active Clydesdales, to that of thoroughbred racehorses. Ireland didn't raise a team to come across to play us.

1879 came round. Things still went on well. The Union flourished. New clubs were joining. A team was sent across to Ireland and again defeated its opponents, but this time by half the former score, and the Irish forward play had improved in a way that promised to give Scotland and England some trouble to hold their own at no distant date. The English International of 1879 was played at Edinburgh. A tough and splendid match resulted in a goal placed by Stokes from a run by Burton being equalised by a most cleverly dropped goal by Ninian Finlay, and the result was a draw in favour of nobody.

In 1880 the Scotch Union prospered, the funds prospered, new clubs joined. There were now 24 clubs composing it, whereas in 1879 there were 21, and in the first year, 1873, there were eight. Ireland came over to Glasgow, and, while showing good mettle, was well beaten in all points of the game, but the Irish had left their souls in the Irish Channel the night before. England had previously been over in Dublin and just escaped being beaten by Ireland. Scotland was thus the favourite – she had never had such a good team. The English team was too old and the men stale. Never was a greater mistake made. The Scotch as usual were fully as good as the others forward, but the backs might, half of them anyhow, have just as well been left in Scotland. Once an English back was past the Scotch forwards the backs seemed suddenly seized with paralysis, pawed him like old women, as if to encourage his onward career, and England won by 2 goals and 3 tries to 1 goal placed by Cross from a try by Sorley Brown.

This was the biggest beating Scotland had yet had on paper, and certainly the sorest disappointment. It was also the least easily explained. England certainly had a magnificent team, admittedly on all hands, but Scotland had also a first-rate team. The men had been doing wonders all the season. Certainly the ground was simply not fit for football, hardly fit for mudpies, and a gale of a wind blowing, but that was the same for both sides. It was just what happens sometimes in a man and in a team – they were not in form and not in luck. They seemed to play with the funk on them, and never played to win. This match is noticeable as the first English International played out of London. It was played at Whaley Range, Manchester, and the crowds that witnessed it surpassed anything hitherto seen at any football match in the three kingdoms.

The match with England in 1881 was splendidly contested. Scotland were the first to score, by R. Ainslie making a good run from the 25-yard line, but Begbie's kick failed, the ball grazing the post. This was all the score in the first half, the play being so equal that it was impossible to award the preference to either side. The Scotch backs now played a defensive game, but Stokes getting the ball chucked to him lowered the Scotch goal by perhaps the most magnificent drop-kick ever seen in the International matches. Immediately afterwards Campbell Rowley romped over the line. The place-kick was a failure. With England a goal in advance, the Scotsmen had little hope of saving the match. Three minutes from time the match seemed a certain victory for England, when J. Brown securing the ball eluded Hornby and grounded the ball between the posts, and Begbie kicked a goal. Thus ended the most sensational International match, the result being a draw, a goal and a try for each side.

The match with Ireland ended in a great surprise. There was a schism in the Scotch Union, and some clubs considering themselves hardly dealt with because so few of their men were selected in the team, resorted to the unpatriotic course of withdrawing those who had been chosen. Thus Scotland appeared at Belfast without her best team, and Ireland won by a goal to a try.

Scottish International Football from 1881 to the Present Time [1892]

In dealing with Scottish football in its relationship with England for the past ten years, we may not have as bright a tale to tell as we might have wished for, and we may find that we have been subjected to one or two rather unpleasant castigations; but at the same time the record for the period is quite presentable, and it contains at least two achievements which outshine any performances in the whole history of the game north of the Tweed. In March 1882, our team at Manchester gained a victory which set the whole country into an ecstasy of delight. Ten years later our men went up to London to meet what was styled one of the finest teams England ever produced, and, to our huge satisfaction, Scotland won by the largest score she had ever compiled in one of these matches. These are the particular bright spots on the roll, but on the other side of the account we have to swallow an unpalatable defeat in 1883, when for the first time we were beaten on our own ground, followed in 1890 and 1892 by two more humiliating downfalls on our native heath. These defeats were more than rebuffs, and they were doubly unpleasant from the fact that we had been waiting since 1877 to see Scotland win at home – and we are waiting still. Old players have a way of marking off years on their fingers' ends, and they will tell you such and such a team was much better than England's, although it lost, while another fifteen which won ought never to have had the slightest chance with their opponents. Such a process is too intricate to follow, besides being apt to lead to people 'begging to differ', and for the sake of lucidity we shall here treat of the teams as the balance of the account in goals and tries stands favourably or unfavourably to

them. To get at the condition of Scottish football in any given year we must examine the positions and performances of the leading clubs. In 1882 Edinburgh Institution football players were at their zenith. The Edinburgh Academicals were at low ebb, and Raeburn Place had lost its monopoly. In Glasgow the Academicals were still a strong team, but they were slowly giving way before the West of Scotland. Naturally, these influences affected our national selection, and it is not surprising to find a strong "Stution' element in the fifteen. Among the forwards we had the brothers Ainslie and R. Maitland, and behind Sorley Brown partnered A.R. Don Wauchope at half-back, with A. Philp and W.E. Maclagan at three-quarter. Our full-back was the sturdy High School man, J.P. Veitch, and among the other forwards were C. Reid, not yet quite at his best, rough-and-ready W.A. Walls, J.B. Brown, and D.Y. Cassells as captain of the team. Our two tries' victory gave unbounded satisfaction in Scotland, and none who saw the game will forget how our forwards cut out the work that afternoon. The Scotsmen seemed to have stones the worst of it on weight, but they had all the best of the pushing, and there was only one team in it in the loose. R. Ainslie added greatly to his reputation by his fine tackling and play in the open. To W.N. Bolton he was most attentive, and the big Blackheath man did not get much time to consider his movements. It is generally acknowledged that R. Ainslie stands out as one of the very best forwards ever we had. His weight was not great, but he used every ounce, and we have never had a forward who came through on to the opposing backs more quickly. One of his strongest points was his tackling, which was always safe and low, and his great speed often brought him within reach of a man who seemed clear of the forwards. When at his best he left Edinburgh for the South of Scotland, and gave up football when he still seemed to have a long career before him. T. Ainslie had most of his brother's points, but not so well developed, and although he played for a much longer period, and was in more Internationals, he was not the same brilliant forward. Still he was a fine all-round player, and belonged to the true type of Scotch scrummagers.

That year we had not a single weak spot in our back team, which included two men who belong to a very limited class of players standing on a platform quite by themselves. No stronger defence than W.E. Maclagan's has ever been seen in Scotland, and we never had a man to make the same electrifying run as A.R. Don Wauchope. N.J. Finlay made great runs in his day, and probably scored as often as Wauchope did, but he was never so difficult to follow, and his movements did not produce the same fever of excitement on a crowd that Wauchope's raised. Although defence was undoubtedly Maclagan's strong point, if he got the ball within a dozen yards of the line he was a most dangerous man in more ways than one, and an ordinary player might well be excused if he took second thoughts about standing up before him when he was bent upon scoring. Roughness has often been imputed to him, and there is no doubt in his younger days he now and again gave exhibitions of his strength which were not good for the subject. More than once he has tossed a man, full pitch as the bowlers would say, on to the little paling at Raeburn Place and made the timber crack. He was one of the most powerful players we ever had, and no man on the football field could put his strength to more use than Maclagan when he cared to, or as Dr Irvine says, 'when he was roused'.

From a splendid victory of 1882 we have to pass to a more than unusually unpleasant defeat. Our troubles in 1883 began with our team, which behind the maul was of a most patchy description, and it is safe to say we were never more poorly represented behind than we were that year. Our team before the match did not inspire confidence, and in the actual play some of the men cut up badly, and as a climax we were beaten for the first time at Raeburn Place. A comparison of the opposing rear divisions will almost tell the tale of our disaster. England was represented by – full-back, H.B. Tristram; three-quarters, W.N. Bolton, H.M. Evanson, and G.C. Wade; half-backs, J.H. Payne and A. Rotherham. Scotland – Full-back, W.D. Kidston; three-quarters W.E. Maclagan and M.F. Reid; half-backs, P.W. Smeaton and W.S. Brown. This we should certainly say was the finest back team England played during the decade under notice, and when we consider that Maclagan, far from well, had practically all the work behind our halves to do, and England had three three-quarters playing against our two, the marvel is that we escaped with a two tries to one try beating. But our forwards as usual did splendid work, and if they did not win the match they saved us from heavy defeat. This was decidedly Bolton's year, and he left an impression which was not soon forgotten. Evanson we had heard much about, but he did not sustain his reputation. Tristram did, however, and many present thought it a little rough on Scotland that she should have reared for England the best full-back she ever had.

Our half-backs in this match did quite their share of the work. P.W. Smeaton's selection had been taken exception to in some quarters, but he proved one of the most useful men on our side, and frequently his punt, which he got in from all sorts of awkward positions, gained us ground when we most wanted it. He had never much speed, but he was always a most tenacious tackler, and nobody ever saw him shirk his work. Probably to this day he is of opinion that he scored a try in this match which would at least have made it a draw. At the beginning of the game an incident happened which may have put into Wade's head a perverted idea of Scottish football, and perhaps influenced his play, for he did very little after it. Getting the ball in good position, the Anglo-Australian was making off, and had just got up a good turn of speed when T. Ainslie came in his way. The Institution representative finding he could not reach his man, deliberately shot out his foot and knocked the Oxonian's legs right from under him. Wade rose looking as if he had been hurt – inwardly, and no doubt he made mental comparisons of football as practised in England and Scotland.

During the season 1883–84 a great many changes took place at home. The two three-quarters system, which had received almost its death blow at Raeburn Place, had not been entirely discarded by the clubs, but in all the Union teams three were chosen. A.T. Don Wauchope, who had been off for a year in consequence of an injury to his knee, returned to active participation in the game.

In club football the Institution had sunk from their high position, and their place was taken by the West of Scotland, who were now the champion team. The Watsonians under J. Tod had sprung into prominence. Edinburgh University were strong, and C. Reid, with M.C. McEwen and J.W. Irvine as young players, was building up for the Edinburgh Academicals a fine team which a couple of years later swept all before it. We have never been better off for players, and after defeating Wales and Ireland we had great hopes of the fifteen that went up to London. Everybody knows that the match gave rise to the 'unfortunate dispute', and that Scotland, after holding out for a long time, gave up her

claim, and allowed England the game rather than be without the match. England's back team on that occasion was exactly that which represented her the year previous at Raeburn Place, while Scotland had – back, J.P. Veitch; three-quarters, D.J. Macfarlane, W.E. Maclagan and E. Roland; half-backs, A.R. Don Wauchope and A.G.G. Asher; forward, J.B. Brown, W.A. Walls, and T. Ainslie remained of the old brigade. J. Jamieson, a West of Scotland man, over whose selection there had been newspaper debates, made his second appearance. J. Tod got his place for the first time, and another new player, C.W. Berry, was introduced. Jamieson may not have been all that his friends claimed for him, but he was a smart, clever player and an exceptionally fine dribbler. Berry was one of the best place kickers ever we had, though in English matches it was always a doubtful qualification to urge on a man's behalf that he was 'worth his place for his place-kicking alone'. Berry, however, was a sterling forward of the heavy class, and was always of great service in the tight work. In this match Wauchope and Asher played together against England for the first time, and continuing to represent us for several seasons, they without doubt constituted the best pair we have had in this decade. Asher was a very fine player, who seldom showed poor form, and if he did not shine with the same brilliancy as Wauchope, he was always of immense service to his side. His running was his weak point, and he was never counted a dangerous scorer. When a man does not shine as a runner, and is strong in other points, his friends at once put in a claim on his behalf as an all-round' player. All-round in this sense is misapplied, and if a man be no runner and scorer he is not entitled to have the term bestowed upon him. Wauchope, in the strictest sense of the word, was an all-round player, as he could not only run, but his kicking, tackling, and general defence were very strong when he saw occasion to exert them. Asher's running was poor, and he therefore cannot justly be considered an all-round man. At the same time he was one of our most successful half-backs. He and Wauchope did splendid service for us in this game.

In 1885 we were without our English fixture, but through a freak of the weather, which interrupted our game with Ireland at Belfast, we unexpectedly had the Irishmen at Raeburn Place on the English date. This match we won by a goal and two tries, and it is memorable for Wauchope's running and Green's play on behalf of Ireland. Among our clubs the Edinburgh Academicals broke the West of Scotland record, beat the Glasgow Academicals in the return by the largest score made in an inter-Academical match for ten years, and finally established their claim to be considered the best team in the country by defeating Watsonians by three goals and a try.

After the lapse of two years we renewed hostilities, and at Raeburn Place had a great game with England, which resulted in a scoreless draw. This, in our opinion, was one of the best matches in the series, and we very narrowly missed winning it. Veitch reappeared for us at full-back, and our three-quarters were R.H. Morrison, G. Wilson and W.F. Holms, while opposed to these were C.H. Sample, back, A.E. Stoddart, A. Robertshaw, E.B. Brutton, halves, with A. Rotherham and F. Bonsor, at quarter. In our forward team were J.B. Brown, W.A. Walls, T.W. Irvine, A.T. Clay, C. Reid, M.C. McEwen, and J. Tod.

England's forwards were strong, and we had heard a deal about C. Gurdon's 'hooking' process, which was said to be most deadly on the line. No English team ever came with such a reputation as this one, and it was said the passing of the backs would bewilder us. In fact they were overadvertised, and if we were not conversant with their strong points, it was not because the southern papers had failed to impress them upon us. As often happens in these cases, the strong points proved weak, and we were very little troubled by the English running and passing. Somehow or other we in Scotland could never come to look upon Stoddart as a great player, and while he was highly esteemed in England, we calculated that we had not much to fear from him – and we were not disappointed. Robertshaw we thought more of, and we never liked his wide accurate passing; but G. Wilson that day did his duty admirably as regards Robertshaw, and frequently the Bradford man, when he was looking for a pass from his half-backs, received Wilson and the ball at the same moment. Early in the game our centre three-quarter got behind, but there is no question about his having 'knocked on' when he was gathering the ball. We missed a grand opportunity of winning the match in the second half, when C. Reid broke away and ran up to Sample, close on the line. Many people believe that had Reid gone on he would never have been held, but seeing Irvine following hard at his side, he no doubt thought to make more sure of it by passing. The throw was a bad one, hard and low, and pitched at Irvine's feet. It was not taken and the chance was lost. Towards the close we were having rather an anxious time, but were much relieved when the hardy little John Tod emerged from the thick of it with the ball tucked under his arm, and resolutely pushed his way to the centre. Tod was always as hard as a bullet, a powerful, tightly knit little player, with no end of stamina, and playing with as much vigour at the end as the beginning of the game. Two men on the English side impressed us that year, C.H. Sample by his fine play at back, and C. Gurdon by his obnoxious 'hook'. This latter feat hardly seemed to come under the category of fair football, and on one occasion when Gurdon was at work, a handling he received from C. Reid was keenly relished by a section on one of the stands, where by the way, one old International man exhausted more of his breath on behalf of Scotland than ever he did on the actual field of play. As with H.B. Tristram, we half grudged having given to England such a good man as Sample. At Edinburgh Academy he played in the same fifteen with Frank Wright, who on another occasion rendered great service to England. Sample at school was a fine drop and a good tackler, but heavy and slow in his movements. When he appeared at Raeburn Place his Cambridge training appeared to have fined him down greatly, and while he still retained his drop, and had the real Scotch schoolboy tackle, he was much smarter in his general movements, and his judgement had greatly matured. It is doubtful if C. Reid ever played a better game than he did on this occasion; and if we consider him not as a great individual player, but as a power in any team, it can be realised what Reid at his best meant to Scotland. He was the forward of his time. There was no man to compare with him in England, Scotland, Ireland or Wales. Neither was there before nor has there been since. Besides the physical qualities which rendered him a dangerous adversary, his football at all points was perfect, and we had no specialist in our team of whom it could be said that in his own particular game he was superior to Reid. His speed was much above that of the average forward, and in many matches he made as big runs as the backs. In fact, in the International under notice, his run in the second half was the best performance of its kind of the day. Roughness has been imputed to him, but the charge is almost groundless, and if on occasion he did use his strength, it must be

remembered in extenuation that he had to put up with all manner of annoying attentions, often aspiring individuals who would have preferred the distinction of having knocked down C. Reid to the honour of half a dozen International caps. We have seen a shaved-headed Yorkshireman in the line-out fix on to Reid like a limpet long before the ball was thrown out from touch, and hang on till he had to be forcibly shaken off. G. Wilson was one of the central figures in this match, and from his play all parties declared him to have a great career before him. As his subsequent performances testify, he failed to fulfil expectations, and it cannot be said that he did not get the opportunity, for no man ever lived longer on one game than Wilson did. He was always a dodgy runner, and often very difficult to hold, but his football was faulty, and he was addicted to mistakes, which were liable at any time to endanger the prospects of his side.

1887 was the year of the foggy International at Manchester, which, from the performances of our team against Ireland and Wales, and the large selection of good men at our command, we had hoped to win. The draw, therefore, was not at all satisfactory, and it was all the more tantalising from the fact that the old story of players, brilliant against other countries, curling up when they came to meet England, had to be repeated. It was this ever recurring failure that prejudiced the national mind against scoring men, and accounts for the estimation in which many of England's backs were held on this side of the border. Had some of our players shown a semblance of their form we should have won the match. At one period we thought we had won it, but for once Maclagan's rush at the line was unsuccessful. We had an abundance of first-rate men in the country that year, and our final choice fell on W.F. Holms, back; G.C.

Lindsay, W.E. Maclagan, and A.N. Woodrow, three-quarter-backs; C.E. Orr and P.H. Don Wauchope, half-backs; with C. Reid (capt.), T.W. Irvine, M.C. McEwen, A.T. Clay Berry, H. Kerr, French, McMillan, and Morton among the forwards. We had beaten Ireland and given Wales a hiding by the tall score of 4 goals and 8 tries. The Welsh match was at Raeburn Place, and G.C. Lindsay spent the greater part of the time running behind. W.A. Cameron, the Watsonian full-back, gained his only International cap upon this occasion, and he certainly has not been overloaded with honours, for he was always a reliable back, who had the correct style in all his actions. H.J. Stevenson was at this time beginning to make for himself a reputation as a three-quarter, and J. Marsh was playing in the Institution. P.H. Don Wauchope, who succeeded his brother as one of our national halves, had much the same style, but was not so effective. He did not possess the same weight and strength, but he was probably as fast, and although not such an inimitable dodger as the elder member of the family, he was a very clever runner, and must have scored a great number of tries during his career. Kerr and French were two of a type of Glasgow forwards who seemed peculiarly calculated to raise the gall of the Edinburgh people. Oceans of ink were spilled over them, and it was needless waste, for French was well worth his place, and Kerr was, at the lowest estimate, the fourth best forward in the country.

During 1888 and 1889 the 'unfortunate dispute' in another phase cropped up again, and robbed us of our great match. In 1888 our pride was much hurt by Wales beating us at Newport. On that occasion we played three centre three-quarters, H.J. Stevenson, M.M. Duncan and W.E. Maclagan with C.E. Orr and C.P. Fraser as our halves. The latter

division were blamed for our defeat, but no section of the team played above itself.

In 1889 we had a great game with Ireland, which almost compensated for the loss of the English fixture. We won by a try, but as the *Scotsman* said at the time, it was 'one of the most exciting and hotly contested games ever seen in connection with an International match'. LeFanu and M'Laughlin left great impressions behind them. LeFanu, as one of the best forwards that has played against us, and M'Laughlin as a most extraordinary worker for a quarter.

The English International of 1890 was a very bad one for us. A great surprise was sprung upon the country in the selection of W.E. Maclagan, and in giving G. Wilson a place the Union made anything but a popular choice. Our half-backs were again blamed for losing the match by not feeding their halves, but it would have been very hard for them to feed without the ball. Where we really lost the game was in the scrummage, where the English took possession of the ball, and held our forwards while Fox and his companion nipped it back to their halves. The match taught us this species of attack most impressively, and when our team went to London in 1891 and scored our greatest victory, the English press complained that we had learned it too well. Our forwards undoubtedly won us this match, and our backs, as they very well might, were seen to great advantage. Our three-quarters, W. Neilson, G. Macgregor, and P. Clauss, were scoring men and behind winning forwards were all that was wanted. Had our Union fully realised in 1892 that we should require our backs who were able to cut out the work for themselves, we should never have lost the game that year. G.T. Campbell, W. Neilson, and P. Clauss made a very poor show, and our half-backs were disappointing.

H.J. Stevenson, M.C. McEwen, C.E. Orr, and R.G. McMillan are the prominent men of the last three years. Orr, in the true sense of the word, is one of our best all-round quarters, McEwen is one of our great forwards, a powerful player, strong in all points of the game. Of Stevenson it has to be said we never had a more versatile player. His defence at three-quarters in 1890 materially kept down the score, and when the Union saw fit to place him at full-back in 1891 and 1892 he filled the position as adequately as any man ever we had. Centre three-quarters, however, is his true place, and in it he has never been known to play a poor game, a fitting testimony to the merit of one of the most remarkable players the country has produced, and a back who will be remembered along with N.J. Finlay, W.E. Maclagan, and A.R. Don Wauchope.

Appendix IV

Extracted from *The Gilbert Story*, published in 1957 by James Gilbert, in which he documents the evolution of the rugby ball.

The Makers of the Rugby Ball

It has been the good fortune of my firm to be identified with the game of Rugby Football since its inception.

My grandfather's uncle, William Gilbert, is reputed to have made the first Rugby footballs when the game started at Rugby School at the beginning of the last century.

William Gilbert, who was one of the boot and shoe makers to Rugby School, first had a small shop in High Street, Rugby, in 1842, within a stone's throw of the school, where the firm has been situated ever since. Nothing much is now known of William Gilbert except the following extract from an obituary notice which appeared in the *Rugby Advertiser*, Saturday, May 12th, 1877.

Death of Old Rugby Tradesman

In another column will be found recorded the decease of Mr William Gilbert of St Matthew's Street, Rugby, at the mature age of 78. Mr Gilbert was a native of Rugby and formerly occupied a small shop in the High Street, but for the last 35 years has resided in St Matthew's Street, where he carried on a business of shoemaker and football manufacturer, chiefly to Rugby School. Like most of the old Rugby shoemakers, his materials and workmanship were noted for their general excellence . . . and as a consequence goods of Mr Gilbert's manufacture, especially footballs, are to be found all over the world. Indeed it is hardly possible to go into a London shop, where footballs of different manufacturers are sold, without observing the superior quality of the Rugby ball.

It will be seen that William Gilbert had established some reputation which it has been the endeavour of the firm to keep up.

William Gilbert was a bachelor. He had taken his nephew, James Gilbert, my grandfather, into the business and who succeeded him when he died.

My grandfather had more or less ceased to take an active part in the business by the time I was able to sit up and take notice and the management was under my father, James John Gilbert. My grandfather was a fine-looking man and much loved by the past and present

Rugbeians of his time. One of the things he delighted in doing when I was a very small boy was to walk in front of a few of us small fry dropping pennies for us to pick up. Once he dropped a two shilling piece, and on my pointing out that I thought he had made a mistake, he promptly exchanged it for a penny. An old Rugbeian, Mr E.F.T. Bennett, who was at Rugby School in the 1860s, writing to me in 1930, says:

Your grandfather was a delightful man and a friend to us (very wild naughty boys I suppose) and a great tweaker maker, but do not tell your son to tweak. He was a wonder of lung strength and (before the pump came in) blew even the big match balls up tight. I wrote an article in Badminton Magazine *about 20 years ago, but have not got a copy. I made sketches of Jim Gilbert's footballs . . . Jim did anything we asked him to do, and I never can remember him being put out by our rough rushes into his shop. His boots were good, and anything he did he did well . . . I trust the Rugby game will never become an inducement to betting and buying good players, for any sport is spoilt by making it a money affair for mere betters. These people in many cases have never played games or hunted or run paper chases . . .*

A tweaker mentioned by Mr Bennett is a catapult and was tabooed by the School authorities many years ago.

My grandfather must have been very clever with his hands when he was a young man because I still have in my possession the small stand which he made for the firm's exhibit at the London Exhibition in 1851. This was made out of wood and leather to the design of a local antiquarian, Mr Matthew Bloxham.

I do not know whether my grandfather ever played Rugby Football, but I remember seeing him kick off once in his old age in a football match on Rugby Football Club ground. Rugby Football Club were honouring him for his long association with the Club and also for his always providing the Club with Rugby footballs free of charge, which the firm has continued to do ever since. He died in 1906 and my father, James John Gilbert, succeeded him in the business.

My father did play Rugby Football for the Rugby Club and had the distinction of breaking his collarbone on three occasions when playing. He was very proud of the firm's reputation of supplying balls for the Rugby game and saw that every ball went out as perfect as possible. I am very grateful for what he taught me. He was a very keen follower of the Rugby game and took me to see my first International Match (England v Ireland) at Leicester in 1902, before the Rugby Football Union had their own ground at Twickenham. He was in failing health at the beginning of World War I and died in 1917 when I was in France.

I suppose with all the background it was only natural that I should want to carry on the good work of manufacturing Rugby footballs. Like other people at some time in their life I once did ask myself 'what is the good of my job'? I found that answer in a certificate I hold when my grandfather's uncle exhibited Rugby footballs in the London Exhibition in 1851, on which it states that the goods were classed as Educational Appliances. I came to the conclusion that if a Rugby football was an article used in education, it must be of some use. There is no doubt the reason why Rugby Football has spread to so many schools throughout the British Isles and Dominions and to other countries, was not simply for the exercise it gave, but for its character building and other well-known qualities. My job has given me great pleasure and I have got to know heaps of Rugby footballers whom I consider the salt of the earth.

In my very early years it seemed to me the firm was exporting more rugby balls than it was making for home consumption. More men had to be engaged about Christmas time and onwards to cope with the export orders and such names as Sydney, Melbourne, Adelaide, Perth, Brisbane, Fremantle, Wellington, Christchurch, Dunedin, etc., which were stencilled on the packing cases intrigued me very much.

The local secondary school which I attended in those days played soccer football, but there were quite a lot of us little boys who were keen on Rugby Football and in the Christmas and Easter holidays we used to go up to Rugby Recreation Ground with one or two Rugby balls, which I had got from my father, nearly every day when it was fine and play games of Rugby (as we thought it was) of five or six a side. If only a few of us turned up we used to practise kicking goals. We would have sides, say three of us standing on one side of the goal and three on the other, each taking it in turn to kick the ball. If the ball was punted over the crossbar it counted 3 points; if drop-kicked 4 points; and if place-kicked 5 points. The kick had to be taken from where it was caught or where it dropped. In this way I got used to handling Rugby balls at an early age and able to distinguish what I thought was a good ball and which was not so good.

Although 'International Caps' were, and are, being gained each year for Gilbert Rugby balls, I am sorry to say I achieved no fame on the Rugby field after leaving school, but I have never lost my keenness for the game. I was once, however, taken for a Rugby footballer. I had gone over to Coventry to see a Rugby Union trial match which was being played there and, as I was having lunch with a party of friends, someone came into the hotel dining-room, slapped me on the back and said, 'Are you playing this afternoon?' I replied, 'No, not this afternoon.' Whom he took me for I do not know. I remember I played one game on Rugby School Close. I thought nothing of it at the time, but today I know players and referees are glad to be able to say they have played or refereed on the ground where the Rugby game was made.

The Evolution of the Rugby Ball

I am constantly asked why and when the Rugby ball became oval in shape. I much regret to say that my firm kept no records in the very early days of its existence, and it is very difficult to answer this question.

In the book published in 1930 entitled *Football Records of Rugby School, 1823–1929* (collected for the Old Rugbeian Society by a subcommittee) the following paragraph appears:

The group photographs in this book show the great alteration which has taken place in the shape of the ball. Though the ball was never round, it was much less an airship than at present. How the School originally came to play with an oval ball is unknown: it baffled even the researches of the authors of the Origin of Rugby Football.

My own researches in this matter are as follows and my chief authority is Mr E.F.T. Bennett, OR, who was at Rugby School in the 1860s and who said in a letter to the *Morning Post* of 22 April 1930:

As I am more than eighty-two years of age and my last football on Big Side was in 1864, I can say something about the ball we used in those days before the india rubber bladder had taken the place of the animal bladders, which Jim Gilbert used to blow tight with his great lungs.

The shape of our ball came from the bladder and was a perfect ball for long drop-kicking, or placing, and for dribbling too.

The modern plum-stone is good for none of these, but seems meant for carrying and throwing or passing between players.

It must be remembered that before the exploit of William Webb Ellis in 1823, football, as played at Rugby, had already a distinctive feature in that a goal was scored by kicking the ball over the crossbar of the goal posts and not simply through the goal posts as in other games of football, and the following passage from *Tom Brown's Schooldays* will be of interest:

Tom followed East until they came to a gigantic gallows of two poles, eighteen feet high, and some fourteen feet apart, with a crossbar running from one end to the other, at a height of ten feet, or thereabouts. 'This is one of the goals,' said East, 'and you see the other across there, right opposite, under the doctor's wall. Well, the match is for the best of three goals; whichever side kicks two goals wins; and it won't do you see, just to kick the ball through these posts, it must go over the crossbar; any height will do you see, so long as it is between the posts.'

Mr Matthew Bloxham, who was at Rugby School from 1813–1820, writes that it was by means of placed kicks that most of the goals were kicked in the very early days of the game, and Mr Bennett in an article he wrote in *The Badminton Magazine*, September 1898, describes how drop-kicking was a great feature of the game in the 1860s. Place-kicking and drop-kicking were therefore very important features of the game in the early days, and it is probably due to these two features that we get the oval ball, as it was found that the best results could be obtained

with this shaped ball – the shape being suggested in the first instance by the shape of a pig's bladder.

Mr Bennett wrote:

The Big Side balls were half an inch larger every way than the ordinary ball (and this is a very vast difference); the ends were well rounded, and seventy yards was not at all an impossible kick: how few now think of trying a goal even from thirty yards.

This shape has been evolved since 1875, as being the best shaped ball for handling and passing in modern Rugby Football.

There is no record as to when the Rugby ball first began to assume its oval shape: probably some years before 1823. In *Tom Brown's Schooldays* in the description of the Big Side Game will be found these words: 'the new ball you may see lie there, quite by itself, in the middle, pointing towards the School goal'. The ball had therefore become oval by 1835, when this game was supposed to have taken place.

Rugby footballs in the early days were made of four pieces of cowhide stitched together in the same way as they are today; and were inflated with pigs' bladders. These unsavoury articles were put into leather cases in their green state, and, usually with the aid of the stem of a clay pipe, which was fastened to the opening of the bladder, they were inflated by lung power. You never see an inflated pig's bladder being used as a football now, but when I was a small boy, it was not an uncommon sight to see one being kicked about in the street by some small boys.

The substitution of rubber for the pig's bladder for inflating rugby balls took place about 1870, when an inflator was also invented. And so the far from salubrious task of inflating pigs' bladders came to an end.

The Rugby Football Union was founded

in 1871 but there does not appear to have been any regulation size of the Rugby ball until standard dimensions were fixed in 1892, which then appeared in the Rules of the Game. The Rule that a Rugby ball should be oval in shape and *as far as possible* (or words to that effect) should measure 25½"–26" in width circumference and 30"–31" in the length circumference remained until 1931, when the width circumference in the Rule Book was altered to 24"–25½", as players had for some years prior to this been demanding balls which were not so fat.

The Rugby Rules have always stated that the ball should be *as far as possible* certain dimensions and this qualification no doubt accounts for the slight variation in the shape of the ball to suit the ideas of the different Rugby Unions throughout the world. New Zealand, for instance, has always favoured a ball measuring half an inch less in the width circumference than the ball used at home.

Rugby balls are made with 4, 6 and 8 panels; the most popular being the 4-panel (*i.e.*, four pieces of leather sewn together as in the original Rugby ball) and it is interesting to note that whereas New Zealand has always used 4-panel balls, South Africa prefers 8-panel balls.

Appendix V

Laws of Football at Rugby School – 1846

1. Kick off from Middle must be a place kick.
2. Kick out must not be more than 25 yards out of goal, nor from more than 10 yards if a place kick.
3. Fair catch is a catch direct from the foot.
4. Charging is fair, in the case of a place kick, as soon as the ball has left the ground; in the case of a kick from a catch, as soon as the player offers to kick, but he may always draw back, unless he has actually touched the ball with his foot.
5. Offside – A player is off his side if the ball has touched one of his own side behind him until the other party kick it.
6. A player being off his side is to consider himself as out of the game, and is not to touch the ball in any case whatever (either in or out of touch); or in any way to interrupt the play, and is, of course, incapable of holding the ball.
7. Knocking on, as distinguished from throwing on, is altogether disallowed under any circumstances whatsoever. In case of this rule being broken, a catch from such a knock on shall be equivalent to a fair catch.
8. It is not lawful to take the ball off the ground, except in touch, either for a kick or throw on.
9. First of His Side is the player nearest the ball on his side.
10. Running In is allowed to any player on his side, provided he does not take the ball off the ground, or through touch.
11. If, in the case of a run in, the ball is held in a scrummage, it shall not be lawful for the holder to transmit it to another of his own side.
12. No player may be held, unless he is himself holding the ball.
13. It is not fair to hack and hold at the same time.
14. No hacking with the heel, or unless below the knee is fair.
15. No one wearing projecting nails or iron plates on the soles or heels of his shoes or boots shall be allowed to play.
16. Try at Goal – A ball touched down between the goalposts may be brought up to either of them but not between.
17. The ball when punted must be within, and when caught without the line of goal.
18. The ball must be place kicked and not dropped and if it touches two hands the try will be lost.
19. It shall be a goal if the ball goes over the bar (whether it touches or not) without having touched the dress or person of any

player; but no player may stand on the goal bar to interrupt it going over.

20. No goal may be kicked from touch.

21. Touch – A player may not in any case run with the ball in touch.

22. A player standing up to another may hold one arm only, but may hack him or knock the ball out of his hand if he attempts to kick it, or go beyond the line of touch.

23. No agreement between two players to send the ball straight out shall be allowed.

24. A player having touched the ball straight for a tree and touched the tree with it, may drop from either side if he can, but one of the opposite side may oblige him to go to his own side of the tree.

25. In case of a player getting a fair catch immediately in front of his own goal, he may not retire behind the line to kick it.

26. No player may take the ball out of the Close.

27. No player may stop the ball with anything but his own person.

28. If a player takes a punt or drop when he is not entitled to it, the opposite side may take a punt or drop, without running (after touching the ball on the ground) if the ball has not touched two hands, but such a drop may not be a goal.

29. That part of the Island which is in front of the line of goal is in touch, that behind is in goal.

30. The discretion of sending into goal rests with heads of sides and houses or their deputies.

31. Heads of sides, or two deputies appointed by them, are the sole arbiters of all disputes.

32. All matches are drawn after 5 days or after 3 days if no goal has been kicked.

Some amendments of 1847

4. Charging is fair, in the case of a place kick, as soon as the ball has touched the ground.

5. Offside – A player is off his side, if the ball had been kicked or thrown on by one of his own side behind him, until the other party kick it, thrown it on or run with it.

26. No player may take the ball out of the Close, i.e. behind the line of trees beyond the goal.

Appendix VI

Edinburgh Academicals FC Rules – 1858

A foreword states 'The following Rules are taken from the Book of Rules used at Rugby'.

1. KICK OFF must be from MIDDLE and a place kick.
2. When the ball is touched down behind goal, if touched by the side behind whose goal it is, they have a KICK OUT; but if the opposite side, they may have a TRY AT GOAL.
3. KICK OUT must not be from more than 25 yards out of goal.
4. FAIR CATCH is a catch direct from the foot, or a knock on from the HAND of the opposite side only.
5. A CATCH from a throw on is not a fair catch.
6. CHARGING is fair, in the case of a place kick, as soon as the ball has touched the ground; in case of a kick from a catch, as soon as the players offers to kick, but he may always draw back unless he has actually touched the ball with his foot.
7. OFFSIDE. A player is off his side when he is behind all the players on the opposite side, or in front of the kicker of his own side.
8. A player being off his side is to consider himself as out of the game and is not to touch the ball in any case whatever (either in our out of touch) or in any way to interrupt the play, and is of course incapable of holding the ball.
9. It is not lawful to take the ball off the ground, except in touch, for any purpose whatsoever.
10. It is not lawful to take the ball when rolling as distinguished from bounding.
11. RUNNING IN is allowed to any player on his side, provided he does not take the ball off the ground, or through touch.
12. RUNNING IN: If, in the case of a run in, the ball be held in a maul, it shall be lawful for a player on either side to take it from the runner in.
13. No player out of a maul may be held, or pulled over, unless he is himself holding the ball.
14. Though it is lawful to hold any player in a maul, this holding does not include attempts to throttle or strangle, which are totally opposed to all the principles of the game.
15. No one wearing projecting nails or iron plates on the soles or heels of his boots or shoes shall be allowed to play.
16. TRY AT GOAL: A ball touched down

between the goalposts may be brought up to either of them, but not between; but if not touched between the posts must be brought up in a straight line from where it is touched.

17. The ball, when punted, must be within, and when caught, without the line of goal.

18. The ball must be place kicked or dropped, but if it touches two players' hands the try will be lost.

19. It shall be a goal if the ball goes over the bar (whether it touch or not) without having touched the dress or person of any player; but no player may stand on the goal bar to interrupt it going over.

20. No goal may be kicked from touch or by a punt at any time.

21. TOUCH: A ball in touch is dead; consequently the first player on his side must in any case touch it down, bring it to the edge of touch and throw it straight out, but may take it himself if he can.

22. No player may stop the ball with anything but his own person.

23. Heads of sides, or two deputies appointed by them, are the sole arbiters of all disputes.

Appendix VII

Blackheath Club Rules – 1862

1. That the game be started from the centre of the ground by a place kick.
2. A fair catch is a catch direct from the foot or a knock on from the hand of one of the opposite side, when the catcher may either run with the ball or make his mark by inserting his heel in the ground on the spot where he catches it; in which case he is entitled to a free kick.
3. It is not lawful to take the ball off the ground, except in touch, for any purpose whatever.
4. A ball in touch is dead, and the first player who touches it down must kick it out straight from the place where it entered touch.
5. A catch out of touch is not a fair catch, but may be run off.
6. Running is allowed to any player on his side if the ball is caught or taken off the first bound.
7. Any player holding the ball unless he has made his mark after a fair catch, may be hacked; and running is not allowed after the mark is made.
8. No player may be hacked and held at the same time – and hacking above or on the knees or from behind is unfair.
9. No player can be held or hacked unless he has the ball in his hands.
10. Though it is lawful to hold a player in a scrummage, this does not include attempts to throttle or strangle, which are totally opposed to the principles of the game.
11. A player whilst running or being held may hand the ball to one of his own side who may continue to run with it, but after the ball is grounded it must be hacked through, not thrown or lifted.
12. When a player running with the ball grounds it, it cannot be touched by anyone until he lifts his hand from it.
13. If the ball goes behind the goal it must be kicked out by the party to whom the goal belongs from in a line with the goals; but a catch off a kick behind goal is not a fair catch, but may be run off.
14. No player is to get before the ball on the side furthest from his own goal; but if he does he must not touch the ball as it passes him until touched by one of the opposite side, he being offside.
15. A goal must be a kick through or over and between the poles, and if touched by the hands of one of the opposite side before or whilst going through, is no goal.
16. No one wearing projecting nails, iron plates or gutta-percha on the soles or heels of his boots be allowed to play.

Appendix VIII

Laws of Blairgowrie, Rattray and Neighbourhood — 1865

1. The maximum length of the ground shall be 200 yards, the maximum breadth shall be 100 yards; the length and breadth shall be marked off with flags; and the goal shall be defined by two upright posts, 8 yards apart, without any tape or bar across.

2. The game shall be commenced by a place kick from the centre of the ground by the side winning the toss; the other side shall not approach within 10 yards of the ball until it is kicked off. After a goal is won the losing side shall be entitled to kick off.

3. The two sides shall change goals after each goal is won.

4. A goal shall be won when the ball passes over the space between the goalposts (at whatever height), not having been thrown, knocked on or carried.

5. When the ball is in touch, the first player who touches it shall kick or throw it from the point on the boundary line where it left the ground, in a direction at right angles with the boundary line.

6. A player shall be out of play immediately he is in front of the ball, and must return behind the ball as soon as possible. If the ball is kicked past a player by his own side, he shall not touch or kick it, or advance until one of the other side has first kicked

it or one of his own side on a level with or in front of him has been able to kick it.

7. In case the ball goes behind the goal line, if a player on the side to whom the goal belongs first touches the ball, one of his side shall be entitled to a free kick from the goal line at the point opposite the place where the ball shall be touched. If a player of the opposite side first touches the ball, one of his side shall be entitled to a free kick from a point 15 yards outside the goal line opposite the place where the ball is touched.

8. If a player makes a fair catch he shall be entitled to a free kick, provided he claims it by making a mark with his heel at once; and in order to take such a kick he may go as far back as he pleases, and no player on the opposite side shall advance beyond his mark until he has kicked.

9. A player shall be entitled to run with the ball towards his adversaries' goal if he makes a fair catch or catches the ball on the first bound; but in the case of a fair catch, if he makes his mark, he shall not then run.

10. If a player shall run with the ball towards his adversaries' goal, any player on the opposite side shall be at liberty to charge,

hold, trip or hack him, or to wrest the ball from him; but no player shall be held and hacked at the same time.

11. Neither tripping nor hacking shall be allowed and no player shall use his hands or elbows to hold or push his adversary, except in the case provided by Law 10.

12. Any player shall be allowed to charge another, provided they are both in active play. A player shall be allowed to charge even if he is out of play.

13. A player shall be allowed to throw the ball or pass it to another if he makes a fair catch, or catches the ball on the first bound.

14. No player shall be allowed to wear projecting nails, iron plates, or gutta-percha on the soles or heels of his boots.

Appendix IX

International Dinner Menu
Glasgow, 3 March 1873

Chairman: Hon. F.J. Moncreiff
Croupier: J.W. Arthur, Esq.

POTAGES
Mock Turtle
Oxtail
Cockie Leekie
Misa's Oloroso Sherry

POISSONS
Salmon with Cucumber
Fillet of Whiting, a la Maitre d'Hotel
Chablis, Steinberg 1857

ENTREES
Scotch Haggis
Sweetbreads, a la Financier
Lobster Cutlets, a la Cardinal
Supreme de Volaille aux Truffles
Fricandeau of Veal Sauce Tomato
Sparkling Hock, Creme de Marcobrun

RELEVES
Sirloin of Beef, Horse Radish
Saddle of Mutton, with Jelly
Roast Quarter Lamb, Mint Sauce
Boiled Turkeys, Macaroni Sauce
Brunswick Ham

Ox Tongues
Pollinger's Extra Dry Champagne 1865

ENTREMETS
Meringue Naepolitaine
Compote of Apricot
Cabinet Pudding
Gooseberry Tart
Blancmange.
Maraschino Jelly

GLACES
Vanilla
Raspberry

DESSERT
Ch. Leoville 1862   Port 1851
Royal Pale Amontillado
Liqueurs

TOAST LIST

The Queen   *The Chair*
The Prince and Princess of Wales and other
Members of the Royal Family   *The Chair*
The Army, Navy and Reserve Forces
                              The Chair

The English Twenty	*The Chair*
	F. Stokes
The Scotch Twenty	F. Stokes
	F.J. Moncreiff
Rugby Football	J.W. Arthur
	D.F. Turner
The Rugby Football Unions	B. Hall Blyth
	A.G. Guillemard
	Dr J. Chiene
The Match Committee	A.G. Guillemard
	B. Hall Blyth
The Chairman	A.St G. Hamersley

	F.J. Moncreiff
The Ladies	Mr Forrester
	Mr Luscombe

The dinner was held following the game between Scotland and England at Hamilton Crescent, Glasgow. At a meeting following the match, the decision was taken to form a Scottish Football Union. Oddly, and despite the fact it was not yet formally constituted, the Scottish Union, and its first president, Dr John Chiene, appear on the toast list.

Appendix X

World Highlights

1823 The alleged birth date of the game at Rugby School in England when William Webb Ellis, 'with fine disregard for the rules of football as played in his time, first took the ball in his arms and ran with it, thus originating the distinctive feature of the rugby game'.

1843 First rugby club formed at Guy's Hospital, London.

1851 A 'Rugby School Football' – an oval-shaped ball – inflated by a pig's bladder – made by William Gilbert was on display at the International Exhibition in London.

1854 Dublin University club founded in Ireland.

1857 Edinburgh Academicals playing and incorporated the following year.

1863 The first recorded club game – Richmond v Blackheath – took place. This is the oldest regular fixture in Rugby Union football.

1870 First rugby game in New Zealand.

1871 The Rugby Football Union founded in London. The first-ever international game – Scotland v England – played at Raeburn Park in Edinburgh.

1872 The first rugby club formed in France in Le Havre.

1873 Scottish Football Union founded.

1874 New South Wales Rugby Union formed in Australia.

1875 First game of rugby in South Africa – Cape Town.

1877 Players in international teams reduced from 20 to 15.

1879 First Calcutta Cup match took place at Raeburn Place.

1880 Rugby introduced to Argentina.

1881 First England v Wales game.

1883 First seven-a-side tournament at Melrose.

1887 International Rugby Football Board founded by Scotland, Wales and Ireland.

1890 England joined the IRFB.

1891 Currie Cup started in South Africa.

1895 The Northern Rugby Football Union – eventually Rugby League – was formed.

1897 Rugby introduced to Japan.

1900 Rugby played in the Olympic Games in Paris – France wins the title.

1905 New Zealand toured the British Isles, Canada and the USA.

1908 First Australian tour of England and Wales – the Australians win the rugby competition in the London Olympics.

1914 Rugby introduced to Romania.

1924 USA win the Olympic title (USA 17, France 3). Rugby has since been discontinued in the Olympic programme.

1925 Phil Macpherson's side win first Scottish Grand Slam.

1931 Bledisloe Cup between New Zealand and Australia commenced.

1933 Australia tour South Africa.

1946 Five Nations Championship resumed after World War II.

1948 Australia, New Zealand and South Africa joined the IRFB.

1949 Australian Rugby Football Union founded.

1958 'Rules as to Professionalism' introduced.

1959 France won outright Five Nations for the first time ever.

1965 Argentina toured South Africa.

1969 First Asian Championship.

1971 RFU Centenary Congress attended by representatives from 43 playing countries.

1974 Amateur Regulations replaced the 'Rules as to Professionalism'.

1977 First Caribbean championship.

1984 Jim Aitken's side win second Scottish Grand Slam.

1986 Centenary meeting in the IRFB. Representatives from 76 countries in attendance.

1987 Sixteen Unions (by invitation) took part in first Rugby World Cup held in Australia and New Zealand. New Zealand defeated France in the final.

1988 Creation of the first full-time IRFB secretariat and office.

1989 Second international meeting of IRFB Member Unions, at which the extended membership of the Board was created and an enlarged Executive Council, to include Argentina, Canada, Italy and Japan, was appointed.

1990 David Sole's side won third Scottish Grand Slam.

1991 Second Rugby World Cup held in the UK, Ireland and France – over 30 teams involved in the preliminary rounds. Australia defeat England in the final.

1992 Inaugural General Meeting of IRFB attended by 49 Member Unions.

1993 Twenty-four nations took part in the inaugural Rugby World Cup Sevens held in Scotland (the birthplace of the abbreviated version of the game). England defeat Australia in the Murrayfield final.

1995 IRFB joined the Olympic Movement as the International Federation for Rugby.

Annual meeting of the Council held in Bristol. Cook Islands and Zambia became members of the IRFB. Sixty-seven nations in membership.

Third Rugby World Cup in South Africa – over 50 nations involved in the qualifying rounds. South Africa defeated New Zealand in the final.

Special Meeting of the IB Council – Paris. The regulations relating to amateurism were repealed.

1996 Northern Hemisphere game in turmoil as professionalism took hold; England were almost excluded from Five Nations following row over broadcasting rights; Scottish Rugby Union signed its first professionals.

1997 Alan Tait (Newcastle and late of Kelso) became the first former Rugby League player to play for Scotland.

People's Republic of China became 76th member nation of International Board.

Fiji defeated South Africa in final of second RWC seven-a-side tournament held in Hong Kong.

British Lions returned to South Africa for first time in 17 years and first time since ending of apartheid.Martin Johnson's Tourists win Test series 2–1 to become only second British and Irish touring side this century to do so. Scots in the party were centres Ian McGeechan and Jim Telfer, fitness adviser David McLean; Tour medic, Dr James Robson; and players Rob Wainright, Gregor Townsend, Tom Smith, Doddie Weir and Alan Tait. Weir returned home injured before the Test series began; Smith played in all three Tests, Townsend and Tait in the first two and Wainright in the third. The Hawick and Scotland centre/wing Tony Stanger played one match for the Lions as a temporary replacement for the injured Welsh wing Ieuan Evans.

Appendix XI

Participants at the IRFB Special Meeting on Amateurism in Paris on 24–26 August 1995

The meeting at which the game was declared 'open'

Peter Brook, John Jeavons-Fellows (England); Fred McLeod, Allan Hosie (Scotland); Tom Kiernan, Dr Syd Millar (Ireland); Vernon Pugh, Ray Williams (Wales); Dr Roger Vanderfield, Norbert Byrne (Australia); Tim Gresson, Rob Fisher (New Zealand); Dr Louis Luyt, Mluleki George (South Africa); Bernard Lapasset,★ Marcel Martin (France); Carlos Tozzi (Argentina); Alan Sharp (Canada); Maurizio Mondell (Italy); Shiggy Konno (Japan); Keith Rowlands (IRFB Secretary).

★ In chair

Bibliography

Football: The Rugby Union Game, Rev F.P. Marshall, London, 1892

The History of Scottish Rugby, Sandy Thorburn, Johnston and Bacon, London, 1980

The Scottish Rugby Union Official History, A.M.C. Thorburn, SRU and William Collins and Sons, Edinburgh, 1985

The Story of Scottish Rugby, R.J. Phillips, T.N. Foulis Ltd, Edinburgh and London, 1925

International Rugby Union: a compendium of Scotland's matches, John McI. Davidson, Polygon, Edinburgh, 1994

One Hundred Years at Raeburn Place 1854–1954, The Edinburgh Academical Club, Edinburgh, 1954

The Edinburgh Academical Football Club Centenary History, Edinburgh Academical FC, Edinburgh, 1958

West of Scotland FC 1865–1965, C.D. Stuart, Glasgow, 1965

Feet, Scotland Feet, ed. Derek Douglas, Mainstream, Edinburgh, 1991

The Flowering of Scotland: Grand Slam 1990, ed. Derek Douglas, Mainstream, Edinburgh, 1990

Fifty Years' Football in Hawick, Hawick RFC, Hawick, 1923

The History of Hawick Rugby, ed. Bill McLaren, Scott and Paterson, Hawick, 1973

Poetical Works of Sir Walter Scott, Globe Edition, London, 1876

Hawick Archaeological Society Transactions, William J. Windram, 1975

Upper Teviotdale and The Scotts of Buccleuch, J. Rutherford Oliver, W. and J. Kennedy, Hawick, 1887

The Statistical Account of Scotland, 1791–1799, Vol III, the Eastern Borders, ed. Sir John Sinclair

Collins Encyclopaedia of Scotland, John Keay and Julia Keay, Harper Collins, London, 1994

Sport and the Making of Britain, Derek Birley, Manchester University Press, Manchester and New York, 1993

The Gilbert Story, James Gilbert, Rugby, 1957

Tom Brown's Schooldays, Thomas Hughes, first published 1857

20th Century Dictionary of National Biography 1901–11

Athleticism in the Victorian and Edwardian Public Schools, J.A. Mangan, Cambridge, 1981

Running with the Ball: The birth of rugby football, Jennifer Macrory, former archivist Rugby School, Collins Willow, London, 1991

A Hundred Years in Black and White: a history of Kelso RFC, ed. Arthur Hastie, 1976

Langholm RFC 1871–1971, by Walter Bell

Royal High School FC Centenary 1868–1968, RHSFP, Edinburgh, 1968

Rugby Football Internationals' Roll of Honour, E.H.D. Sewell, 1919

Glasgow Academical Club Centenary Volume 1866–1966, Blackie, London and Glasgow, 1966

The Daily Telegraph Chronicle of Rugby, ed. Norman Barrett, Guinness Publishing, London, 1996

The Buildings of Scotland: Edinburgh, John Gifford, Colin McWilliam, David Walker and Christopher Wilson, Penguin Books in association with the National Trust for Scotland, 1984

British Lions, John Griffiths, The Crowood Press, 1990

The History of the British Lions, Clem Thomas, Mainstream, Edinburgh, 1996

Springbok Rugby, Chris Greyvenstein, New Holland, London, Cape Town, Sydney, 1995

The Herald; *The Glasgow Herald*; *The Scotsman*; *The Oval World*, official magazine of the International Rugby Football Board, issue five, Spring 1997; *Bell's List*; *The Merchistonian*.